An Actor's Guide to Getting Work

Fifth Edition

An Actor's Guide to Getting Work

Fifth Edition

Simon Dunmore

methuen | drama

Published by Methuen Drama 2012

Methuen Drama, an imprint of Bloomsbury Publishing Plc

1 3 5 7 9 10 8 6 4 2

Methuen Drama
Bloomsbury Publishing Plc
50 Bedford Square
London WC1B 3DP
www.methuendrama.com

Fifth edition 2012

Copyright © 2012, 2004, 2001, 1996, 1991 Simon Dunmore

Simon Dunmore has asserted his rights under the Copyright, Designs and Patents Act 1988 to be identified as the author of this work.

Fourth edition 2004
Third edition 2001
Second edition 1996
First edition published 1991 by Macmillan Publishers Ltd

ISBN: 978 1 408 14554 8

A CIP catalogue record for this book is available from the British Library

Available in the USA from Bloomsbury Academic & Professional,
175 Fifth Avenue /3rd Floor, New York, NY10010.
www.BloomsburyAcademicUSA.com

Typeset by Margaret Brain
Printed and bound in Great Britain by CPI Group (UK) Ltd, Croydon CR0 4YY

Contents

'More than a practical guide through the terrors of the audition minefield, Mr Dunmore's book is so positive and encouraging in its approach that it must be essential reading for any actor setting out on this perilous career.

If it's true that "Luck gets you there; talent keeps you there", then Mr Dunmore goes a long way towards explaining the mystery of "luck".'

Dame Maggie Smith

Acknowledgements

There are numerous people whom I would like to thank for their contributions and comments.

First, I must thank all the students, teachers, actors, directors, casting directors, agents and all the other professionals I've ever met; you have each given something to this book.

Second, a special thanks to the following who cheerfully allowed me to pick their brains: John Ainslie, Laura Albery, Mark Allen, Pat Armitage, Iain Armstrong, Adele Bailey, Osian Barnes, Laurie Bates, Sophy Boreham, John Bowler, Carole Boyd, Chris Bramwell, Tracey Briggs, Robin Browne, Alex Caan, Amanda Caswell-Robinson, Jacquie Charlesworth, Mary Churchward, Roy Civil, Martin Cochrane, John Colclough, Ruth Cooper, Janine Cowie, Tim Crouch, Angus Deuchar, Stephen Douse, Katie Draper, Alan Dunnett, Richard Evans, Nicky Furre, Nicholas Geake, Marsha Gorbett, Louise Grainger, Tina Gray, Bob Hamlin, Vicky Hasted, Jan Haydn Rowles, Chris Hocking, Phillip Hoffman, Ed Hooks, Bill Hughes, Cameron Jack, Anna Koutelieri, Beccy Lamb, Sarah de Larrinaga, Iain Lauchlan, Steve Lawrence, Maggie Lloyd-Williams, Nichola McAuliffe, Peter McCarthy, Elizabeth McKechnie, Sally Marshall, Mike Maynard, Terry Meech, Peter Messaline, Richard Moore, Alex Nash, Janet Nelson, Tom Nordon, Pilar Orti, Bert Parnaby, Andrew Piper, Mark Pitt, Fiona Power, Janet Rawson, Rachael Rena, Hannah Rothman, Denni Sayers, Nigel Seale, Nik Simmonds, Guy Slater, Sharon Small, Amy Stoller, Alison Taffs, Barbara Thompson, Jude Tisdall, Annie Walker, Chris Wallis, Malcolm Ward, Ben Warren, Eric Watson, Liz Whiting, Tana Wolf, Peter Yapp and Lesley Young.

Third, similar thanks to those who contributed but preferred their input to remain confidential.

Fourth, enormous thanks to the following who not only gave me insights but whose especial contribution deserves separate mention: Maev Alexander, Tim Bentinck, Don Gilét, Wyn Jones, Stephanie Pack and Michael Tucker.

Fifth, apologies and many thanks to anybody I've inadvertently missed out of these credits.

Sixth, many thanks to my original editor, Susanna Wadeson, for kicking me into making sense on the page and to Dame Maggie Smith for her generous endorsement.

Introduction

This is a book of advice containing lots and lots of details based upon my long experience of employing and teaching actors and input from very many others.

One of the most frequently asked questions that I get is: 'Where did you train?' I try not to give a sixteen-hour outpouring of my tortuous route into my decades in professional theatre. I try just to focus on my degree in physics and maths – and how those brilliant disciplines are at the heart of the way I work. I might summarise thus: pay attention to details and in time big things could happen. Lack of attention to those details will significantly reduce any chance of success. My heroes are largely not actors – although I will always love good acting. My real 'heroes' are the great scientist-communicators like Carl Sagan, Jacob Bronowski and Max Born. All three gave me incredible and inspiring insights into science and humanity. Through their communication skills, I learned and understood so much . . . What have they got to do with acting? Much more than you might believe! A significant part of good acting is about communicating – underpinned by detail.

Careful consideration of every detail is an investment in your future. With so many actors available and so few jobs going, any little thing can count against (or for) you. I am constantly amazed at how careless so many actors are with the details of their marketing processes – a perfect analogy would be actors only learning the lines that they like. Only a tiny, fortunate minority simply sail over all the hurdles set up by the acting profession. Talent is only part of what's necessary to be an actor; self-discipline and sales technique are also vital to success.

You have to be a survivor. You have to recognise the seemingly fickle nature of the whole business – its short-term memory (long for miscreants) and its frequent ability to seem almost inhuman. You must keep up the need to be an actor and believe in yourself or you won't survive. On the outside you have to acquire a durable veneer of resilient rubber to cope with the constant rejections and bounce back every time. You will be knocked down many, many more times than you are picked up. On the inside you must keep all the sensitivity that is fundamental to the job of acting. No other profession relies so much on its practitioners' ability to use the painful and difficult parts of their personalities to work in it. As an actor you need to be vulnerable; as a salesman for yourself you need to be invulnerable. You also have to be organised – ready for the unexpected at any time. 'Chance favours the prepared mind' (Louis Pasteur – another scientist). And you have to be mentally prepared for the 'unexpected' not to happen for some time.

Finally, the advice that follows is not a philosopher's stone for success. You should take what you need, use your instincts and use it in your own way.

1: *If you* really *want to be a professional actor*

People who aspire to become professional actors are of all ages and backgrounds, ranging from those still in primary education to those who have held steady jobs for decades but still have yearnings for the profession. Each group of people has different things to consider, so I will deal with them in chronological order.

Those of school age

The performer is in most young children. (The onset of puberty, and the awful consciousness of self that this brings, eliminates many.) For those wedded to the idea, remember that it is one thing to perform in front of people you know and in familiar circumstances; very much another to do it before those you don't in a previously unknown venue.

So what is the best course for the child who won't let go of the idea of being a professional actor? There are numerous full-time private stage schools and a few publicly funded ones – however the former are expensive (with a few scholarships available) and the latter will often require the child to live away from home and don't usually provide accommodation. There are also numerous part-time schools (part of national franchises and locally based). Such schools (part- and full-time) are often allied to agencies which promote their children for professional productions, but it is a fact that many child stars do not succeed as adult actors. There are notable exceptions – Nicholas Lyndhurst, Dennis Waterman, Jodie Foster and Jenny Agutter, for instance – but they are the exceptions that prove the rule. I also wonder whether a childhood largely devoted to performing is entirely healthy – what about learning about life? It is also important to note that employment of children is very strictly regulated.

Generally the best thing for the stage-struck child is to send him or her to one of the numerous youth theatre groups and drama workshops that exist in almost every town and city. (Many of these are members of the National Association of Youth Theatres

<www.nayt.org.uk>.) Public productions are often the last priority of such groups – especially for the younger ages – but a terrific amount can be learnt by the young from what seem like simple make-believe games. Children in such groups won't learn many of the technical skills necessary to acting, but they will learn a lot of important social skills and the fundamental business of 'interacting' that is so important to an acting ensemble: that it's not just what you can create that matters, it's what you can create with other people. Many managements will choose to use the freshness and spontaneity of such 'not formally trained' talent for their productions. They will audition hopefuls but not always through public advertisement; usually they directly approach appropriate youth theatres or conventional schools with strong drama departments.

For serious aspiring actors in their teens it is well worth audition-ing for the National Youth Theatre <www.nyt.org.uk>, the National Youth Theatre of Wales <www.nyaw.co.uk/e_nytw.html>, the Scottish Youth Theatre <www.scottishyouththeatre.org>, the National Youth Music Theatre <www.nymt.org.uk> or Youth Music Theatre UK <www. youthmusictheatreuk.org>, all of which run extremely good workshops in school holidays as well as mounting excellent productions.

Drama/Theatre Studies exams While success in these can lead on to a university course, they are not necessarily a good idea for a genuinely aspiring actor. Although they contain some practical content, they are predominantly theoretical – and this concentration on looking from the outside can be confusing for someone wanting to become a professional actor with its concentration on working from the inside. (They also pay little attention to important acting techniques like how to use your voice properly. This doesn't necessarily mean learning how to speak with an educated accent; more how to use your voice to its full potential.) The study of alternative subjects can be more beneficial in the long term because they can broaden the student's horizons in finding alternative work when not acting.

Other early training Elocution lessons may enable someone to speak beautifully but they can be damaging to a future actor as their method is directed towards recitation of words with little account of the feelings behind them. Correction of a speech defect is better done by a qualified therapist. The well-established Speech and Drama examinations tend to have very little to do with modern acting.

These, as one drama school maintains in its prospectus, are 'judged on entirely different criteria' from those for entry to full-time training.

School-leavers

It is essential to get a proper training at a recognised drama school – perhaps doing a conventional degree first! It used to be possible to become an actor without formal training – and why not? An awful lot of what is fundamental to acting is that indefinable instinctive something which you either have or have not. In the past, doing menial tasks and watching the professionals at work could teach aspirants all they needed. Nowadays, it's increasingly difficult to progress in the profession without doing at least a year at drama school.

That is not to say that it is not worth trying to get work experience in order to observe and learn from others; that experience can be very valuable for the future.

The mature entrant to the profession

If you are one of these, you have far more going for you than your younger counterpart. This is principally because professionals of your age, if you are over about 30, are fewer on the ground (many drop out in their first decade for financial and domestic reasons) and those that are around tend to become more choosy about what work they will accept. Therefore, there is not quite as much competition and it is easier to find those small parts that are the essential first step in an acting career. Also, there is great value in having life experience before training, which brings me to the primary question:

To train or not to train? You'll hear endless stories of famous actors who didn't formally train. They were fortunate enough to have learned through being part of repertory theatre companies for long contracts. These hardly exist any more. In order to sustain a career almost everybody needs the bedrock of a proper training.

Most of the actors I know who have successfully made the transition from a conventional career to one in acting have been to drama school. Often they've found it difficult to adjust to the 'school' disciplines after so long. Many have also found the immaturity of some of their fellow students hard to cope with for the first few months. However, through patience and by standing back from the herd and ignoring any ageist attitudes, they have found their respective niches and have often got a lot more out of the training than the younger students. As a mature student you should have a much better idea of how to learn, how to organise your life and how to sell yourself.

It is a common phenomenon for maturing dancers – as their bodies decrease in flexibility – to wish to continue performing, albeit less athletically. It is essential to get proper acting-training: you have got to unlearn those bodily positions which people do not use in real life, as well as learning how to use your voice properly.

Incidentally, I've met several people who have gone to drama school in their 40s and even one who started her training at the age of 59. It's never too late! If you're not sure that full-time student life would suit you, then try a part-time course, but you'll find it much harder to crack the nut of gaining a toe-hold in the profession as it is generally the full-time schools where agents and casting directors search out new talents.

Note: Contrary to rumour, drama schools are not biased against more mature students.

Amateur theatre as a training ground Some people think they know it all through amateur work. This is almost invariably untrue. I am not saying that all amateur theatre is bad (or that all professional theatre is good), but there are numerous techniques and professional practices which amateur theatre cannot teach you. For example, performing the same role for three weeks or more (even for several years) requires much more stamina and technical skill than the four or five performances which are the norm of amateur theatre. Amateurs aspiring to be professionals should find out what further training they need – and can get – and audition for drama school.

Preliminary training

Nowadays, it's increasingly difficult to progress in the profession without doing at least a year at drama school. However, there are courses (see details in *Actors' Yearbook*) which can help you on your way.

Short-term, foundation and part-time courses There are numerous examples of such courses, some of which are run by drama schools. They cannot be seen as a complete training; they can only really touch the tip of the iceberg. However, they can be a good grounding for those who want to go on to full-time training – especially the one-year, full-time Foundation courses.

Warning: There are a growing number of such courses being established by private individuals – check very carefully before accepting a place on such a course.

Intensive part-time courses There are also courses that operate for a similar number of hours to a full-time course, but are scheduled (evenings and weekends) so that students can also earn their living from non-acting work. These are a viable, but much more difficult way into the profession – you've got to be extremely fit, disciplined, organised and prepared to all but give up your social life for a while. A few of these courses are gradually gathering good reputations within the profession; with continuing funding problems, more may come along and the whole idea receive its whole-hearted validation. Once again, you should check very thoroughly before accepting a place on such a course.

Unfortunately, the vast majority of these courses are concentrated in London.

University acting-oriented degree courses These are rarely any longer a passport into the profession. It used to be the case that any degree from one of the more prestigious universities made potential employers look twice at a CV, but this is generally no longer true. This is because the actual acting training is only part of the course and, generally, is inadequate. (Some of them specifically state that they are not training you for the profession. One senior university lecturer told me that his department wouldn't even interview anybody who said that they 'wanted to be an actor' in their personal statement.) Today's graduate should try to get a place on a National Council for Drama Training (NCDT; established in the mid-1970s to monitor standards) 'accredited' postgraduate course (preferably a two-year one): these tend to be extremely hard work as they usually embrace much of what is contained in the full three-year courses.

Full-time training

Whatever your age, level or acting ability, if you want to be a professional actor you have to have proper training at a drama school. (Most won't admit you until you are 18.) You should obtain prospectuses and see which schools you think might suit you best. Audition procedures vary and you will have to pay for the privilege – between £35 and £55 for each school as of Autumn 2011. In addition a minority of schools require applications via UCAS <www.ucas.ac.uk> – which is an additional cost. Then there are the travel costs and, if necessary, those for overnight accommodation. Even for someone living in the London area (where half the drama schools are based), these costs can easily total around £400 for half a dozen applications.

Note: A few schools take a higher proportion of men on their three-year courses. This is not fair, but does represent roughly the proportion of work available. The gender balance of numbers of applicants is in the reverse proportion.

Drama schools At the moment, there is a core of established schools which belong to an organisation called the Conference of Drama Schools (CDS). Most of these run courses that are 'accredited' by NCDT. This organisation assesses courses every few years and decides whether each is up to a sufficient standard – a process called 'accreditation'. (At present, individual courses rather than the schools themselves are 'accredited'. Check the NCDT's website for the latest details.) Essentially, it is better to get on to an 'accredited' course. There are two reasons for this (apart from the obvious one of checks being made): (a) you will stand a much better chance of getting funding than you would for a 'non-accredited' one and (b) directors, agents and casting directors are far more inclined to pay attention to graduates of 'accredited' courses.

A complete list of CDS courses, called *Guide to Professional Training in Drama & Technical Theatre*, is available free of charge to all UK addresses from French's Theatre bookshop (<www.theatre@samuelfrench-london.co.uk>). You can also download it and access all the CDS's member schools' websites via <www.drama.ac.uk>. In addition, you'll find lots of useful information on funding on this site and on that of the NCDT <www.ncdt.co.uk>. The latter also contains a useful guide to the whole application and auditioning process entitled *An Applicant's Guide to Auditioning and Interviewing at Dance and Drama Schools*. Other schools are listed in *Actors' Yearbook*.

Note: At the time of writing, there is much discussion about changes in the way the 'accreditation' system works. No conclusions had been reached by the time this book went to press, but I'm assured that the principles will remain the same.

Drama school degrees Nowadays, most three-year, 'accredited' courses have BA status – in spite of the fact that there is little or no written component to the courses, let alone formal, written exams. Some one-year courses have MA status – these do require some written work. (Historically, the schools took the degree route to help students get funding on the same basis as those following conventional academic courses.) Degree status actually means very little in the acting profession and courses with degree status are not necessarily better than those without it. Some schools have been quite vociferous about not wishing to become embroiled in the whole philosophy and bureaucracy that is fundamental to degree education, believing that joining with a university would compromise the purely vocational character of their courses. One such adds: 'Universities are academic institutions and the intelligence required of an academic is different from that required of an actor. Whilst some are blessed with both kinds, many talented and intelligent actors are of indifferent academic ability. We would not wish to exclude them.' BA status will enable you to go on to a higher degree and enhance your employment prospects outside the profession – but not within it.

Duration of training For the school-leaver there's no question that three years is essential. (I would advocate a year out before starting training – simply to gain some life experience away from educational institutions.) Most mature students seem to go for a one-year training course, but from my observations that is usually insufficient. Of course, many will have to fund themselves and one year is significantly cheaper than three, but I would like to see more 'accredited' two-year courses for mature students (there are currently only three to my knowledge). While these are still scarce, I don't think there's any question that three years is much, much better than one for the vast majority of aspiring actors.

Specialist training Every CDS school (and others) offers an acting course. A few also offer courses specialising in musical theatre. Since the start of the millennium there has been a growth in alternatives – courses which have acting-training at their core but specialise in certain aspects of drama, for instance, contemporary theatre, physical theatre, radio, film and television. If you're applying for any such course, it is important to be clear in your mind that this is what you really want. The plain fact is that only a minority manage to sustain a career in a single specialist area of acting – with the possible exception of musical theatre.

Choices

Where to apply Seek advice from teachers, youth theatre leaders, drama advisers and anybody else you can find who knows about today's profession. Never rely on the word of just one person – get a consensus of opinion. The best advice will come from those with recent contact with drama schools, not from those who trained decades ago and have no idea of current trends in those establishments. A drama school is only as good as its current teachers: a list of famous graduates (and/or patrons) or a glossy prospectus with smart graphics doesn't tell you what it's really like now. It is also wise to be cautious if you encounter an overuse of names like Stanislavski and terms like 'The Method' – both have been considerably refined for today's actors. There is no one absolute system of good acting; 'You act how you act,' as a friend expressed it.

It is essential to read prospectuses properly to get a feel for each possible school and their courses. If possible, see productions at each and talk to past and present students at the drama schools you are interested in. Also, look at <www.theessentialsguide.co.uk> for a very well thought through list of what to look for in a training.

Note: In the main, it is wise to ignore public statements made by famous actors about their training – both positive and negative; invariably things will have changed since they left.

When to apply Some schools encourage you to apply early – before Christmas. However, contrary to widespread mythology, this will not enhance your chances of getting a place. However, it is important that your repertoire of audition material should be ready before you send off your application forms. Be aware of the application deadlines of the schools you are interested in!

Schools offer places progressively throughout their audition processes which continue until May or June. Some schools finish their auditions later than others. When the last schools make their final offers, there is a domino effect around the drama school circuit as a fortunate minority with more than one offer change their minds. (Even the most prestigious schools are turned down by around ten per cent of their first offers during this process.) Each change of mind can take a few days, which means that offers are still being made until early July. (This is later for many one-year courses.) In short there is no advantage in applying early.

Don't apply to just one school! Unlike almost every other form of further or higher education there are only minimal (if any) academic qualifications for an applicant trying to gain entry to drama school. The decision on whether to accept you or not is based on what you can do in audition, not on what you've done before in an examination room. Of course, someone who has had good tuition from school, Youth Theatre, and so on, stands a better chance; but that 'good tuition' is not nationally regulated and is available only randomly around the country. Also, you may never have auditioned before in your life and all the practical experience of auditioning you can get will help. Apply to as many schools that you feel suit you as you can afford. The competition is extremely fierce. Figures vary, but only a tiny percentage of applicants actually get accepted into the principal drama schools – and numbers applying have risen significantly in recent years.

Some fundamental considerations

If you enjoy acting and feel the need to take it up professionally, there are several other crucial factors, apart from training, to consider:

1) Will you be able to cope with having a fluctuating income which, unless you are extremely lucky, will probably be less than the average industrial wage? A recent survey revealed that fewer than 10 per cent of actors earned more than that statistical average and two-thirds earned less than £5,000 a year from acting – that is, roughly 20 per cent of the current average industrial wage which, in itself, is barely enough to live on in the London area.
2) Are you prepared to work unsociable hours and stay away from home for much of your working life?
3) Are you prepared to pay higher insurance premiums, be refused credit, and generally be regarded as unreliable and disorganised? I know that this is grotesquely unfair – actors have to adhere to the most incredible disciplines in their work – but that attitude among other people is a fact of our working lives.
4) Are you able to keep sufficiently fit in mind and body in order to work? Essentially there is no time available for you to miss

any rehearsals except under extreme circumstances, and only the bigger productions can afford the luxury of understudies during performance. In television, film and radio the days for recording are set far in advance and any absenteeism will cause an earthquake of disorganisation. A reputation for absenteeism, however reasonable the causes, will count significantly against you in the jobs market.

5) Do you have the personality to go out and sell yourself to other people – possibly several times a week?

6) Can you organise the funds to pay for all the equipment necessary to start out on an acting career? (See 'An actor's toolkit', pages 68–70.) I estimate that you'll need £1,000 at the very least for these essential items before you start earning any money from acting.

7) Are you aware that being an actor can seriously change your life? That perhaps should have read: 'As an actor it is difficult to be a normal human being.' But perhaps that's part of the reason why you want to be an actor – because you don't want to be Mr/Ms/Mrs Normal. It is a gypsy life – and like that minority you will be persecuted with lack of understanding from non-actors and suffer constant rejections. Being an actor puts a terrific mental and physical strain on you and your family and friends with its extremes of ups and downs. Your life will never be regular and ordered. Sometimes you will be on cloud nine, at others you will be deeply frightened and lonely as the months of unemployment seem to drag on for ever. If you really feel that you will be able to cope with such extremes of emotional temperature then perhaps you have the chemistry that can make you a professional actor.

Early preparations

If you are thinking about becoming an actor, read plays and read about acting (I have listed a number of suitable books in the Bibliography). Don't just read books; they can't give you up-to-date trends and happenings. Read *The Stage* (published every Thursday) for information, and publications like *Theatre Record*, and explore the internet for serious critical comment. Compare what they say with your own views. Ask other people what they think and, above all, watch acting critically. Examine television, theatre and films – don't just sit back and watch them mindlessly. Constructively criticise what you see. It is no use just saying you didn't like a production or an individual performance – work out why for your own future use.

If you want to be an actor in order 'to get up late and do funny walks in the evening' (Dan Leno) and lead a glamorous life – forget it. It's much, much harder work than is generally realised. On the positive side actors are usually among the kindest, warmest and most helpful of people. Cheap fiction (including some newspapers and magazines) will have you believe that the profession is riddled with vice and back-stabbing. This may be true among a small band of publicity seekers, but it is not true of over 99 per cent of this profession. You may be down and out of work, but you will always find a friend.

A drama school applicant's toolkit

Once you've decided that full-time training is for you, it is useful to plan ahead. I suggest that in the summer prior to submitting applications – that's over a year before taking up your place – you should:

1) Get as much information about potential schools from their websites in order to get a feel for where you might apply – and which courses. Also get a copy of the CDS's *Guide to Professional Training in Drama and Technical Theatre* from their website <www.drama.ac.uk>. This is updated every year (usually in late summer/early autumn) and it's well worth waiting for the most recent version before finally deciding. The same is true of individual drama schools' prospectuses.

2) Draw up a personal list of the parameters of each individual school you might apply to – audition requirements, funding systems, application mechanisms and deadlines. You'll find a downloadable list of these practical basics on my website. Note that occasional details of these change every year and it is essential to double-check with each and every school you're thinking of applying to.

3) Search for the audition speeches and songs that you're going to use. It's important that (a) they fit within the guidelines that the drama schools set, (b) they suit you and (c) they cover a range of types. *Important note:* These guidelines vary quite widely between schools. Usually you will be asked to prepare at least two audition speeches – often one from a 'classical' and one from a 'modern' play. Check carefully how each defines these terms as there are wide variations. Sometimes 'classical' simply means Shakespeare (1564–1616); more often his contemporaries (Fletcher, Jonson, Middleton, Marlowe, and the like) are included. A few schools

stretch the time period further with 'before 1800' (or similar), which opens up the possibility of the Restoration playwrights – that is, post-1660 and including Vanburgh, Sheridan, Farquhar and Wycherley. Currently, one school has 'written before 1900' – which opens up the option to include the likes of Ibsen, Wilde and much of Chekhov. Definitions of 'modern' (sometimes called 'contemporary') range from 'written after 1830' to 'written within the last twenty years' – with other schools specifying (one of) after 1870, 1900, 1945, 1950 or 1960. A few schools ask for three speeches; some give you a set list of 'classical' speeches to choose from; some ask for just two 'moderns'. A few offer advice: avoid certain speeches, character types, don't use speeches directed to the audience, for instance. Specialist courses (musical theatre, for example) also have other audition requirements.

4) Find, read and absorb the plays and shows that your selected speeches and songs come from. Also start the background work on each of your characters – allow at least three months for this!

5) Research the details of the funding systems of each course for which you might apply. Although most three-year courses are funded much like conventional university courses, a significant minority use the Dance and Drama Awards (DaDA) system. One-year courses are either self-funding or DaDA. If you're going to have to raise money to pay for all (or part) of your training, it's a good idea to start early. Some courses require applications via UCAS <www.ucas.ac.uk>. A few of these will accept applications directly or through UCAS. However, if you get offered a place at such a school and you've taken the former application route, you will still have to go through the UCAS bureaucracy. This can be very slow, so it's usually better to take the UCAS route in the first place to minimise any possible delays in getting your funding. Application deadlines vary from mid-January to the end of May – and some one-year courses have deadlines that are even later.

6) Start writing your personal statement. Most people find this very hard and it's important not to put it off until the last minute – more details on these in the next chapter.

'What are audition panels looking for?'

This is probably the most frequently asked question by drama school auditionees and some schools try to define this on their websites. In my opinion many of these are quite dry and uninspiring. Among the more evocative are: 'how connected you are', 'ability to create and sustain a character within an imagined world' and 'evidence of thought and feeling behind the actions and words'. There's also: 'spontaneity and immediacy' and 'openness and responsiveness to others' . . . In my experience of watching tens of thousands of audition speeches, I think the most vital qualities are spontaneous communication of (your) truth throughout each of your characters' journeys and your openness to change – that is, find a new truth at the slightest suggestion. Perhaps a simpler way of expressing this is: always be in the moment – never get stuck on railways lines. Each speech should be subtly different every time you do it – depending upon the immediate circumstances.

2: *Applying for training – the details*

The paperwork

Every drama school is different and it's important to be clear about each one to which you decide to apply. Although a minority require you initially to apply through UCAS (just one form and one deadline), all have their independent application forms, deadlines, audition requirements, etc. It can be useful to compile your own checklist.

Application deadlines You need to check these for each school. Around two-thirds have deadlines between mid-January and the beginning of March for three-year courses. Others are later and those for some one-year courses extend into the summer. It is also important to check with each school if there's a deadline for application for funding.

Application forms It is important to fill these in clearly, accurately (with correct spellings) and without exaggeration, let alone invention. Once again, it's what you can do in audition that matters most. Also, don't send off the forms until you have thoroughly rehearsed your speeches (and, if necessary, songs) – you could get called to audition at very short notice, though you might have to wait several months.

Note: If you have an illness or disability, be honest about it. CDS states that, 'All members of the Conference of Drama Schools are committed to a policy of widening access, to reflect the social and cultural diversity of society.' Some drama schools have more detail on their disability admissions policies on their websites.

Personal statements These are many people's nightmare, but they are important and it's a good idea to allow yourself plenty of time to write yours.

A few guidance notes:

- Don't go overboard about why you want to be an actor.
- Don't exaggerate – be grounded and straightforward.

- Don't just focus on the acting you've done. Acting is about recreating other people's lives, so all other experience is useful.
- Watch sentences don't become too long with lots of sub-clauses. Break them up into shorter sentences!
- Make sure that you spell proper names (play titles, writers, etc.) correctly.
- Titles should have capital letters at the start of each word – unless it's a joining word like 'in', 'the', etc in the middle of that title.
- Watch out for spellings that are correct according to a spell-checker, but have completely different meanings. For instance, 'there', 'their' and 'they're' are completely different words.
- Make sure that you use acceptable grammar and correct spelling.

It can be very useful to (a) get someone experienced to read your personal statement and (b) read it out loud to those you feel that you can trust for an honest reaction.

Audition speeches

For drama schools these are at the core of their decision-making processes, and not just for conventional acting courses. They are also important in the profession – although not as high a priority – and you can be expected to provide one without notice. 'A pet is not just for Christmas, it's for life', is also true for audition speeches. (One actor was told at a commercial casting, 'I just want to see some more.') Decades of watching people (in drama school and professional auditions) led me to research what makes an audition speech – acting without set, costumes, lighting, sound effects, an audience and other actors – succeed.

Many argue that doing audition speeches is a desperately artificial way of having their worth assessed. I would tend to agree but, however much you may hate them, you have to do them. Of course it's an artificial situation, but isn't acting about making artifice seem real? There are ways of making them work. (Think of Bob Hoskins in *Who Framed Roger Rabbit* and Steve Martin in *Dead Men Don't Wear Plaid* – both acting with beings who weren't really there.)

Essentially audition speeches should be self-contained, well chosen, well researched, well staged and well gauged for the space you are in and for whoever is watching you – just like a good production of a play. In fact an audition speech should be a 'mini-production' (of a 'mini-play') in its own right.

Overall, success comes through connection with the playwright's words, not simply your ability to learn them. You should think of characters in plays as real people, and remember that people say things because they have a need to do so. You should study each speech (and the play it's from) and work on the character's thoughts and feelings without learning a line. If you do this over a period of time, you'll gradually find that you learn the lines naturally, by absorption – even with a 'classical' speech.

Note: The commonly used term 'monologue' means a one-person play, which is slightly different.

Sources of speeches Don't just rely on plays that you know. You should be steadily expanding your knowledge of dramatic literature: seeing, reading, sitting in libraries and bookshops (especially second-hand ones and those in theatres like The Royal Court), even picking up an audition book to find inspiration for a playwright (previously unknown to you) whom you could explore further. Look in novels, at less well-known films and good journalism (for instance) for material that could be made into good drama. For example, Shakespeare copied (almost word for word) Queen Katherine's wonderful speech beginning 'Sir, I desire you do me right and justice . . .' (*Henry VIII*, Act 2, Scene 4) from the historical record. I have taken this idea further and found for my students a dramatic description of a mass killing, a musing on the pleasures of working with wood by the playwright Arthur Miller, a description of the hellish fighting at the siege of Stalingrad by a Nazi soldier, and many more. I found most of these by listening to Radio 4 and reading the quality newspapers. It's an almost limitless field that is well worth exploiting.

It's generally inadvisable to write your own speech(es). This rarely works because very few actors are good playwrights. However, if you are an exception and do decide to use a self-written piece, it can be a good idea to use a *nom de plume* (pen name) – you're promoting yourself as an actor, not a playwright. You should also be prepared to talk about the whole play, even if you haven't written it yet.

Note: There is a list of playwrights worth exploring for audition material on my website. There is also a wonderful website <www. doollee.com> which lists over a hundred thousand modern (that is, post 1956) plays with their writers, publishers and other details.

Books of audition speeches These are the main resource for those who don't yet know enough plays. An editor has done the hard graft of seeking out good speeches for you, but once you've fixed on a speech from one of them, get a copy of the whole play! This is where the problems start as they often come from plays that are out of print or, although performed, were never published. The other problems with these books are that (a) too many people use the speeches from them (which can become tedious for auditioners) and (b) many of the speeches that they contain are far too long and need cutting. You will probably be safe with a selection from a new book, but after a few years auditioners will have seen the bulk of its contents many times – and seen them done brilliantly.

I believe that the best use of these books is to discover more playwrights whose output you could explore further for audition material.

Note: See the 'Bibliography' for details of my *Alternative Shakespeare Auditions* books. Although they've been available for over a decade most of the speeches they contain are still not widely used on the audition circuit.

The original speech It is always useful to have 'original' pieces (that is, ones rarely used in audition), provided they're good and meet all the requirements listed elsewhere. There is no doubt that a good performance of a well-written unknown piece can advance your cause significantly. This is simply because if we've never seen it performed before then we have no benchmark against which to assess you – and assessing good acting is a highly inexact science – even for experienced auditioners.

Finding 'original' speeches It can be hard to know where to start when faced with all those shelves full of plays. Try focusing on the writers of speeches (from an audition speech book, for example) you've liked – they almost certainly wrote other plays.

It is possible to find out-of-print plays via libraries or book-finding services and by combing second-hand book shops. Some publishers (even a few playwrights' agencies) will organise a photocopy – for a fee. Also, The British Library (in theory) has a copy of every play ever performed in this country but there can be complications in actually getting hold of a copy. Start with your local library if you're determined to find a specific play; if they don't have it they may well be able to get it from another library (via the inter-library loan system), but be prepared for it to take a long time.

What types? 'Types' can mean, happy or sad, dark or light, weak or strong, and so on. As you become absorbed in your search for speeches, it can be terribly easy to find that many of what you've selected so far are close to just one of these. Periodically, do a review of your collection to check for sufficient variety in order to satisfy that common audition requirement – 'contrasting'.

Note: There are some wonderful monologues (that is, 'one-person plays') written by well-known writer-performers like Victoria Wood and Alan Bennett. It is generally better to avoid these as they were specifically written to be performed by the writer or another well-known performer. It is very, very hard for the viewer not to compare your rendition with the original. You'd be better off looking at monologues by less well-known (but just as good) writers like Peter Barnes, Michael Frayn, Ella Hickson, Jane Martin and Don Nigro.

The popular speech There are certain speeches (from Shakespeare, for instance) that get used a lot for audition. They usually meet all the requirements previously mentioned, but you can all-but guarantee that any auditioner has seen them done brilliantly on a previous occasion – either in audition or production. It is almost inevitable that your rendition of such a speech will be compared with that 'brilliant' performance, usually in an unfavourable light. However, if you are committed to such a speech and feel you consistently do it very well, then go for it. If unsure, you can test the water by giving your auditioner several alternatives including the popular one to choose from (but see 'You choose', page 31). If they have already seen eight speeches from Jim Cartwright's *Road* that day, you'll probably be asked for one of your other options.

Note: You will find lists of popular Shakespeare speeches on my website. I will not attempt a similar list of modern speeches as these change constantly – you'll have to ask around to discover whether a speech is currently in this category.

Shakespeare and the classics Unfortunately, too many people perform these indifferently. Too many renditions seem as dead as their writers. The problem is that they are remote – in language and in content – from our direct experience and therefore usually require much more research, thought and preparation than a modern speech.

On the plus side there is no doubt that Shakespeare not only had a great understanding of mankind but also managed to communicate it in the most wonderful language. Many of his contemporaries (and those that followed) are also worth exploring for something 'original' – especially for women.

'Modern' and 'classical' (and 'period') You'll find a wide range of definitions of these terms – and it's important that you're clear about what's required for each audition.

I'd like to add my own definitions. To me, 'modern' means a speech in which the language is easily comprehensible to the modern ear; 'classical' where it's not immediately so. By these definitions the dividing line lies somewhere around the middle of the nineteenth century. I suggest that we need another, in-between category: 'period' – that is, plays written in 'easily comprehensible' language, but from a time when the general social mores were very different from now. It is wise to check specifically what will be required.

Note: A modern translation of a foreign 'classical' play is not usually acceptable under the 'classical' heading.

Content Too many people fail because they choose to do an indifferent speech – that is, one that is badly written, doesn't make sense without a knowledge of the rest of the play, lacks content, etc. Essentially you should go for pieces that have good 'journeys' – just like a good play.

It can be useful to find speeches that enable you to show your special skills (singing or juggling, for instance), but don't try to cram so much in that the sense is lost in a firework display of technical virtuosity. At the other extreme, avoid something that requires performance at one pace or on one note.

Never set out to shock deliberately through content and/or crude language. That is not to say that you shouldn't use speeches with shocking content; rather, don't set out with the specific idea of 'shocking' your auditioners as many people seem to intend. We've heard most of it before. I cannot describe how mind-numbingly tedious audition days can become when peppered with such speeches.

Warning: There is now a lot of free audition material available on the internet. Much of it is indifferently written; however, I have come across the occasional gem.

Shape Make sure that each of your pieces has a decent shape. Once again, it should be 'like a good play', with a beginning, middle and ending. Generally, avoid choosing something which is a section taken from a longer speech; such pieces tend to do nothing for you because they usually don't have a good shape. This is not always the case, but it is often better to take snippets out of a long speech so that the essence, or overall journey, is still there. Don't be beguiled by beautiful language; be ruthless in order to achieve that shape within your target time. Your speech should be a 'mini-play' in its own right.

Length An audition piece should be about two minutes long (that's roughly 300 words), which feels very short while you are doing it. (It is considerably shorter than the three-and-a-half minute average in a mini-survey I once carried out.) You may argue that there is no way you can show enough of your skills as an actor in such a short time. True, you can't show everything, but you can give a very good indication of your potential – like a good television commercial. And you don't want to use up too much of the overall time allotted to you on one thing.

It doesn't matter if it's less than two minutes, provided it's self-contained. In fact it is probably better to aim for less, but don't compromise your speech for the sake of brevity. Doing it fast, simply to crack the two-minute barrier, will get you nowhere. The impact of a short speech (even one lasting just a minute) that meets all the requirements listed elsewhere in this section can be tremendous. Also, auditioners can generally tell if you are of interest to them within the first thirty seconds or so.

If you time your speech yourself, you are probably about 10–20 per cent under the actual playing time. The sheer act of self-timing makes most people speed up.

Stick within your 'playing range' Your speeches should be within your 'playing range'. At school/college, etc. you may well have played all kinds of parts, in many different age ranges. For auditions it is important to select characters who could be within a few years of your actual age.

Accents If you choose to do a speech written in an accent not your own, make sure you can do that accent well enough to convince a native. Some people choose to translate such a speech into an accent with which they are more comfortable, and this can work. However, in doing this be careful that you are not sacrificing too much of the quality of the original language. Some auditioners can be quite purist about this, and will only countenance speeches done in their original accents – particularly well-known ones.

An example of a famous writer who doesn't seem to 'translate' is

Tennessee Williams – something to do with all that heat and humidity. And there are many others.

Note: It's very tedious to see comedy Shakespeare speech done in a 'cod' West Country accent. If you can genuinely do one of the many variants of this accent, then that's fine, but his language works in every other regional accent in which I've heard it done.

Stringing together It is possible to make a complete speech by 'stringing together' short speeches from a piece of dialogue, but make sure that the end result no longer relies upon responses from other people. It is absolutely useless to leave pauses while you say the other lines in your head, yet people do it. I've known the odd eccentric think it all right to ask the auditioner to read in the other person's lines, and one who threw them in, like asides, himself.

It is legitimate to change the order of dialogue so used, provided it makes a complete and comprehensible speech. However, the art of such editing is quite difficult and can take some time and experiment to get right.

I've also seen a wonderful rendition of a speech that was constructed from three characters talking with each other via intercoms. The actor very excitingly switched instantly back and forth between characters.

Tip: It is a good idea to retype an edited speech, so that you see it as a complete speech in its own right – and not as a collection of crossings-out, interspersed with the words you're going to say.

How many? I suggest that you should build up a repertoire of at least six completely different pieces (if not more) of which you are very sure. This might seem rather a lot, but you need at least that number to ensure a good range to choose from. (When Janet McTeer first auditioned for The Manchester Royal Exchange, she eventually did six speeches because they 'liked her so much'.) Even if you're only asked for two or three, you never know when an alternative might be useful – such as when someone does one of your speeches brilliantly immediately before you. Also each time you work on a new speech, you'll gain deeper insights into acting. Overall, I suggest finding (at least) three modern and three classical speeches – plus any from lists you're required to select from.

Note: It is usually not a good idea to use those 'list' speeches (see 'The popular speech', page 18) at other auditions – unless you can perform them brilliantly even when you're feeling terrible.

Trying on Try reading any speech that looks good to you (on the page) out loud in front of someone else before you start rehearsing it – a teacher or youth theatre leader, perhaps. If you do this, you'll get an even better idea of whether each speech really suits (and grabs) you. It's a bit like buying clothes: you see a pair of trousers (say) that look good on the hanger but sometimes you will feel completely different about them when you try them on. The opposite can also occur: you feel indifferent about a speech on the page; you read it out loud and it feels much, much better.

Read the whole play You must read and absorb the whole play, not just to inform the particular speech you are doing but also to be able to discuss it afterwards. It can be useful to read (or see) a few other plays by the same playwright.

Tip: When reading a play, read with your ears as well as your eyes. If necessary, read sections out loud. You'll be better able to get inside what's going on underneath the words.

Research You must also get a sense of the world that each of your characters lives in. This is not to suggest that you write an academic thesis, but to provide imaginative stimuli that will give more life to the world of the play. For instance, a room lit by oil lamps feels completely different from one filled with fluorescent light. (I'll never forget my grannie talking about the introduction of mains gas to her family home in the 1890s: 'We got rid of those smelly old oil lamps.' She didn't get mains electricity for over another decade.) Don't just research facts of living but read novels and look at paintings from the period. For plays set since the invention of photography, sound and video recording, there are even more useful imagination stimulators available. Also, if possible, visit locations where each character could have lived.

Rehearsing your speeches

What are you bringing on stage? You must bring your character's life history (gleaned from the play and supplemented by your imagination) into your performance. As the character (i.e. in the first person), write notes of all the bits of information (big and small) that you find (and invent) in order to build his/her life. Most of what you bring won't be obvious to your auditioner(s). However, it will be immediately obvious if that 'life history' is not present. Just as 90 per cent of an iceberg is underwater, a similar proportion of a good performance is also hidden but must be there, underneath, to support that performance.

It is particularly important to be clear about what actually provokes the character to start speaking – the ignition that kicks your engine into life. Try running a brief film in your imagination, culminating in the event (for instance, a statement or a gesture from someone else) that is your cue.

Your invisible partner(s) If you choose a speech addressing another character, then it is vital that that other person (and how they are reacting through the speech) is clear to you. It is generally better to imagine an adaptation of someone you know rather than 'borrow' someone you've only seen on a flat screen – there can be a huge difference in how we perceive others between two and three dimensions.

It's not just them (and how they are reacting); it's also important to be clear about your relationship. As well as imagining what your character's lover looks like, you must also know the feel of their touch, their smell, and so forth – and many more personal aspects.

If there is more than one other present, you have to be clear about each one. If it's a crowd, it can be useful to imagine a few individual faces – and their reactions.

It is also important that any other people, places and events mentioned in the speech are similarly clear in your imagination.

Your invisible circumstances You should also bring the location, clothes and practical items with you – in your imagination. (*Note:* I could have written 'set, costumes and props', but I believe that it's important to think of everything being real and not items constructed for a production.) I believe that auditionees neglecting these is the cause of a high proportion of failed and indifferent speeches. It's not just the visual images, it's also what the other senses give you – the brush of a summer breeze across your face, for instance. Auditionees tell me that this is hard – I don't see why this should be. Plays are not performed in real rooms (there will be at least one wall missing) and every play has at least one non-appearing character mentioned – these absences are filled by the actors' imaginations. Do the same with these 'absences' in the audition circumstances.

It isn't just the major features that you should think about, but also the apparently minor details – for instance, that mark on a wall that suddenly catches your character's eye. It can be a good idea to draw a map (or groundplan) so that the whole geography of your circumstances is clear to you – and fill out your imaginary location with as much detail as possible.

Interpretation As you are creating a 'mini-production' of a 'mini-play' (the 'child' of its 'parent play'), I believe that it's legitimate to make changes to the given circumstances of the speech when it occurs in the play, especially if such changes enhance your audition performance. (After all, a child can never lose the genetic code of its parents, but he/she will evolve their own personality, which will be different.) However, be prepared to justify it – and don't get defensive. There's usually no harm in honest disagreement.

Journey There will often be some variations between characters as they appear in the play and as they appear in your speech when it has been separated from the play. The journey travelled in that speech within the context of the play will be different from the journey you have to travel when doing the speech on its own.

That voyage of discovery Be aware of the 'voyage of discovery' that shapes your speech. Don't anticipate the end at the beginning. This is a common fault in rehearsal, which is easily corrected – but a remarkable number of people fall into this trap when performing their audition speeches.

It can be very useful to write out a speech with each sentence (or even each phrase) on a separate line. It then appears less of a 'block' of words on the page and more a series of separate, but connected, thoughts and ideas. It is also a good idea to leave sufficient space between each line to write notes on what the impulse (or shift in thought) is to go on to say the next thing, and the next, and so on. (Also see 'The "need"', page 33.)

All of this also applies to classical verse – where sentences can span several lines. Not only will you get a clearer idea of the whole sentence (and what relates to what within it), but it'll also be easier to see where each new 'impulse' occurs. Some purists maintain that turning verse into prose is a kind of literary crime. What I'm suggesting is only a temporary measure. Once you've understood properly how the sentences work, simply go back to the verse form.

Beginnings If you start your speech nebulously, your auditioner(s) probably won't take in what you are doing for the first few seconds and may miss vital information that could make the rest of it a complete puzzle to them. You need to find a way of starting your speech that will grab their attention from the very beginning. This doesn't mean that the beginning has to be loud, simply that it should be positive and effective – almost as if the house lights are dimming and the curtain rising on . . . you!

Note: It can also be very useful to incorporate a simple movement to start a speech – a turn of the head, for instance.

Endings It's also important to be clear as to why a character stops speaking after talking for two minutes. You need to be clear what your character's final thought is – crucially stopping his/her flow.

Shakespeare Many people find his works daunting (even alien) and difficult to connect with. I believe that this is because:

1) he and his plays have been put on an academic pedestal to be worshipped – and take exams in;
2) the way that he used language is unfamiliar;
3) his characters and plots seem so remote – even, silly/naïve – to us.

In order to give you a perspective:

1) Shakespeare wrote – not for future academic study – but to engage audiences. He did this to make some money for himself. We don't know much about his life, but we do know that he died a wealthy man.
2) Just as word usages vary across the country (and the English-speaking world) nowadays, they varied across centuries. For instance, read Dickens. The way his characters speak may be closer than Shakespeare's to how we speak now, but it's still different. Recently, I watched a modern play set in a remote, rural part of the USA – the words were modern yet phrased very differently from current English usage, but still engaging and communicative. I could quote zillions of other examples. If Shakespeare had written in language that felt 'alien' to his audiences, they would have stopped paying to come to see the plays.
3) Shakespeare's world was so very different from ours. It was a

world where democracy barely existed, education, medicine and sanitation were primitive – and there was no mains gas, electricity or water. (*Note:* It's only within the last century-and-a-bit that all these now commonplace essentials have become the norm in the civilised world – some more recently than others.) It was a world in which what we'd now regard as unfair was normal; a world in which what we'd now regard as unreal was regarded as possible; a world in what we'd now regard as obvious was not necessarily the case. Nowadays, we easily accept (for instance) that Mary Poppins can fly unaided – in a film, so why not 'easily accept' that Puck can fly around the earth 'in forty minutes' – also 'unaided'? Nowadays, we can feel fairly sure that a sudden death will be investigated – in Shakespeare's time it could easily be concealed. Nowadays, we take it for granted that we can travel thousands of miles in less than a day – in Shakespeare's time it was only the rich who could travel a hundred miles in a day. There are thousands of other huge differences between then and now . . .

Worry less about big events of Shakespeare's world! Get inside the real lives and circumstances of those who lived four centuries ago and you're part way there.

Warning! Never, ever try to copy another's performance! Mimicry is not the same as acting.

Some practical considerations

New speeches It is essential to try a new piece in front of someone else first. If you don't have a friendly director to help you (and even if you have, be wary: directing a play is different from directing an audition speech), almost anybody else in the profession will do as a first-time audience. A speech always feels different when done in front of an audience – just like a play.

The last-minuter Don't try to get a new speech together at the last minute. An audition speech, like a performance, needs a good gestation/preparation period to come to full fruition. The rehearsal time needed varies from person to person and from speech to speech, but the 'last-minuter' rarely succeeds. A half-known, half-prepared speech – however suitable – will waste everybody's time and put you right out of the running. I would suggest that a new speech needs at least a month's preparation – conscious and subconscious – before its first airing.

Staging Once you've done all the work set out in the previous paragraphs, you need to think carefully about how you stage each piece. Too many people seem inclined to put in extraneous moves either to compensate for the lack of the other character(s), or because they think the speech is boring if it doesn't contain enough movement. If you are properly connecting to character and circumstances, the moves will follow naturally from each impulse. However, much of the effect of your performance will be dissipated if your auditioners don't see enough of your face and especially your eyes. In general (unless it is an address to the audience), they should be able to see three-quarters of your face for at least half the duration of the speech. To achieve this, orientate the other character(s) and circumstances to suit each audition situation. For instance, place the imaginary person to whom you're talking at around 45 degrees to left or right in front of you. If your map (or groundplan) is clear in your mind, then it should be simple to angle it appropriately. There is no point in placing a chair specifically to mark another character or using a mark on a wall – or even the hat-stand which I once saw used as the object of some singular passions. If you do use such objects you'll usually find yourself concentrating on that object rather than your partner(s) – they should be clearly lodged in your imagination so that the auditioner can see them through you. Also, don't think that you have to stare at one place continually just to make it clear that he or she is there. Remember: it is only in certain circumstances that we look directly at someone for extended periods.

Chairs A warning about chairs. There is a common variety of chair, as familiar as the bollard is to the motorway, that inhabits many popular audition venues. It can serve all kinds of functions as well as the simple one of being sat upon. However, don't rely on the well-known weight and balance of these plastic and steel functionaries for crucial elements of your well-prepared speech. You may suddenly find only chairs with arms or a room filled with wobbly ones. Be prepared to adapt to whatever form of seating is available.

Tip 1: Do a brief check on the mechanics of your audition chair before you start your speech. For instance, you don't want to be thrown by the fact that the back is lower than that of the chair you rehearsed with.

Tip 2: If your audition chair represents a different type of seat (a low, backless bench, for instance), sit on the chair as though you're sitting on that 'bench'. You can achieve the feel of this by placing your bottom near the front of the seat and having no contact with the back.

Props Avoid using props. As you haven't got a proper set, costume or lighting, too much of the visual emphasis goes on to the prop and consequently away from you. It is amazing how riveting even a small piece of paper produced for one of the numerous 'letter' speeches can become. Props can be mimed: that mime doesn't need to be brilliant. And think how much easier it is to put down an imaginary glass on an imaginary table, without making a sound at the wrong moment. In using any imaginary prop, remember not just the shape as you hold it in your hand but also its weight and its impact on your sense of touch. The only exception to this can be a prop introduced briefly and then quickly discarded. Even then, make sure its impact doesn't take the focus away from the rest of the speech. Some find it useful to have some kind of token secreted on their person to help connect with the character.

A service and an MOT Be careful your speeches don't go stale. (The better the writing, the more chance of them staying fresh; there will always be more layers of that 'subtextual onion' to peel off.) Audition speeches, like cars, need regular servicing or reassessment. If a favourite old 'banger' has done you good service in the past, make sure it's still roadworthy before you bring it out again. If not, trade it in for something new. However, unlike cars, you can sometimes find new life in a speech neglected for a while – say, a few months.

Essentially, each time you do a speech it should still have that freshness, that need to communicate and that willingness to give blood that personifies a first night. A second-night performance will not do. It is no excuse to blame the cold ambience of the room you are doing it in.

'Should I take a copy of my speech with me?' Some like to carry a copy of their speech with them as a security blanket. Most auditioners won't want to know about it. However, there are occasions when one is asked for, so it can be handy to have a copy of such a speech with you; even better, take the complete play with you.

Finally Ask yourself: 'Is my speech and my presentation of it a good piece of theatre – that is, a good "mini-production" of my "mini-play"?'

Performing your speeches

Each presentation of a speech has to have the raw energy of a first performance. Unlike a first night where the only new factor – at least, in theory – is the audience, you have to face numerous new and possibly unexpected factors when doing your audition speech. You need to be not only well rehearsed but also well prepared for how to cope with all the peripherals that are other people's responsibilities when you are actually doing a production. You are your own stage management, wardrobe department, front-of-house manager, and so forth.

'Act in here?' I don't think any audition room is entirely satisfactory. They can be dirty and unkempt, too hot or too cold, too big or too small, have inconvenient echoes, have barely adequate waiting facilities and/or be hard to find down a maze of corridors. You'll be very fortunate if the whole session has only road traffic as a background noise. You have to be prepared to adjust the presentation of your speech(es) to each context – for example, by fractionally slowing down and enhancing your diction slightly if there's an unavoidable echo or scaling down your movement in a small room.

It's your space You should regard the space in which you are doing your speech as your stage with which to do whatever you wish – as long as you have due reverence for the fabric of the building, for your auditioners and their goods and chattels. Move the chairs if you need to, take your shoes off if that's necessary, and so on – but don't ask if it's all right to do so. It can get very tedious for an auditioner if you keep on asking permission every time you want to change something. Providing it doesn't affect your audience directly, just get on with what is necessary for your performance. Don't ask where to stand; your actor's instinct should tell you the optimum place for what you are about to do. Especially, don't ask permission to start, even if it's only with one of those pathetic little enquiring looks – another way of undermining yourself in your auditioners' eyes. Once you've been given your cue, it's all yours and in your own time. (See 'A pause for thought', page 32.)

Natural hazards Be aware of natural hazards in the room: for example, a low afternoon sun pouring through the windows that blinds you as soon as you happen to turn into it. Don't, however, stand in the deepest shadow; nobody wants an auditionee who cannot find his or her light. Your auditioner will probably be sympathetic if the unexpected suddenly interrupts you, but it really is your responsibility to spot this kind of thing beforehand and adjust accordingly. If it is something impossible to anticipate, then aim to recover as quickly as possible and get back into your speech. After all, if something goes wrong during a performance, you don't just stop until it's put right – you continue as best you can, and 99.9 per cent of the time nobody in the audience will notice that anything went wrong.

Explanations Minimise explanations about your speech. Ask yourself if you need them at all. In fact the best speeches are self-contained and don't need explanation beyond the character's name and the title and the writer of the play. Whatever their individual faults, most auditioners do know a lot of plays, the characters within them and who wrote them. Be careful not to insult auditioners by telling them what they already probably know (for example, 'Hamlet from *Hamlet* by William Shakespeare'). However, make sure you know the title and writer of more obscure plays and be prepared to discuss them. Sometimes, in the process of getting inside the character, auditionees forget to give these basic details. I don't think this matters (I enjoy trying to work them out for myself), but some auditioners have a nasty habit of interrupting auditionee's preparations with demands like 'What are you doing, then?' If you do forget and are interrupted in this way, don't be so thrown that you rush into your speech.

Tip 1: It is a good idea to incorporate the seemingly simple task of announcing what you're doing into your rehearsals. Then it will become ingrained in your performances.

Tip 2: It can be helpful to do your announcement from a neutral place, then use the walk to your acting space to help get into character.

Your auditioner as the other character Some people try to use their auditioner as the other character for the purposes of their speech. This is not necessarily a good idea. It can work but is fraught with pitfalls. First of all, do you need to ask permission beforehand? Politeness dictates that you should. After all, you are asking the auditioner to do the job of being in your play. He or she may say, 'Yes, of course,' but has probably been asked the same question in every other session of the day; it can get very tedious. Even if it is all right, the auditioner may well want to drop out of character to write notes and consequently won't be a consistent partner. Even if everything seems fine, your auditioner certainly won't react the way you'd always imagined – which could throw you. A sympathetic director once volunteered to be Brutus to a friend of mine's Portia, even going as far as to stand up and move with her (*Julius Caesar*, Act 2, Scene 1). She'd rehearsed Portia starting by approaching from behind. The director dutifully turned his back, and she started. After one line he turned round, totally throwing my friend who had envisaged Brutus turning at a later point. They started again. My friend, then only just starting in the profession, was getting quite nervous by this time, and when the director turned after the third line – again too early! – she was a heap on the floor and could not for the life of her go on. The director was still sympathetic. 'But', he said, 'I've got to watch what you're doing!'

So, in general, don't use your auditioner – unless you feel it happening naturally during your speech. (I've enjoyed being part of a number of speeches in which this has spontaneously occurred.) Finally, if your speech has sexual intent, be especially careful about using your auditioner as the object of your character's passion. This can lead to irritation and embarrassment. Some men seem to take great delight in pointing speeches of male sexual superiority straight at a woman in the room. That is very stupid. *Note:* Very occasionally auditioners will request that you address a speech to them. If this is the case, you should be responsive to what they give you.

'You choose' Auditionees sometimes come up with several alternatives on being asked: 'Well, what speeches have you got?' That's good – they are well prepared – but they often trip up when they cannot make up their minds which one to do. This may not matter – the auditioner may enjoy choosing one for you to do – but don't then suddenly say: 'I don't feel like doing that.' If a speech is not going to feel right for that particular ambience, don't suggest it. Be crisp and positive about the decision-making.

Preparation Do give yourself a moment to check your chair (if needed) and the geography of your performance in this particular space.

A pause for thought Do give yourself that moment of thought before starting a speech – a moment to immerse yourself within your character and circumstances. Almost everybody understands that it can be hard to change gear from chatting to acting. Don't think that you are wasting time – it'll only be a few seconds, and your auditioner will almost certainly have something else to write down before concentrating on you again. (For most auditionees a 'few seconds' feels much, much longer in these stressed circumstances.)

However, don't take too long to prepare for your speech with lots of heavy breathing or pacing about or even just standing quietly in a corner. That may be what you have to do before you go on stage, but most auditioners, however understanding, will begin to wonder what kind of lunatic you are and whether you are going to take up precious rehearsal time with these warm-ups. Your 'pause for thought' should be as brief as you can make it without showing your inner turmoil. Properly done, this can be riveting to watch.

Starting One of the hardest aspects of doing a speech is starting it from cold. If you are onstage at the beginning of a stage production (especially on a first night), you'll experience an immense – and, for some, terrifying – feeling of excitement and power as the audience goes quiet. You should aim to recreate this feeling just before you start your speech. It'll give you tingles up your spine and put a real 'kick' into your speech. This will communicate to your auditioners and make them really look at you – even if they've had their heads down scribbling in the preceding seconds.

Tip: To help stimulate this process, get the smell of dust into your imagination – it's the pervading smell of any theatre.

Communication and clarity You may well 'feel' your speech, but are you communicating it? You may be in a small room with only a couple of auditioners and your character needs to speak quietly, but are the words reaching your audience? Are they clear to that audience? It's not just about adjusting your volume – it's also about your clarity. I'm not suggesting that you should focus all your energies into enunciating every word carefully but that you should aim to 'tweak up' your clarity (especially those hard consonants like 'd's and 't's) – just as you would when trying to communicate to officialdom in urgent circumstances. It can be a good idea to articulate through the words of each of your speeches (without thinking about the acting) a number of times. When you go back to acting, you'll find a sufficient level of clarity embedded within them.

Overall, you should make that room your theatre with your auditioners sitting in the best seats in the stalls (the ones reserved for the critics on a first night) with the rest of your imaginary audience ranged in front of and behind them – and aim just beyond the limits of that space.

Don't blast your auditioners out of their seats either. In prior conversation, listen out for any echoes. If you detect one of these, simply aim to be slightly clearer and don't shout.

The 'need' There is a 'need' that drives any speech: two minutes is a long time for someone to keep on talking. A long speech is a series of connected thoughts and ideas; underneath there has to be the 'need' to talk at such length. We all know people who 'go on' too much in everyday life – the odd person is able to sustain attention because of the energy and 'need' to communicate. The same is true on stage and in the audition.

Remember that your character hasn't usually planned to say so much. Essentially, the circumstances provoke the 'need' for them to add more, and more, and . . . (Also see 'That voyage of discovery', page 24.)

Your whole body Another trait of auditionees is to forget about their bodies. Maybe it's because of the artificiality of the situation and they wouldn't do it on stage – but how is the auditioner to know that? Just because you haven't got the proper costume, props and furniture it doesn't mean your body isn't part of your speech.

Stopping If you do need to stop during a piece – it's started badly, for instance – do it positively and calmly, and do it without a grovelling apology. You may feel terrible but you have to get yourself out of the mess without becoming embarrassing. You can even capitalise on having handled it well. A brief (and positive) 'Sorry, I'll start again' or whatever won't be held against you.

Don't stop, however, if you still feel connected to your character and circumstances – even if the lines are going wrong. If you are connected a momentary pause is all you need to find your words again.

'Where from?' If you do have to go back a bit, don't ask 'Where from?' The auditioners almost certainly won't know the exact words of the speech, with the odd famous exceptions. Make your own decision.

Again, be in control of your stage area and solve your own problems without recourse to your auditioners. You wouldn't ask an audience what to do if something went wrong during a performance.

Clever tricks If you've got a novel way of introducing your speech, make sure you really can carry off this trick and don't leave your auditioners so bemused that they aren't taking in the first thirty seconds or so of what you are saying. For instance, one woman started her speech outside the room. She simply said, 'Would you excuse me a minute?' and walked out of the door. She suddenly started yelling – at her imaginary husband, as it transpired. It was all so real that none of the four of us quite realised that this was her speech, in spite of the fact that she'd been given her cue. She'd have been better advised to start inside the room – probably with her back to us – and then all would have been clear. Or she could have simply said, 'I'm starting from outside the door.'

It is probably better to have a novel way of finishing. For instance, I once auditioned someone who did one of that day's 'Ritas'. Her first attempt was very inhibited, so we discussed it for a few moments before I asked her to try it again. Very quickly she started to fly, and I found myself roaring with laughter. Her *pièce de résistance* was to jump up and sit on my table to punctuate the end of the speech. It was very exciting. She claimed it wasn't premeditated, that it simply came out of the new impetus she'd found in the speech. Whatever – it worked! Not every auditioner would have been happy about that. You should assess very carefully whether you can do such a thing to your auditioners. And be careful of their precious – and confidential – pieces of paper.

Finishing When you finish you should keep the final thought in your mind and gently freeze for a moment, just as you would if you're left onstage at the end of a scene in a play. Then fade the imaginary stage lighting (and close the curtains) at a suitable rate. (That 'moment' should last about a second. If you're unsure, say a multi-syllable word like 'Mississippi' in your head.) Then, without looking your interviewer(s) in the eye, relax back to your normal self, ready to move on to whatever your interviewer wants to do next. Many find the 'not looking your interviewer(s) in the eye' difficult, and a few even think that it might seem rude. However, if you do make eye contact at that crucial moment, you'll probably start to feel very vulnerable – and give out the vibe that you're not confident about your performance. Whatever you may really feel about that performance, there's nothing else that you can now do, except wait.

There may be a silence; your auditioners may well want to write notes on what you've done. Just settle down and let them get on with it. Don't be thrown by that aching pause. You should wait quietly. The ball is now very definitely in the auditioners' court to restart the session.

Tip: After you've been through the 'finishing' process don't make eye contact until an auditioner speaks.

Pitfalls on finishing Some auditionees opt for a 'Thank you', or 'That's it', at the end. Sometimes this is combined with a smile; with others it comes across as sheer arrogance (watch the way some actors do curtain calls). If you've got a good enough ending, it'll be clear that you've finished. The auditioner may not respond immediately, but you should have clearly established that the 'ball' is now firmly in his or her 'court'. It's much better to say nothing.

Too many auditionees tend to give an apologetic little smile to indicate that they've finished their speech. That smile can seem like an expression of how badly you think you did the speech. You may feel you have done it badly, but that's your subjective view. Let the auditioner(s) be the judge and find a positive way of becoming yourself again.

A friend offered the following analysis of this: 'The English are not supposed to show off. Performing at an audition is different from performing on stage in that the audience at a theatre is listening to the contents of a play rather than making too many value judgements about the acting. The audition speech should be a "mini-play", and involve the auditioners as audience, but the actor feels the difference and artificiality, hence the "apologetic little smile".' I understand this, but it doesn't alter the fact that 'the apologetic little smile' is a particularly undermining phenomenon to any actor's credibility.

'Thank you' There may be a vague 'Thank you' or 'Right', even 'Mmmm' from the auditioners at the end of your speech. Don't read anything into these vague expostulations. If you do you'll start to undermine yourself. We auditioners are usually thinking about what we're going to write down about your efforts. That thinking process is dominant and what comes out of our mouths is merely our acknowledgement that you've finished – an attempt at politeness that doesn't come out quite right. (I hear myself doing this constantly, but have never found a way round it.)

Switching off It is respected that it can take a few seconds to come back to reality, particularly if it's a very emotional speech. Don't worry about this. A few moments' recovery should be respected. However, don't overindulge! I will never forget a woman who did a wonderfully passionate speech from Arnold Wesker's *Four Seasons* and ended up in floods of tears. She had done it extremely well but when it was over she simply could not stop crying and had to be taken from the room and given time to recover. What would have happened if she'd had to get similarly emotional on stage and then immediately go on to do a comic scene, as can occur? This is an extreme example which exemplifies the need to look very carefully at how you change back to reality.

'Why did you choose that speech?' This is probably one of the most common questions afterwards. Often, it's simply the auditioner's way of continuing the conversation and sometimes it's because the speech seems radically different from your perceived personality. Whatever the motivation, it's much better to have some positive explanation beyond the often limp 'I like it' or 'My teacher suggested it'. Anyway, your speech choices should have been reached through long research for what suits you.

'Why don't you try that again – differently?' Don't get so stuck into a way of doing a speech that you cannot do it in any other way put to you. Some auditioners like to work on speeches. You should understand the insides of each speech so well that you could do it in whatever 'different' way is suggested – however absurd it may seem.

'That was dreadful' It is rare for auditioners to tell you exactly what they thought of your efforts – even rarer for somebody to say: 'That was dreadful.' If you know, without paranoia, that you've done your speech (or reading) badly – and know you are capable of doing it very well – and the auditioner is on the verge of saying 'Next, please', try to find a way of discussing your failure positively. This is very hard to judge properly, but it is worth looking for the opportunity without seeming pushy or paranoid. (There may even be time to do it again.) You could climb some way back into their esteem.

Encore! If there's time, and the auditioners are inclined, you might be asked to do an extra speech. Your auditioners may well feel that they have learnt enough from what you've already done – this is not necessarily a bad sign and can in fact bode well. Anyway, an extra speech will take up more precious time.

If you are asked to do an extra speech, make sure it's sufficiently contrasting. If the idea isn't mentioned, don't suggest it! And don't, as I have seen several people do, go straight from one speech to another with hardly a pause between – let alone asking whether another was wanted or not.

Tip: If you are asked to do an extra speech it's a good idea to make the staging as different as possible from your first efforts.

Advice Some auditioners give constructive advice. In general, take that as a compliment, even if they are critical. Nobody will waste time and energy giving notes if they didn't at least like some aspect of you and your work. However, one auditioner's constructive notes can become another's criticisms. In rehearsal an actor will take a note and try it out. Sometimes it doesn't work, and the moment has to be looked at again. Maybe it was only half-right. In an audition there is usually no time to rehearse that note to see if it works for you. So, when you do try it, and it perhaps doesn't quite work, you have no recourse to its originator for further amplification. Take such notes as suggestions to be utilised or discarded as suits you and your speech. That's how rehearsals should be anyway.

Audition songs

Much of that which applies to audition speeches also applies to audition songs.

Selecting and preparing your songs

A singing audition doesn't mean just standing there and hitting the right notes in the right rhythm at the right moments. You have to think and prepare carefully in order to succeed – and ensure that you act them well.

Your repertoire If you're applying for musical theatre courses, you should have at least six (if not a lot more) suitable and varied songs well prepared. In general your selection should be from musicals. Pop songs past and present (even the beautiful Palestrina piece I once heard) are almost always unhelpful in the assessment process. Here is a list of categories on which you could base your repertoire (if you're applying to other courses, I'd suggest that you opt for at least two songs):

1) a slow ballad (the ultimate singing test) – to show range and vocal quality – from a show like *Nine* or *Secret Garden* (but be careful; if you can hit a top C on a good day, then remember that an audition is rarely a 'good day'. Play safe and go for an A);
2) an up-tempo song – to show energy, rhythm and character – from a show like *Sweet Charity* or *Hair*;
3) an up-tempo, more modern rock song from a show like *Tommy* or *Rent*;
4) a slow modern rock ballad from a show like *Fame*;
5) a patter or comedy song, for example, Noël Coward, Gilbert and Sullivan, Tom Lehrer, Victoria Wood – a definite option for those with limited ability;
6) a song within which you can show off any special abilities that you have – like speaking Russian, playing the trombone or tap-dancing.

Note: The above-mentioned songs are well-known examples. I suggest that you don't actually use them – they're done a lot. As with audition speeches, don't try to write a song yourself or do one written by a friend unless you're supremely confident of it. An indifferent song can make you seem indifferent. Also, make sure each of your choices will make a good piece of 'theatre'; if they come from good musicals, then they should do.

The accompanist Not all accompanists are good sight-readers so make some of your songs ones that are not too complicated if they're not generally known. For example, obscure Sondheim, Bernstein, Weill or Jason Robert Brown songs are intriguing but are probably out for all except the most accomplished accompanists. That is not to say avoid these composers completely, but select the less complex of their songs – 'Send In the Clowns' or 'Being Alive' would be fine in this respect. (Again, these specific songs are done too much.) Some of these more complex songs have had their arrangements simplified when reprinted in songbooks – but beware: 'simplified arrangements' can be banal. Essentially, if a specific song makes the accompanist 'glaze over', have a simpler one in reserve.

Length Make sure your songs are not too long. There are some wonderful songs from *A Chorus Line* but they go on for five minutes or more. Like speeches, songs can be cut. They should be no longer than two or two and a half minutes – and preferably less.

Interpretation Don't just copy the famous performance of a standard or the interpretation of a current hit – it will show singular lack of imagination on your part. For instance, as a devotee of early Elvis Presley I get very bored with people who do pale imitations of his songs. There is absolutely no point in trying to imitate the inimitable. However, I once heard a marvellous – totally original – rendition of 'Heartbreak Hotel' that led to a job for that actor. Aim to make each song your own without just being quirky or showy.

Acting Give the acting of your song as much thought as you would your speeches – if not more. There is no point in just singing it, in an acting vacuum. You must think about the lyrics and what they are saying – and aim to make them truthful. As with classical verse, write out the lyrics as separate sentences (rather than verse layout) – and separated from the tune. Once you've done all the work described in 'Rehearsing your speeches' add the music back in and see how that can help your acting even more.

Some auditionees believe that they've got to move more than is natural because of the music; others just stand there frozen to the spot focusing entirely on hitting the notes correctly. Make sure each song is well acted, and not over-acted. You can help yourself by choosing songs you feel are actable in the first place.

And remember, you should be connected to your character and circumstances before you indicate to the accompanist that you're ready to start. Even if there are a few introductory bars, they are part of the song and you should be connected through them.

If your singing voice is limited, good acting can still keep you in the running. There are plenty of people who are brilliant at hitting a vast range of notes accurately, but who can't act and/or move.

Also see 'Communication and clarity' on page 32.

The 'dots' You should think of the sheet music (or 'dots') as the accompanist's map – he or she will have to drive the piano at the same time as reading the music. So you must take the sheet music in the right key. (Transposing may be a simple mathematical process, but it is hard to do while playing.) It must be in a convenient form for the accompanist to read and easily turn the pages – with one hand. If your music is in loose sheets it can be a good idea to stick them together. It is essential that you do this neatly so that the page-turning can be accomplished with ease. And make sure that the resulting 'concertina' is not too long.

If you are not singing the whole song, mark very clearly where you are starting and finishing and what you are missing out. A friend not only sticks her music on pieces of card so they don't flop about, she also photocopies any repeat and inserts it at the repeat mark so that the accompanist doesn't have to turn back. The way in which you present your 'dots' also reflects on your professionalism.

Don't fold your music (to fit in a pocket or bag) either: it can tend to want to return to its former compressed form at the wrong moment. It's wise to keep it flat in a folder to avoid any possibility of structural collapse.

Note: Don't forget to take the 'dots' of all the songs you might use to each audition.

Final preparation Of course you will rehearse each song with a teacher before exposing it to the rigours of audition. Even if you can read music, a song always feels different when performed with accompaniment. It is advisable to refresh every song you might use before each subsequent audition. This can get expensive, but could make the difference between success and failure.

Don't try to get a song together at the last minute. Amazingly, a lot of people do. Perhaps they believe that it is only necessary for them to demonstrate their vocal capabilities in isolation. This is not true. The actor who doesn't know the words to a song won't get far. As with audition speeches, you should periodically 'service' your songs (see 'A service and an MOT', page 28). As well as 'servicing' the vocal side with your singing teacher, periodically take another look at the acting – that could also go stale. Look for new songs and get rid of old ones that you no longer feel happy with. At regular intervals revise and add to your repertoire to cope with any situation.

Performing your songs

Warm-ups If you know that you'll need to warm up, make sure you arrive in sufficient time to do what you need to do. Don't feel embarrassed about having to do this in a corridor, toilet, car park, and so forth – such seemingly eccentric behaviour is normal around audition locations.

The popular as opposed to the 'pop' song As with audition speeches, there are a number of very popular audition songs. The same parameters apply. If you can sing 'Summertime' extremely well, then go for it, but have a viable alternative if you see dark clouds of 'Oh, no, not again!' passing over the corporate faces of your interviewers.

It is highly likely that you will be able to hear the previous auditionee's effort. If you have prepared the same song, forget it instantly – unless you feel you can do it significantly better – and dig another suitable one out from your repertoire.

Alternative accompanists Don't bring a recorded accompaniment, your guitar or electronic keyboard, or sing unaccompanied (a cappella) – unless invited to do so. They will want to know whether you are capable of following tempi that are given to you; a surprising number of people may be able to hit the notes and sound good, but are wildly inconsistent with tempi given by someone else. Singing, like acting, is not just about what you can do but also about a creative partnership with others.

The tempo Give the accompanist a good indication of the tempo you want beforehand. It doesn't matter if you haven't been quite clear to start with – just stop and quickly and calmly rework it with him or her if necessary.

'Where shall I stand?' This question gets asked too often at singing auditions. Don't be a wimp! You need to stand where everybody can see and hear you properly – and where you can easily (and clearly) indicate to the accompanist that you're ready to start. As with audition speeches, you should be aware of natural hazards that might interfere and don't be so close that you blast your interviewers out of their seats. There may be an interesting echo at some point in the space. Look to avoid it. It'll probably be somewhere in the middle.

'Don't shoot the pianist!' Don't criticise the accompanist. He or she will have some influence on your success – or otherwise. In my experience the problems that arise come from (a) unreadable sheet-music taped together into a too-long and unmanageable concertina and (b) the appalling condition of some audition-room pianos.

Do thank your accompanists – especially if they have had to cope with both those problems.

Dance auditions

These are only usually required at musical theatre auditions. However, there is sometimes a dance element at recall stage for other acting courses. Unlike speech and song auditions (where advance preparation is essential), much of a dance audition is about learning and performing in the room. All you can do is take some classes beforehand in order to remain fit and supple, but there's nothing specific you can work on. However, you can prepare yourself in other ways.

Suitable clothing You must wear suitable clothing for the kind of movement or dance required. Basically, the freer the movement form, the more flexible your clothing needs to be. Short of being naked, leotard and tights are the only clothes that give your body full freedom to express itself. It is also well worth being neat and stylish in your appearance to help the impact of your presentation.

Be ready on time Come suitably dressed or arrive early enough to give yourself time to change (and, if necessary, warm up) before your appointment. You'll probably be learning a routine with around twenty other people – and sometimes more. Organising that number of people can take more time than you might think, so it's important that you are also properly prepared, relaxed and ready to listen for instructions – in good time. 'Faffing around' at this stage – through becoming absorbed in conversations with other auditionees, for instance – can count against you.

Warm-ups You'll probably do a quick warm-up with everybody else before being taught the routine. This may not be a formal part of your assessment, but any lack of commitment on your part at this stage will be noted.

All those other people Don't feel insulted by the fact that there are lots of other people, and don't be put off by the specialist dancer with hankerings to act who seems to pick up the routine in thirty seconds flat. Don't get angry with yourself when you just can't quite get it together. That dancer is probably not nearly the actor or singer that you are, and any anger sours the atmosphere for everybody else. Nobody wants an actor who might waste time in rehearsals through self-defeating anger and frustration.

Can you see? Make sure you are standing in a good position where you can clearly see the steps being demonstrated and hear the teacher. This is your responsibility. Don't ask the teacher to ask the person who is masking your view to move. Sort it out yourself. There is no strategic advantage to any specific position in the room – front or back, side or middle. Choose a place that suits you. Good teachers ensure that they can see everyone – so there's no hiding either.

You can ask the teacher to go back over steps you've not quite grasped. However, if you keep on asking – especially if you've not placed yourself properly – it'll count against you. A remarkable number of people don't seem to be able to get themselves organised in this simple fashion.

Time There should be enough time to go through the steps and run the routine two or three times before the teacher sits back and watches everybody go through it to make his or her assessments. You may feel you've not had enough time to learn that routine, but that you could get there given time. Well, I'm sorry; there's limited time in classes and rehearsals as well.

Continuous assessment Don't think that this final go is the be-all and end-all. Yes, it is your chance to put everything together into a performance on which judgements are based, but the teacher will also have been watching each person through the teaching of the routine – and so may teachers of other skills. After all, they don't just want good performers, they want to be sure that you would be good to work with. Dance may seem cut-and-dried to the non-specialist, but musicals require performers who can give and invent as well as receive instruction.

Sell yourself Having learnt the routine, perform it. Don't just mindlessly go through the steps you've been taught; that's almost like just reading the words out loud with no inflection in a reading. There is nothing more dull on stage than dancers just going through a series of steps with nothing behind the eyes. You may be in that majority of actors who've only done a basic dance training (if any) and have to concentrate extremely hard on what your limbs are doing. If this is so, you will enhance your chances if you perform the routine with style – and, if you go wrong, go wrong with style. Have a positive purpose behind what you do. Sell yourself!

Movement, improvisations and self-devised audition pieces

These are generally part of recall sessions – but not always. There are several essential matters to bear in mind:

1) Listen very carefully to the brief that you're given – and ask for clarification if necessary.
2) Don't try to show off – focus on being real.
3) Don't try to take sneaky looks at your auditioners – focus on the task in hand.

A few courses require you to devise your own audition pieces. They'll give you a brief. Once again, absorb the brief very carefully, don't aim to show off, and be real in your presentation!

Sight-readings in drama school auditions

Most drama schools ask you to do one of these at a recall stage, although a couple have recently introduced them into their first rounds. Sometimes you're given a solo piece; at others you'll be asked to work on a scene you're given.

There's a lot more advice on these in chapter 7, but the most important things to remember are:

• Sit or stand openly – that is, open to the auditioners or your scene partner(s).
• Hold the script somewhere at your side so that it doesn't act like a barrier to the auditioners or your scene partner(s).

- Aim to communicate the words clearly.
- Use the punctuation to find the thought changes (however slight).
- Don't try to impose acting too much – let the words inform your acting.

Interviews

You'll find a lot more about these in chapter 7. What follows are the important aspects for drama school auditions.

Why do drama schools incorporate them in their audition processes? (*Note:* Not all do. A few learn about you through the dialogue involved in workshops.) They want to get to know the real you in order to assess whether you will be able to function well as part of a group. A drama school is a very tight-knit community working long hours very closely together. Therefore it is very important that there are no negative influences. The interview is also an opportunity to see if you have your own independent personality – and that you're not just full of what you've been told. That tight-knit community will only flourish and grow if everybody gives and receives constructively and imaginatively.

Note: Most interviewers are largely not conscious of these objectives. They feel them instinctively through long experience of being in acting communities – in drama schools and in the profession.

Your general approach/attitude Overall you should aim for a friendly exchange of information and ideas. Bear in mind the following:

1) There is no such thing as a right or wrong answer – so long as yours are honest. There is absolutely no harm in healthy disagreement. ('I disapprove of what you say, but I will defend to the death your right to say it' – attributed to Voltaire.) There is also no harm in not having a specific response – provided that you respond in a positive manner. An upbeat 'I'll need time to think about that' is far more engaging than a limp and apologetic 'Dunno . . .'
2) Keep positive even when talking about something negative – for instance, the production that went disastrously wrong. Try to bring out positive aspects while being straightforward about the negative(s).
3) Never leap in immediately to answer a question! Too often you'll start coming out with a confusing jumble. Always take that tiny

(but vital) moment to think about what you've actually been asked. The human brain processes incredibly fast. A moment to absorb (digest) the question and evolve your response can make an enormous difference. Think of it like playing catch games with a small child. The 'ball' is the question: you 'catch' it and then 'throw' it back – in a spirit of co-operation. There is a tiny moment between 'catching' the question and 'throwing' your response. That moment is your chance to absorb the question – not only to begin to formulate your response, but also to store it to refer back to in case you start deviating too far from where you started.

4) Try not to deviate from the original question too much. This is a very common failing and is easily avoided if you keep the original question in mind. You can tie yourself up in embarrassing knots ('dig holes' for yourself) if you deviate too far from where you started.

5) Try not to talk too much about any topic. You probably only have about ten minutes (if that) and it's much better to cover several topics. It should be a dialogue – not another monologue!

6) Don't be too brief either! For example, if you're asked 'What was the last production you saw?', don't just give the title. Add one or two other details.

7) Don't concern yourself with what your interviewers are writing – you'll just start getting paranoid. Anyway, the moment a pen hits the paper will be at least several seconds after the provocation to write occurred, so there's nothing you can do.

8) Do share your responses with everyone on the panel. It may only be one person who's asking the questions, but everybody there will have input in the decision-making.

9) Try to relax as much as possible – and be open. Sit in your chair without wrapping your limbs tightly round each other and/or your chair. Being physically relaxed will help you be more mentally relaxed and receptive to whatever is 'thrown' at you.

What will they ask? You can never be quite sure of specific questions, but you can be 99 per cent certain that they will focus on you, your acting and acting in general. Obviously you can't prepare specific answers, but you can help yourself by making mental lists of what you should know. It is amazing how even the most relaxed interviewee can go blank when asked the simplest of questions like, 'What was the last part you played?' or 'What was the last production you saw?' Don't worry! Almost everybody does this at some time or other – and not just in interview circumstances. If this happens, your interviewers will probably be sympathetic to this common human failing. However, it can start to make you feel awkward and embarrassed – which can easily escalate. Much better to have that mental checklist available.

You will also be asked subjective questions – about a production or a specific actor's performance, for instance. Once again, you can't prepare specific answers, but you can develop your thinking about why certain productions and actors appealed to you – or not. Other subjective questions can include why you're applying to this school, why you enjoy acting, your choice of audition speeches, and so forth. You had good reasons (at some point in the past) for all these personal decisions. Take a little time to think them through again before your audition.

Those 'plonker' questions Unfortunately, a minority of questions that crop up are extremely difficult to answer easily. 'Why do you want to be an actor?', 'Where do you see yourself in ten years' time?', 'How do you think your speeches went?' are among the ones that have been reported to me. I would argue that these are almost impossible to respond to straightforwardly in a short space of time. If you feel it expedient, try to divert slightly from such questions in your responses.

There are others like 'What will you do if you don't get a Drama School place?', 'Where else have you applied and how did you get on?', 'How do you intend to pay for the course if you don't get funding?' and so forth – which might seem difficult and embarrassing. However, previous lack of success (if that's the case) and financial difficulties are common phenomena. These are topics that are best dealt with briefly, simply and honestly. Then you'll have time to be taken on to pleasanter pastures.

Finally Be aware that the questions cited above may be phrased slightly differently in each interview. The main content of your response will be the same, but your phraseology should accord with the specific question asked. For instance, 'What was the last production you saw?' is slightly different from 'What productions have you seen recently?' The latter opens up more possibilities that you might prefer to discuss . . .

And, after it's all over, you'll think of some better answers you could have given. However, there's nothing you can do about that now. Do the best you can and don't beat yourself up afterwards with what you could have said or done. Aim to learn for the future!

Audition days

For the day of an audition you have to be prepared . . .

Arrangements It is important to be relaxed for your audition. Apart from proper preparation of your speeches and songs, it is essential that you are organised – in respect of appropriate clothes (suitable for everything that you're going to be required to do), travel arrangements and overnight accommodation if necessary. If the date and time offered is awkward, then contact the school to change it as soon as possible – most schools are flexible if you give them sufficient notice. Don't leave it until the last moment except in extreme circumstances. If you are perceived to be disorganised, even at this early stage, it could well count against you in the highly competitive audition system.

What to wear? It is always important to feel comfortable and at ease for auditions. Therefore, wear clothes that make you feel like this. Go dressed to work, not to impress through your outfit. Avoid anything that will catch the auditioners' eyes too much (bright colours, excessive patterns, slogans, etc.).

Ensure that your shoes allow firm contact with the ground – and heels should be no more than an inch.

Make-up and accessories should be minimal. Once again, don't wear anything that catches the auditioners' eyes too much.

For the dance component of musical theatre auditions (and the more vigorous movement sessions some drama schools stage at recalls) it is essential to wear appropriate clothes. Such schools will inform you if such clothing will be necessary.

Waiting around distractions Unfortunately, most auditions involve a lot of waiting around. Of course you may well get involved in conversations with other auditionees, but be wary of becoming too involved in these. It is essential not to lose focus on the main task at hand. Take your iPod, novel, crossword puzzle – anything that helps you remain relaxed and focused.

Note: Conversations with other auditionees seem to be where a lot of the mythologies that buzz round the audition circuit germinate and fester.

Travel arrangements It is essential to allow yourself sufficient time to (a) allow for travel delays and (b) find the actual building if you've never been there before. It's better to arrive early in order to acclimatise and relax.

Before the audition Upon arrival at the appointed place, you should find a reception or registration area. You may have some kind of briefing from a member of staff and/or another form to fill in. In spite of your nervousness about the new environment and your actual audition, listen carefully to what you're told and fill in the form clearly, honestly and carefully.

You will be shown round by staff and/or current students – even if such people don't observe your audition, it's possible that their opinion may be sought.

After your induction processes, you may have to wait around before auditioning (several hours in a few regrettable instances), so have something with you to distract your attention sufficiently.

Audition formats These vary from school to school, but broadly break down into two types: group and solo. 'Group' auditions tend to last several hours (if not a whole day) and usually involve a warm-up, voice and movement classes, improvisations (and sometimes sight-readings), and so forth – as well as everybody's audition speeches. Also, it is very common for people to be eliminated as the session progresses. 'Solo' auditions are simply an interview and your speeches and possibly a sight-reading and/or song. If a school uses this methodology for their first auditions, it is almost certain that you will go through the 'group' version if you are invited for recall(s).

Nerves There is one extra factor that is important to bear in mind: nerves! After all, auditioning is a very strange idea to those not used to it. In my experience the most overtly nervous people are those auditioning for drama school. Too often desperation takes over and all that careful preparation flies out the window, leaving a shuddering wreck trying to spit out lines that seem meaningless. Audition speeches are harder because you are all on your own with no support from anyone else. Added to that, you will be in a strange place with strange people who won't smile very much and will spend a lot of time writing notes and not looking at you – apparently not a very sympathetic audience. In fact they are concentrating on you very hard (hence shortage of smiles) and wanting you to succeed. It is not wrong to be nervous. A calm actor will often give a boring performance. However, when your nerves become too disordered and chaotic your whole concentration goes and your limbs become numb. You have to find a way of focusing your nervous energy on your speech and not on the fact that the tension is growing. Tension, once you are aware of it, can escalate out of control very quickly. Don't even begin to contemplate it. Do something else! For instance, actors, while waiting in the wings on a first night, will often jump around and wave their arms about to get the blood circulating and counteract the terrible numbing effect that nervous tension can bring. Other tricks are to imagine that you are doing your speech at home in front of your friends or that the whole audition panel is sitting there stark naked. You have to discover what suits you and your nervous system. Remember also that you know something that your auditioners do not in your individual interpretation of your speeches. Focus your nerves on that advantage and don't let your need to become an actor turn into a numbing chaos of nervous desperation. Above all, aim to enjoy performing your speeches (whether happy or sad) and try not to think of it all as an examination.

If these ideas aren't good enough for you, try some Alexander Technique classes – these should do the trick. I cannot recommend any medication as a solution (beta-blockers, for instance) unless specifically prescribed by a doctor.

Recalls Most schools operate recall systems – that is at least one extra session (sometimes on the same day as the first round) in which you will have to display your speech(es) again, and possibly a variety of other aspects of your talents. Different schools have different methodologies, but the one thing they have in common is that you will probably be seen by many more people than in the first round. You should aim to communicate to them all in spite of the fact that some of them don't speak to you.

The other factor to bear in mind is that the gap between first audition and final acceptance/rejection can vary between the same day and six months.

After your auditions

If you get a place

Some schools will make offers on the day, some will phone, others will use post or email. Whatever the mechanism, don't immediately say 'Yes!' – this can be legally binding.

If you do accept and then don't take up the place, you could well be legally liable to pay the first term's fees – so read any contract offered very carefully. The exception to this is if you accept a place in a CDS school and subsequently receive an offer from another one. You can take up that second offer instead (with no penalty) provided that you do this before a specified deadline (usually the end of June).

'Any place is better than no place at all' Before accepting a place, do some further and more investigative research on the school. Ask around, go and see productions, hover in the bar to pick up vibes, try to talk to current students, bear in mind how you felt treated at audition, even ask if you can watch classes. Look again at what it says about its training methods. Is their entire focus on theatre? Do they have sufficient radio and television classes (and reasonably up-to-date facilities for these)? Think about the location: living costs (parts of London are much more expensive than anywhere else), local amenities and the ambience of a school's premises are all very important considerations when you'll be working such long hours. You should also balance up the relative prestige of a school: those higher up the scale will attract more prestigious professionals to final productions and showcases. If you find too much inauspicious information about the school's current state, don't formally accept their offer of a place and continue auditioning elsewhere.

Formal acceptance Read the paperwork carefully and take particular note of what you could have to pay for before you even start (let alone get your student loan) – a deposit in advance of your fees, books, special clothing, and so on.

Reserve/waiting lists

With most applicants applying to at least three or four schools (if not many more), it is inevitable that a minority receive more than one offer. However, with auditions going on to within a few weeks of the CDS deadline, it is inevitable that some of that 'minority' will be changing schools at the last minute. To accommodate this, schools have 'reserve/waiting' lists. If you're on one of these, you still have a chance of acceptance – even weeks after that deadline. Some schools keep those in whom they're interested in a pool to be selected from at the end of their audition processes.

It is important to note that there is a lot of switching of acceptances in the few weeks before the CDS deadline. Each of these switches can take a few days while individuals make their decisions. (I know someone who was offered three places in a single day.) In consequence, a few places are offered after that deadline.

Funding your training

As soon as you start applying for drama school, start looking into funding. Training actors is a very expensive business because of the high number of teaching hours and the necessity for small class sizes – not because the teachers are overpaid. It is important to be clear about how much you will have to pay up front (usually at the beginning of each term) in fees and add on potential maintenance costs – accommodation, food, transport, equipment, books, and so on. If you get no outside financial help, these costs can amount to around £70,000 for a three-year course. If you are eligible for financial help from the government, much of this will be in the form of loans which are repayable after you finish your course. It is important to be clear about the financial implications for you, up front and long-term. After all the effort you've put in to winning your place(s), it is horrible to have to say 'No, thank you' because you can't afford it.

Government funding This has a chequered history: from the 'discretionary' grant system (when it depended upon where you lived to have a chance to be eligible) to the Dance and Drama Awards (DaDAs, introduced in the late 1990s), which are much fairer but do not yet 'allow the maximum number of the most talented students to attend the best schools'. The principle that funding should be fairly available (along the same lines as that for conventional university courses) has finally been acknowledged by central government – recognising that the performing arts are a vital part of the UK economy and our image abroad. It will continue to be tough to get funding, because there persists (in some minds) a belief that acting and the other arts do not constitute proper work. It is important that you ask about funding arrangements for each course that you apply for, as they currently vary (including whether or not you would be eligible for a student loan to cover maintenance costs), and study them carefully to see what action you might need to take. Also, start working through the ferocious funding application forms and keep an eye on the schools' websites and those of the NCDT and the CDS for future developments in funding arrangements.

Warning: Some authorities are not very good at keeping up with the changes in drama-school funding arrangements. Drama schools are a tiny part of the massive higher education (HE) cauldron – and operate *differently*. If you're having difficulties, get advice from the school whose offer you've accepted.

Other funding Even if you do get funding and a student loan to cover your maintenance (which is currently barely adequate), like university students you will need more money to support yourself while you study, as well as having to pay off the loan at the end of the course. The problem for acting students is that the long and varying class/rehearsal hours, not to mention those required for preparations, mean that it is difficult to plug the financial gaps with part-time work. It is also important to ensure that you will not be so exhausted from work or training that you are unable to do either properly.

If you anticipate significant financial problems (especially if you can't get funding and/or a student loan) it is important to talk to the administrator or registrar of that drama school. Some have acquired a great deal of expertise in helping students towards finding some of their funding. In addition some drama schools have scholarships to be won, there are a few nationally awarded bursaries for drama students and there are charities which can be tapped. (*Note:* almost none of these will cover the full costs of an entire course.) The other obvious thing to do is to write to famous actors – and many have been very generous over the years. However, this area of support seems to be reaching saturation point and it can be a better idea to look for local individuals and businesses who might be persuaded to support a future star. In short, guided by your drama school you need to explore every possible funding avenue in good time before you start your course. Getting funding still has its anomalies and unfairnesses, and talent is only one of the requirements. You have to be determined; don't be put off at this early stage.

Fund-raising tactics It is important to prepare the ground for your fund-raising tactics early – it's a time-consuming process.

1) Make lists of everybody who might be sympathetic (school friends, family friends and any other good contact you may have made). Even if they can't help financially, they might be able to put you on to someone who could.
2) Make lists of charities who might help – your local library will have directories that list thousands of them – and check the NCDT and CDS websites. It is important to check (a) whether each charity will fund a vocational acting training and (b) that there are no restrictions (where you live, for instance) that would rule you out.
3) Prepare the letters you are going to send. These could contain your connection to the recipient and a brief explanation of what you want to do (and why) and what they might get in return – a quarterly newsletter, for instance.
4) Prepare the material that you are going to send out with your letters. For example, a printed leaflet with photos, reviews, character references, messages of support, fees, living expenses – anything that could further your cause. It should all be clearly expressed and well laid-out, and the end result should not look too glossy (you're short of money, remember). Also see chapter 6 for further thoughts on promoting yourself on paper.
5) Open a separate bank account for the money you receive and keep accurate records.

Some of the most successful fund-raisers I've known have helped their causes through activities using their acting skills for the benefit of others. For instance, I know someone who set up and organised her own youth company as a public relations exercise (touring old folks' homes and hospitals). It was so successful that she got financial support from several local businesses and a significant (and unexpected) bequest from someone in one of her audiences. Previously she'd written lots of letters asking for help and received very few replies, let alone any money. So she deferred her place for a year (not all drama schools will allow you to do this; some insist that you audition all over again) and worked at doing something positive rather than write 'yet more whingeing letters'.

Notes:
1) Don't treat (3) and (4) above as a mathematical formula. There are many variations and if any potential donor starts receiving similar format appeals, he or she might start looking elsewhere to spread their generosity.
2) Always say 'Thank you', even for a small donation. Not only is this a common courtesy, but neglecting to do so could queer your pitch (and that of others) on a wider field than you might imagine – you'd be surprised at who knows who, who knows who, who . . .
3) It is essential that you are not seen to 'fritter' any money you receive – the consequences could be far worse than the above. I know of a student who gambled the thousands from one funder in an attempt to improve his situation further. He lost both his place and his school's reputation with that particular funder.

If you prepare all this in parallel with doing the audition round, you'll be up and running with your mail-out immediately you're offered your place.

If you don't get a place

Most drama schools won't tell you why they rejected you. If they did it for one person, they would have to do it for everybody and that would take more time than they can afford. Specific explanations are usually far too complex to be communicated briefly. However, a few have started to give written feedback. Unfortunately, this is often not very useful (and sometimes barely comprehensible) if you're not able to discuss it with those who wrote those comments – or put marks in those boxes. However, if you'd like whatever feedback is available, simply contact the school to see if they'll provide it.

Dealing with rejection This is a fundamental part of an actor's life, and the worst thing you can do is to feel that this is the end of any possibility of being an actor. If you are determined, then you must go on and try again, and again, and . . . I've known lots of aspirants who have had to spend several years auditioning before gaining places – and one who took seven years.

Each drama school, like each professional employer, has different views on what it looks for in a student. If one doesn't think you have potential, another may disagree. Principally, try to learn from each experience without drowning yourself in a sea of regret at what you might or should have done. Try to learn from your rejection(s). Discuss them with someone you trust; it is all useful for the next occasion. Determination and persistence are prerequisites for being a professional actor.

Preparing to try again After a period of recovery, you'll need to start the whole process over again – deciding what to change, trying part-time/short-term courses, and so forth. I think the most important thing is to do something else as well – preferably outside your existing comfort zone. This has two advantages: (a) you can gain some valuable life experience essential to the actor's craft (I was not sympathetic to the third-year acting student who explained his failure over a particular part with 'I've no real emotional experience to take from'); (b) you could start to gain insights into the other job you are going to do to earn a living in those inevitable periods of being out of work. (That dreadful euphemism 'resting' is completely misplaced; I would personally like to strangle whoever invented it.) If you can afford it, I suggest travelling as the most beneficial 'something else'.

Summary

There's a terrific amount of work outlined in this chapter. If you find it too daunting, then go for something easier than acting as a career. You may protest that it's as though you're being asked to be a professional before being trained. It's more that you have to be able to show a professional attitude. It's even tougher in the profession!

3: *The training*

You've got over the first big hurdle – getting a place at drama school (and funding it). Your focus will be on classes and productions (initially internal ones), but there are many other things you should start thinking about and preparing for.

Being at drama school

Drama-school training is incredibly demanding – physically, mentally and emotionally. The hours you spend in classes and rehearsals are much, much longer than those of your contemporaries studying other disciplines. You won't have nearly as much written work to do, but you'll still need to do a huge amount of homework if you're to make the most of your hard-won training. An acting training is not simply 'learning different walks and changing your voice' (a very honest first-year student), it is an immensely complex (and punishing) emotional and physical re-examination and re-working of your self. It isn't easy and cannot be approached in a casual fashion – it's a serious business. You cannot just borrow someone else's notes in order to catch up on classes you've missed. As in the profession itself, there isn't time to be ill or absent for any but the most catastrophic of reasons. It is essential that you arrive, and stay, mentally and physically fit.

Chaos theory Contrary to its popular image, acting has to be highly organised in order for it to seem spontaneous.

Self-motivation One of the principal problems I have found in drama schools is that many students who have come straight from a conventional school lack self-discipline, initiative and the ability to use their own imagination. This enhances my argument for doing something else first, to begin to learn some 'life skills' before taking up your place. Fundamentally: (a) the more you put into learning, the more you will get out of your teachers and (b) drama schools sometimes get asked for recommendations from agents, directors, casting directors and managements. If you 'queer your pitch' too often, you will not only get less than full value from your training but you could also prejudice your early career chances.

Self-organisation Given the above-mentioned assault on your body and psyche it is very important to ensure a good base. Boring things like budgeting, tidiness, eating and sleeping properly are very important. Too often (especially early on) students tend to neglect these essentials and their work suffers – sometimes irretrievably.

Self-discipline It is essential that you go along with the basic disciplines of your school and the individual teachers. Acting is a group activity and it is incredibly destructive to have a class or rehearsal disrupted by latecomers, mobile phones going off and irrelevant private conversations. Losing scripts, rooms littered with festering food and drink remains, and so on, are all destructive to your group as a whole. Good schools are quite specific in their required disciplines – they're not being petty-minded; those rules are there for very good reasons.

The disciplines There are numerous aspects to an acting training (movement, voice, and so on) – don't treat them as entirely separate entities. They're all fundamental to good acting. You should look to bring things learned in your movement classes, say, into your acting classes.

Different teachers in the same discipline might well work in different ways and have different ways of expressing things. Don't think that only one is right and the others are wrong. Think of them as different perspectives and try to make connections – and work out what's best for you.

Ask questions! The majority of the teachers who work in drama schools are not 'tired old has-beens' as some students seem to think. ('Only those who can should teach.' Uta Hagen.) In them I find more passion about the art and craft of acting than in any theatre. Many teachers will go out of their way to give extra help – with acting and career advice – to those who ask good questions. And remember that in acting, instinct often counts as much as (and periodically more than) intellect.

Fully exploiting your acting skills Explore fully all the possibilities for employment as an actor – or, as a friend put it, 'Look to broadening your work-base.' Actors' skills are being deployed in more and more areas (use of role-play has grown rapidly, for instance – see chapter 9), and there are probably some that haven't even been thought of yet. Some are very technical, and art seems irrelevant, but at least they pay. Too many students think of a repertory theatre company as the first step in their career: this used to be true, but is now rarely possible.

Imagination is the engine of acting. Use yours to create new projects, often with contemporaries, that might benefit you later on – at the very least, they'll be a welcome addition to your CV.

Drama-school jargon Like any institution, drama schools have their own jargon. For instance, I've come across the terms 'modules', 'workshops' and 'showings' to describe internal assessment productions. Such terms are all but irrelevant to a potential employer. Find straightforward ways of expressing your abilities and achievements on your CV and in interview. Also, if you are fortunate enough to win one of the prizes that drama schools give, bear in mind that – however prestigious within your school – they generally mean very little to the majority of employers. Use your winnings wisely and don't be 'miffed' if many in the profession don't recognise the kudos attached. National awards like the Laurence Olivier Bursary (which helps talented and needy students) and the Carleton Hobbs Award (for radio) do impress the professionals.

Bitchery Drama school is where you will make your first professional contacts: not just teachers and directors, but among your fellow students. Some of these latter you'll get on with famously; others you'll find intensely annoying (even apparently incompetent); some you may take months even to notice because they are so unforthcoming. It is very important to keep negative personal opinions to yourself and work at getting on with everyone – not only because harmony is very important to a close-knit community like a drama school, but also because you never know who might go places. Anybody could be a contact for future work.

Leaving early Dissatisfaction with casting, a rock band taking off, a girlfriend in New York and job offers are just a few of the reasons I've encountered for students leaving drama school early. (Running out of money is another, but that's a different problem.) If you still intend to become a professional actor it is invariably stupid to leave early unless the reason is an extremely positive professional one. It is important to discuss such a decision with the school's 'powers that be'. Bear in mind too that you may be asked to pay some of your funding back – wherever you got it from.

Planning ahead It is terribly easy to get so immersed in classes and productions that many find themselves in a mad scramble to get the business side of their careers organised in sufficient time. CVs, letters and photographs, and so forth, take longer to research and prepare than most realise – and it is vital that you have these essentials in place before you're submerged in rehearsals for your first public productions. 'An actor's toolkit' (at the end of this chapter) lists the vital ingredients of being a professional actor – with details considered elsewhere in this book. However, there are two matters of special relevance to those about to start the final year of their training:

1) *Your entry in the* Spotlight Graduates *book.* This is a once-in-a-lifetime opportunity to advertise yourself in a widely-read publication which contains only those about to graduate – that is, about 5 per cent of all the adult actors in *Spotlight*. The casting fraternity eagerly scan through these new faces for saleable fresh talent. The deadline for submission of your entry (if you're on a two- or three-year course) is mid-October with publication in the following February. If you're on a one-year course, the submission deadline is late November.
2) *Your professional name.* It is vital to decide upon this before your first public performance and to get it right. Your professional name represents you and your public image and must suit your personality. If you do have to invent one, start from names within your own family – and have several alternatives in case your first option is already being used by someone else. Once you've got some ideas (and it is well worth discussing this with teachers and others) you must check with Equity – whether it is real or assumed – that there is nobody else registered under that name. (Don't simply rely on checking in *Spotlight*, as there are plenty of Equity members working in performance fields not covered by *Spotlight*.) You should also make sure that everybody (parents, flatmates, drama-school switchboard operator, and so on) knows who is being referred to when a phone rings professionally for you; changing your name later can cause damaging complications. *Note:*

Remember that you will have to give your real name (if different) to any employer for use on your pay cheque and your national insurance contributions. There is more detailed advice available on both the Equity and Spotlight websites.

Special note for those about to start on one-year courses: although your *Spotlight Graduates* book deadline is late November, it is still quite a short time after the start of your course. It is therefore useful to do what planning you can beforehand.

Your first public appearances

The best advertisements you will have early in your career are the public productions at the end of your time at drama school. It is essential to get your letters, CVs and photographs organised before the first of these – say, a month before opening night – ready to be sent as opportunities arise. A greater concentration of professionals with influence will come to these productions than to anything else you do for quite a while: it's a fertile hunting-ground for saleable new talent. Even if you are playing a small part or one way beyond your own age, such 'cognoscenti' will be able to pick you out if you are of interest to them – I've seen this happen so often. ('There are no small parts; there are only small actors.' Stanislavski.)

Your directors Final productions will probably be directed by outside directors. Use what they have to give you. You may be deeply frustrated by aspects of the school and its teachers, but don't take those frustrations out on the outsider. It's nothing to do with them, and it is very important for you to come over well in those final productions. An outside director also provides an opportunity for a fresh start, for you not to feel weighed down by previous criticisms. (I'm not advocating ignoring those 'criticisms', simply putting them in better perspective.) Also, these directors are links with the profession and good contacts are very important to your career. ('It's not what you know, but who you know' is often true.) You should keep in touch with the ones you get on with and you should see those you find difficult as positive learning experiences – there's no mileage in blaming someone else for a failure.

'They left in the interval' This is one of the commonest complaints I hear from actors about agents and casting directors who've come to see them in a production. It doesn't necessarily mean that they hated you. Such people see a lot of productions, have been working all day and will probably have to work all day tomorrow. And they can often learn all they need to know in one brief appearance. It has been suggested to me that when inviting you could add, 'I don't mind if you leave in the interval.' I'm not so sure if this is a good idea; it sounds a bit pathetic to me. Much better simply to face up to the possibility and accept gracefully any subsequent apology.

'They didn't even turn up!' It so often happens that after all the effort put into letter writing (and so on), let alone that put into your performance, you find that very few (perhaps none) of those levers into the profession have seen you. Don't despair! It's a simple fact that there are far too many productions for agents and casting directors to cover while doing the rest of their work. You simply have to persist and be inventive with your invitations. You have to keep up the propaganda campaign. Somehow, somewhere, something will happen if you keep on steadily trying.

Non-appearance can even occur if you managed to extract a promise of attendance – something more pressing has come up. In these circumstances try to carry forward that 'promise' for the future, without embarrassing them. Something like, 'I'm sorry that you weren't able to get to [production name]. I'm next appearing in X.'

Showcases All drama schools stage showcases where all the graduating students are given opportunities to briefly show off their talents to a concentration of directors, agents and casting directors. Different schools have different ways of approaching these, but generally the onus will be on you to find the material with which to show yourself off. Start thinking about this early and find something 'original'! However, don't choose something with the idea of it being a challenge. Find potential material that will show you off well – as you appear to be. A good choice of 'original' material, well executed, will definitely help you stand out from the crowd. Go back on all that research and reading you did to find your audition speeches.

An agent's approach I have often stood in theatre bars after show-cases and seen groups of students who don't quite know where to put themselves, indulging in almost farcical non-conversations. In among the rest of the crowd are unfamiliar faces, some of whom are agents and others with casting clout. Eyes flick everywhere for the approach of someone new . . . It is a horrible situation – because there is no consistency of approach. A few agents like to stay on and approach people directly; others much prefer to rush off anonymously and then phone, text or email those they find interesting later. Some fear monopolisation and many know they can't afford to be away from their offices for too long. In these circumstances, try and wipe any thought of a possible 'approach' out of your mind. I know it's difficult, but try to focus on my guesstimate that only 10 per cent of approaches occur in person immediately after a showcase. After your showcase performance, it's very important to measure your eating and drinking. I've known several instances of students messing up an agent-approach through guzzling the free wine and food to excess.

Note: It is generally better not to accept any offer of representation until near the end of your training – there may be someone better waiting in the wings.

Adrenalin After a live performance you will be more adrenalised than members of your audience – which may contain somebody of influence. Should you encounter such a person in the bar afterwards, be wary of gushing all over them as they won't be on the same high.

'What did you think?' If you do meet someone of influence in the bar afterwards, don't put him/her in an embarrassing situation by asking this. I know it can be good to 'cut through the crap' and maybe get some constructive notes, but it's hard work giving constructive criticism. You may get more than you bargained for and you don't know who that person knows. Discretion is the better part of getting work.

It's different in the real world Students of any subject emerging into their chosen professions – even if they are going into the profession for which they were trained – will find a welter of new technical terms, working practices and unspoken rules that they never encountered in college. In the fierce competition for acting work, nothing is more likely to mark you down than the precious time an employer has to spend on teaching what has become as fundamental as breathing to him or her. If you can get as much practical experience as possible, where you can observe the pros at work – as a dresser, a follow-spot operator or an usher, for example – before leaving, you will have given yourself a head start. And if you can find a way to learn more about the workings of television and radio – maybe simply as an observer – that can be extremely useful. Don't simply rely on those television and radio courses.

It's also useful to note that things tend to move faster in the 'real world'.

Your first professional steps . . .

Advice An actor's career is very like a life-long game of snakes and ladders – with far more (and longer) snakes than ladders – for the vast majority of the profession. You'll get plenty of career advice, both formal and informal, and some of it will be contradictory: for example, different people will like different photographs from your selection. Finally you have to make up your own mind by using your own instincts – often by going back to your first gut reaction.

Directors You may already know a few professional directors from shows you've done at drama school – you may even be given your first break by one of them – but don't think that all directors are like the ones employed by your school. Most of these are not only experienced directors but they usually also have the patience to help you overcome the acting problems you encounter along the way. In the profession there isn't the time to do this, and some directors just don't have this facility for patience in their emotional make-up. (This is a piece of tact on my part.)

Don't let your technique show Of course there is a wide variety of directors (and agents and casting directors) and a wide variety of methodologies, but most do have a common denominator: they don't really know how the techniques of acting actually work. This may be galling to you after all the sweat to get your breathing right, your received pronunciation correct, and so on, but it's generally true. Ninety-nine per cent of an audience won't have the faintest idea, so why should the director? I have seen too many actors, especially those recently out of drama school, concentrating on these techniques to the detriment of the final product – making it look like a series of mechanical operations. You have to climb beyond the essential mechanics and fly.

Early interviews Some people fall into the trap of just talking about their drama school and its whole philosophy. That simply exaggerates your lack of experience. Some even go so far as to claim that they have 'learnt nothing' from their training. That sounds very arrogant and doesn't say much for your loyalty. If you came straight from school into training, you may feel that you've not done anything else worth talking about but you must have done something that could help illustrate more of yourself. Think about it! (See chapter 7 for much more detailed discussions.)

Be warned that prejudices (mostly based on long out-of-date information) exist about many drama schools. Be prepared gently to disabuse any such notion as appropriate.

Early work (and the lack of it)

In your first few years it is very important to carry on acting and not lose all the momentum you built up in your final months at drama school. Also, drama-school audiences tend to be dominated by other students and friends – they can give a misleading impression. Your teachers will tell you what they think, but nobody but a real audience drawn at random from the general public can really tell you whether you're communicating or not. And communication to those you don't know is at the heart of acting.

Outside productions A student (in between her second and third years), recently returned from a moderately successful sojourn at the Edinburgh Festival Fringe, said to me: 'It's so good to perform somewhere else.' I believe that doing a production outside your school environment while training can be a very valuable learning experience. However, you must make sure that your school is happy for you to do this – a few aren't.

Your first proper job Don't feel you have to take work for work's sake – even if it is your all-important first properly paid acting job. In the early stages career enhancement should be your chief objective. For example, a tempting long tour in the chorus line will probably do very little for you; don't take it unless you're really sure there is nothing else. There is a limit to how much you can learn working with the same group of people and you could be missing out on other opportunities by being away too long. It is important that early jobs have reasonable publicity value for your career and provide good opportunities to start learning about how the profession works. (A good agent will guide you in this.) Aim to get something positive from each one.

Ideals However, don't be too purist about what you would like to do. There is no point in crossing musicals off your list because you prefer straight theatre (or vice versa). You have to look carefully at each job opportunity and see what it might do for you. It may not advance you – indeed you may feel you could be sliding back down the ladder – but don't forget your bills. Ideals are not wrong, but you mustn't let them blind you to immediate realities. Keep them in perspective – for the long term. In spite of what media coverage of individual actors' lives may suggest, virtually nobody consistently gets the kind of work they most want.

Jaded professionals I'm afraid that a minority of experienced professionals waste time and/or mess around while working. I'm not talking about those bits of harmless (but responsible) fun that we all need periodically when working hard; it's those silly attempts to catch others out – by trying to make you 'corpse' on stage, for instance. Do your damnedest not to join in these futilities; if you do, you – with less experience – will probably be the first to get caught out.

An actor's job is to communicate the story to the audience; messing about in performance is not only unprofessional, it is also alienating to that audience.

Good intentions and broken promises One of the hardest things for newcomers are promises that come to nothing. I'm afraid the profession is rife with these – you simply have to face the fact that, because there are too many actors to choose from, you will often be let down. However, most people who break such promises do feel at least a little bit guilty and your aim should be to find ways of letting them off the hook and utilising that 'promise' in the future.

Kicks in the teeth In spite of all my (and many others') warnings, most students seem to avoid taking on board what the profession is really like. For a (very) few it is a comparatively simple process of being spotted by an agent in a final-year production and the agent pointing the student in the correct direction towards their first job. But in the cattle market of final-year productions and showcases, it is impossible for any agent to cover everything. And even if one does see you and like you they won't necessarily leap on to the phone with an instant offer of representation – let alone have a job waiting for you. Looking for new talent is only a part of an agent's working life. Their main focus has to be on their current clients and not so much on future investment – there aren't enough hours in the week. An agent may have liked you in something, but his/her attention can easily be distracted and you disappear from the memory. It is a fact that if you are male, have a strong singing voice and a saleable regional accent (Scouse, Geordie or Glasgwegian, for instance) you stand a much better chance of being snapped up than if you're female, wouldn't claim to be a strong singer and have an ordinary, natural accent.

I know of two contemporaries fitting the above descriptions: he got more than twenty offers of representation; she got none. She, with encouragement, sat down, gritted her teeth and phoned agents who had seen their West End showcase. She got varying degrees of short shrift from most, but after much hard graft is now ensconced very happily with a good co-operative agency. Many of their contemporaries are still wandering around wondering why it's not happening for them – and not doing anything about it.

I'm not trying to frighten; I'm trying to give you a realistic outlook so that you are able to cope better with the kicks in the teeth that you will undoubtedly receive – and have to bounce back from.

Extra work If you can get work as an Extra (you will also come across the terms 'Walk-on', 'Supporting' or 'Background artiste') it can be a very valuable learning experience. (You can find specialist agents listed in *Contacts*.) But if you become known as an Extra, you'll find it difficult to move into the conventional acting sphere. People still do come out of the chorus line and make a career for themselves in theatre, but it's more difficult to come out of a screen crowd to do likewise. Being part of a crowd that is intended to be seen as a group and not as readily identifiable individuals is a different discipline from playing a part which needs specifically to shine through the screen. It is a fact that many television directors and casting directors are prejudiced against people who do Extra work, thinking they can do nothing else.

Screen or stage? One of the most frequent drama-school debates is about the relative merits of work in these environments. For the lucky few who have the option I strongly suggest that it's important to get good stage experience at the outset of your career – balanced with the considerable exposure that a media appearance can give you. The stage is where you find out what works (and doesn't) and learn about real audiences – that is, ones not dominated by friends and fellow students. A performance does not finally exist until it is placed in front of an audience, and that audience will change it if the actor is responding properly. A silence speaks just as loudly as laughter. This understanding of 'real audiences' is very important for media acting when you have to imagine your audience. For a television sitcom you may have a studio audience, but its reaction is not always'real because of the constant breaks in recording and because that audience can see everything else that's going on – cameras moving about, floor-managers talking intensely into headsets, actors waiting out of shot picking their noses, and so on. The audience has also been warmed up beforehand by a professional warm-up artiste, and audience reactions during the takes are cleverly amplified in the final editing stage after everybody has gone home.

Note: There is a counter argument that claims that a camera can see more deeply inside you and acting for screen is an even more challenging task – you have to be even more truthful than on stage. I believe that radio can be equally challenging.

A deafening silence Of course you'll be looking to create chances wher-ever possible, but that first job does not just appear – and no agent seems interested in you. Extra classes will keep you in trim, but there is no substitute for actually doing productions to complete all that training. If you can't get a legitimate job, try the Fringe and/or short films – with all the caveats listed in chapter 8. It can also be fulfilling to look for other ways of exploiting your training – by setting up a drama group or organising play-readings or workshops, for instance.

An actor's toolkit

You need to organise the following essential items before you even get your first interview, let alone an agent and/or your first job. You should start planning for all these in good time, before the end of your training – ready for your first public production.

1) Join Equity! You can join (very cheaply) as a student member (see <www.equity.org.uk/about-us/join-us>) and, for a small extra

fee, reserve your professional name: details of how to go about this are on the website.

2) A good, strong professional name. If you can't (or don't want to) use your real name, it's important to select an alternative that you're completely comfortable with.

3) Well-designed headed paper. Beatrice Warde, the passionate typography expert, said, 'Typefaces are the clothes words wear.' Find a typeface that dresses your professional name well.

4) Secure reliable telephone and internet connections for professional use. *Note:* It is very important that your outgoing message and email address sound professional and not like hangovers from your adolescence.

5) A reliable computer with a good-quality printer. *Tip:* Laser printers provide a much crisper quality when printing text – and laser toner is much cheaper per page than ink.

6) An up-to-date copy of *Actors' Yearbook*. *Tip:* It is worthwhile not only reading the rest of this book to get a feel for how different parts of the profession function, but also reading through websites.

7) A good set of photographs and sufficient copies.

8) A well-laid-out and up-to-date CV. *Note:* It's important to understand how to convert your CV into Portable Document Format (PDF) for email transmission.

9) A good standard letter that you can adapt for individual circumstances and use in emails.

10) Half a dozen (or more) varied audition speeches.

11) Half a dozen (or more) varied audition songs.

12) A mental list of subjects (not just acting) you could talk about in order to respond to the almost inevitable question(s), 'What have you been doing recently?' and/or 'Tell me a bit about yourself.'

13) An entry in *Spotlight* – details at <www.spotlight.com/join>. *Note:* An entry in *Spotlight* is strictly limited to professionally trained and/or professionally experienced performers, and applications are always vetted.

14) A reasonable selection of clothes for interviews and auditions. Essentially, you need to feel comfortable and appropriately dressed for each individual occasion . . . and you will face a wide variety.

15) An up-to-date passport – jobs which require travelling abroad at short notice are becoming more frequent.

16) A budget. The costs of the above can accumulate quite quickly, before you've earned a penny, and there are many other minor things not listed: postage, Equity entry fee and annual subscription, subscriptions to *The Stage* and other professional publications, travel costs to interviews, and so on. All the above items can easily add up to much more money than you might think: you need to calculate your potential professional expenses and budget for them.

    Note: Although many of the above are allowable against tax, don't forget to include your potential tax bill! Also, at the outset of your career, consider carefully the cost-effectiveness of items like personal websites, showreels, etc. These are only worthwhile if you have sufficient high-quality material that makes you look professional.

17) Sources of non-acting income that are flexible enough for you to drop at 24 hours' notice. At an educated guess, only about 10 per cent of the profession earn a living solely from acting and, even for those, incomes can vary widely – from £200 one year to over £20,000 the next, to quote just one example.

18) A working knowledge of the nation's transport systems (especially for Londons): you will often not know where you might be required for audition/interview (even work) until very late in the day. *Tip:* As a general rule it is wise to double your estimated travelling time to allow for the almost inevitable hold-ups.

19) A great deal of patience, persistence, determination, cunning and resourcefulness.

20) A stoical source of solace for the bad times. *Tip:* Find another activity that absorbs you as much as acting does.

21) A copy of this book for reading at any time.

Slog

The odd person leaps straight out of drama school into continuous work. It can take most who persevere at least a year to get their first properly paid job; it probably takes most at least five years to find any credibility within the profession. Even then it's an extremely up and down life. It is a lifetime's slog but with a lot of hard effort in selling yourself you will find work, learn, and within three to five years – maybe sooner – be at one with those who've been forty years in the profession. Their only advantage over you will be that they have more stories to tell in the coffee breaks and in the pub.

And I'll end this chapter with one of my favourite quotes:

'If life doesn't have that little bit of danger about it, you'd better create it. If life hands you that danger, accept it gratefully.'

Anthony Quayle

4: *Equity and Spotlight*

There are two major organisations that are at the heart of the acting profession – Equity and Spotlight. They were established within a few years of each other (between the two World Wars) and although they have different functions, they have some things in common.

It's important to join both. Joining either is not a legal requirement, but you stand the chance of committing professional suicide if you don't – for very different reasons.

Subscriptions to each may seem like a large annual dent in your finances but they are within the price range of such staples as the television licence and annual car tax.

Both develop new initiatives all the time so it's important to keep up to date with their respective websites. My summaries below only cover the basics as new initiatives will be online throughout the lifetime of this book.

Both encapsulate others working in the performing arts as well as actors.

Both have WC2H postcodes. Make of that what you will, but I can assure you that they continue to liaise closely over matters of mutual concern. For example, look at the advice on choosing your professional name on both websites – there are only minor variations in wording.

It's of paramount importance to keep your contact details (including any changes in agency) up to date with both.

Equity

Contact details: Equity, Guild House, Upper St Martin's Lane, London WC2H 9EG; (020) 7379 6000; website <www.equity.org.uk>.

Once upon a time there were stars and there were other actors. On stage the stars would dominate and the others would have to fit in around them. The stars could command high fees, the others would take what they could get. (Young actors would even pay West End managements to play small parts in order to get noticed.) In 1929, with the support of some famous names, the actors' trade union Equity was established in the UK. Although the stars, with their considerable ticket-selling power, can still command high fees, at least the others are being paid much better and work many fewer hours than their pre-Equity counterparts.

The Union Equity is an organisation surrounded by misleading myth and legend. Essentially, it exists to look after the interests of not just actors but also performers in many other fields – from opera singers to stunt people, from ballet dancers to ventriloquists and many more. It also represents production staff like stage managers, directors, designers, etc. – indeed a recent survey showed that actors only constituted 50 per cent of the Union's membership.

Its principal function is to negotiate minimum pay and conditions agreements in all areas of work – and there are far, far more of those than you might imagine, with new ones being invented all the time. Under current employment legislation a management cannot refuse to employ somebody who is not a member of the Union, but there are Equity/Management agreements which state that the latter will endeavour to employ people with previous professional experience – that is, Equity members. (*Note:* This includes newcomers who have completed a course at a CDS school.) And it generally makes more sense for managements to employ those with 'previous professional experience' rather than someone with none at all. Equity is not an all-powerful monolith, obstructing aspiring actors: entry is not tightly restricted as so many seem to think. All the Union requires is some evidence of professionalism to be eligible for membership.

Student membership If you are on a full-time higher education course (HND or above) lasting for a year or more, which is preparing you for work in many areas of the performing arts, you can become a student member of Equity. For a small annual fee (of under £20) you get regular information on what's happening in the industry and the Union, the option to reserve your professional name (as long as it is not already in use by an existing member), opportunities to meet experienced performers, special discounts on insurance and other concessions, and eligibility to join the Actors' Centres around the UK. On graduation you can move up – subject to other qualifying rules – to full membership, and the amounts you have paid as a student member are deducted from the costs of joining. If you aren't immediately eligible for full membership you can continue at the student rate for up to two years after graduating. As soon as you can provide proof of professional work, you should be able to become a full member. All the up-to-date details are on the website.

The Equity card There are numerous other routes to joining and eligibility has eased significantly in the past few years. The details of the whole system are too complex to go into here; it is best to contact the Union for up-to-the-minute details. Guides to entry are available from their offices; there is also a list of membership criteria (and how to join) on their website.

An Equity card is only a passport for, and not a guarantee of, getting work, but it will give you a better chance of getting interviews and auditions. It's not that employers (and agents) won't see non-members, but they are generally disinclined to do so. It is possible to get non-Equity work; there are numerous companies (with no agreement with the Union) who employ non-members, but they commonly pay under the negotiated rate for the job and some have been known to vanish without paying at all – Equity has a very long list of miscreants. Sometimes it can be worth working with such a company to gain experience, but it might not be quality work and after paying your expenses you will certainly not make much money. (There are Fringe venues that are very good shop windows but currently outside any agreement.) More importantly, most legitimate acting work is indifferently paid already and managements who exploit actors' need to work and the actors who work for them are undermining the profession as a whole. Actors need to stand together in order to fight for fair treatment in pay and conditions.

Equity's other work Apart from negotiating (and renegotiating) a whole range of contracts, the Union provides numerous other services: the Job Information Service, specialist legal aid, insurance services, an advice service on tax and benefits, and so on. It is also highly proactive – campaigning for better theatre funding, for instance – all for one of the lowest subscription rates of any trade union in the country (see the website for current rates). Equity now not only has informative leaflets covering all aspects of its work, it also has an excellent and easily navigable website where you can find out an enormous amount.

Who runs Equity? The Union is run by a Council of (currently forty-six) volunteer members who are elected by the membership. There are also elected committees representing specialisms and geographical areas who focus on the problems and needs of their particular remits. Backing all this up are the full-time staff (led by the General Secretary) who do the day-to-day work and who advise the Council and committees.

Equity's image In the UK, Equity is too often seen as 'doing nothing for me', 'weak', and so on. This is fundamentally not true. It *is* true that dealing with all the problems that blitz the organisation every day badly overstretches the existing staff. Combined with this is the fact that there are too many individuals willing to undercut agreements simply in order to work, thus undermining those hard-won agreements. It can sometimes seem like a very uphill struggle. However, if you are a member with a problem that no one else can solve you can be sure of the best advice and support from Equity. Even better, get involved with your local branch, constructively express your opinions and things can be made to happen.

How to use Equity In general an actor with a contractual or legal problem should first contact his or her agent – there are clear-cut agreements over nudity and broadcasting extracts from productions, for example, which a good agent should know. Beyond this, your next recourse is the Equity Deputy (often known as the 'Equity Dep'; under the agreements every company should elect one of these), who should contact the Union for advice. If you do find it necessary to contact Equity directly, (a) don't leave it until the last minute and (b) try to avoid Monday mornings and Friday afternoons. You, the actor, have to try to solve your own problems as far as you can, often with the help of your agent and/or your fellow actors, but when you do have a genuine problem that is beyond you, you will receive very good support, expert advice and positive action.

Non-Equity work There are some areas of work where Equity has no management body with which to negotiate (most training films and corporate videos, for example). However, Equity has evolved (and continues to do so) many sets of guidelines and forms of engagement which are well worth asking for when such work arises. Equity often has no real power in these areas but can offer expert advice and considerable clout. They will even try to assist where the work is unpaid (or expenses only) if a significant problem arises.

Spotlight

Contact details: Spotlight, 7 Leicester Place, London WC2H 7RJ; (020) 7437 7631; website <www.spotlight.com>.

Spotlight is a small organisation with a massive output. It is 'the hub of the industry' (Clive Swift) – where you advertise yourself, whether you have an agent or not. The organisation's two major annual publications are the *Spotlight Directories* and *Contacts*. (It also publishes specialist directories of Children, Graduates, Presenters, Stunt Performers and Dancers.) Although Spotlight was founded in 1927, it is no dinosaur. It moves very much with the times and has a massive, constantly updated website – including actors' photographs, agents, personal skills, physical attributes, languages, accents and abilities, which can be accessed in seconds if someone has a specific casting requirement. As part of membership it also offers other services including the Spotlight Link (Spotlight Link Board) via which some casting breakdowns are accessible. For more details on this and other services see their website.

***Spotlight* book and web pages** These are commonly known simply as *Spotlight* and it is essential that you are in it – it is the first port of call for virtually everybody who is casting productions. Some actors get interviews simply on the basis of what they look like in their *Spotlight* photograph, but more often than not that image of you serves as a reminder of your existence if you've already met, or if they've seen you in something.

The book forms are published annually and the internet version is continually updated. They contain photographs, contact details and other information for some 30,000 adult actors and actresses. For the price of an entry (costing about the same as an annual colour television licence) you'll have adverts on employers' and casting directors' desks all around the world. Before you can enter you have to satisfy them that you have professional experience and/or acting training. If you fulfil these 'professional' requirements, they will send you an application form. You can find entry forms (and a lot more) on their very informative website.

The application form It is important to fill this in as fully as you can – too many blanks will lessen your chances of being found when a reader is doing a search (using specific criteria) on the internet version. It is also important that you write clearly and make absolutely sure that all your spellings are correct – it is insulting to find a director friend's name (for instance) wrongly spelt in such a widely accessed source.

Some sections are self-evident; others are worth thinking about more carefully:

Height and weight Most people fill these in, so if you don't the reader will start to wonder how much out of the ordinary you actually are – especially in respect of height. If you feel that you need to bend the truth a little, don't go overboard by telling an outright lie; it will count against you.

Hair and eye colour These are important, especially if the black-and-white photograph (in the book version) cannot convey them properly: for example, red hair or green eyes.

Age band normally cast This is often also referred to as 'playing range' – see my thoughts on this on page 20.

Skills It is important that you can actually accomplish everything you list – essential if you claim to be 'highly skilled'. Watch television, film and commercials carefully and you'll see all kinds of 'skills' being used. As there is usually no time to rehearse, casters are on the lookout for a wide variety of abilities – sports and athletics, for instance. In theatre, musical skills are especially important.

Your credits Most people only flick through these quite quickly (probably reading only the first half-dozen or so), so it's important to make these brief, uncluttered and straightforward – and not weighed down by pedantic detail. (Your web page will probably be printed out, so it is a good idea to ensure that each credit doesn't take up more than a single line on that piece of paper.) For instance, if you played more than one character in a production it's only necessary to list one. However, I think that it is a mistake to omit dates in this context. Most people do include these and any omissions serve to imply that you are trying to conceal something. For more ideas on how to approach the contents of your CV (correct spellings, for instance), see chapter 6.

How to contact you If you're represented by an agency then you should list them. If you aren't, it is better to put Spotlight's telephone number rather than your own, as yours may change but theirs doesn't. (*Note:* They will vet any enquiry for you before passing on your contact details.)

The date of your photograph Omitting this can make the reader wonder what you might be trying to conceal. 'How long ago was this picture taken and what is he or she trying to hide from me now?'

Your photographer Don't forget that your photographer owns the copyright of your photograph and must be credited (see 'Copyright' on page 131).

VERY IMPORTANT If you miss the deadline for entry in the book version, you will have to wait for up to 18 months before your new photograph (and/or agent) will be published in it, and the book is still used by a lot of people.

> Actors' deadline (with new photograph): mid-October (published in the following April)
> Actresses' deadline (with new photograph): mid-April (published in the following October)
> Graduates' book deadlines: mid-October (for those on two- and three-year courses) and late November (for those on one-year courses) (published in the following February)

Note: You can get an entry on the website at any time of the year. Your details will appear on the internet within a few weeks and will automatically be published in the next edition of the book.

Your *Spotlight* web page This contains a great deal more of the above information than the printed version. Casting directors, and others, can access lists of actors using their chosen parameters – in any combination they like. For instance, they can click 'French' in the 'Language' box and get a complete list of those who filled in the fact that they speak the language. The user can also do a search specifying 'native' next to the language (or an accent). Further refinements could involve finding French-speaking actors in a particular age range, hair colour and height – whatever combination might be desired. It's all quite mind-boggling. What's important from your point of view is that you list everything on the application form that you genuinely can. Remember that it is essential you provide good quality photographs, accurate credits and other details, and keep these up to date at all times.

Thanks to the internet, you can:

- change, or update, details of your entry at any time – Spotlight provides each entrant with a confidential 'update' PIN number;
- pass on a 'view-only' PIN number to anyone whom you'd like to view your entry at any time;
- add extra photographs – in colour or in black and white;
- add voice-clips (see chapter 6) of up to two minutes for a one-off additional charge;
- add a showreel (see chapter 6) lasting up to five minutes (and made up from up to four separate clips) for a one-off additional charge.

Note: Spotlight (quite rightly) insists that you must have written permission from the copyright holders of the material that you use in your voice-clips and showreel – for more details see their website.

Alternatives to *Spotlight* There have been periodic attempts by other companies to offer similar advertising services for actors – in book form. The turn of the millennium saw a sudden rise in alternative casting directories on the internet – without the book option. Most are cheaper to enter than *Spotlight*, but none has yet reached the same level of professional respect. The expertise and contacts that Spotlight has built up over the decades will take anybody else a very long time to catch up with – if they ever do. Go for entry in *Spotlight* first and anything else, if you can afford it, after your other essential outlays.

If you are thinking of also going for one of these alternatives, get opinions from those with current experience of them and consider the following:

- Read the small print of the application form ('terms and conditions', or whatever) carefully and look out for hidden charges – some that claim to be 'free' start charging after a trial period and some have grades of membership, for instance.
- Many are not just for actors; they also contain models, entertainers, presenters – sometimes all mixed in together, which can make it very confusing for the viewer.

- Is there too much extraneous advertising which could frustrate a viewer?
- Are the credits of individual actors well laid out and easy to read? Also, check the standard of spelling.
- Is the overall design pleasing to the eye and is the site easy to navigate?
- Does the site download reasonably quickly?
- Will it survive the test of time? Many dot-com companies go out of business quite quickly.
- Do you want the hassle of having to update your alternative(s) as well as your *Spotlight* entries?

Contacts This is Spotlight's other major annual publication. It is updated every October and is an industry-wide list of contact names. The profession has a highly mobile population of people you need to contact, so some details are quickly out of date. You should update your copy annually. It is available in some bookshops, via the sales hotline ((020) 7440 5026) and through their website.

Note: Actors' Yearbook (updated every September) is more actor-specific – that is, it doesn't contain listings for companies and individuals who offer services actors are unlikely to need. It also contains more detailed information than *Contacts*.

5: *Directors, producers, agents and casting directors*

Actors have probably existed since before the invention of writing; actors' agents have only been around since the invention of the telephone, just over a century ago. Prior to this, work-seeking actors had to make themselves known in person to potential employers – for instance, certain hostelries in the Covent Garden area of central London were well-known talent-spotting haunts. Actors would also catch a ride with one of the touring companies in the hope of proving themselves to the manager – and then being put on the payroll. Others would pay actor-managers to let them play small parts, in the hope of being noticed. All this meant a lot of hard work and/or expense (let alone the time needed to earn his/her living by other means) for the pre-electronic-age actor. The invention of actors' agents seemed to fill a vital gap.

Then came casting directors – a job previously done by directors and producers until many found that they didn't have enough time to do actor research. This is not because the latter don't want to see productions (in all media), it's the time each takes up. And almost everybody needs time – with friends, families, pets, etc. – in order to de-clutter the mind and sleep. I'm convinced that most directors, producers, agents and casting directors care deeply, but are severely short of time.

Who's who in casting

In most cases it is the director of any production (across all media) who makes the casting decisions. The exceptions include commercial theatre productions, television and films where the names will be cast by a producer (possibly with the help of a casting director) and the director employed by that producer. Also, commercials and smaller parts in films are sometimes cast by the casting director alone – who is also employed by the producer.

Directors

'I suppose you'll be having a bit of a rest now,' says the solicitous actor after the triumphant opening night. Kindly meant, but somewhat insensitive to the relieved but tired director. Apart from keeping an eye on the production, there are piles of paper demanding attention – among which is your precious letter, CV and photograph along with those of your peers. There will be others from freelance directors seeking work, and several unsolicited scripts from aspiring writers demanding to be read. However, this creative section is only a small proportion of the new paperwork to be dealt with. There are the messages insisting on urgent action, details of yet another complex funding scheme, letters of complaint from the public about the four-letter words in the last production or poor service in the restaurant or smells in the loo . . . The list is endless. Apart from all this there are papers to prepare for the Board of Management meeting, internal planning and policy meetings, the eternal energy-sapping battles with external bureaucracies – yet another long list of things to do.

Who on earth would want to run a theatre/production company? Well, some people do – probably for similar crazy reasons to those that made you want to be an actor. (Max Stafford-Clark, when Artistic Director of the Royal Court, said: 'I now run a business that occasionally puts on plays.') In some theatres the Administrator (or General Manager or Chief Executive) is senior to the Artistic Director, but even in these cases a lot of the director's time will still be taken up with urgent matters of administration which will have much greater priority than your sales package. Similar external (to actor concerns) matters exist for those in other media. Someone once said, 'The bigger the budget, the less you find yourself caring for the non-starry actors.'

I have tried to give you a perspective on a theatre director's life not for sympathy, but so that you have a better idea of whom you are trying to reach. They may vary as individuals but all have the above in common. And this kind of pressure governs the life of every kind of director – television and film directors coping with the mind-boggling organisation that is necessary, and freelance directors looking out for their own next jobs let alone yours. Actors are obviously important to directors, but because you are not in short supply other matters take a much greater priority. That is an unchanging fact.

The power brokers of the acting profession all work very long hours, have constant demands made on them and find it impossible to focus properly on each and every actor who communicates with them.

Producers

These are the 'top dogs' when there's real money involved – generally in films, television and commercial theatre. They will usually cast the stars and sometimes be involved in interviews and auditions for other parts.

Note: The term 'producer' is often used for the director of radio comedy and sketch shows.

Casting directors

It used to be only the biggest theatre companies who, along with most television and film companies, used the services of casting directors. The last couple of decades have seen a considerable growth in their numbers – both full-time and freelance. It's worth checking production credits for names, and you can find the CVs of some on the website of the Casting Directors' Guild of Great Britain and Ireland (CDG) <www.thecdg.co.uk>.

In fact the title 'Casting Director' is somewhat misleading as they usually only facilitate casting; it is usually the director, and sometimes the producer, who actually 'directs' the casting decisions. Their precise functions vary, but broadly they are the link from the director to the actor (usually via an agent) and take on a lot of the 'nitty-gritty' work involved in casting. This is not meant to give the impression that they just do the dirty work; they are expected to come up with bright ideas for casting that can take ages to formulate. An empathetic, intuitive and imaginative casting director has immeasurable value to both actors and director – and can be just as anxious about where their next job is coming from as you are.

It is important to remember that in an interview a casting director especially wants you to succeed and may even give you hints about what the director wants or give you some advice about how to approach the interview, because your performance in the director's eyes will reflect on the casting director's ability to make good suggestions. And the director is the casting director's employer.

With their growth in numbers there has been a rise in actors' cynicism about casting directors of the 'They never go and see productions; they cast from the television' variety. All the ones I know go to see at least three or four productions a week, keep careful notes about anyone who interests them and have a passion for finding new talent. I have heard stories of 'power-crazy rotten apples', but like their director and agent counterparts they are in a distinct minority.

The mechanics of casting

For a director, casting a production is as traumatic as a first night – I'm told that it can also be very 'fraught' for casting directors and producers. It is full of agonising decisions, disappointments as well as triumphs. There is no one definite methodology, and there are some variations between media – for instance, smaller parts in TV and film are sometimes cast by the casting director without the director's personal involvement. Generally, before even thinking about casting, the director gets to know the script, talks with the writer (if available), and begins discussions with the designer and anyone else who is part of the whole evolutionary process of a production (producer if it's a commercial production, musical director and choreographer for a musical, for instance). In television and film there are many more people with whom to start discussions and logistics to consider. Meanwhile, at the back of the director's mind ideas for potential casting will be fermenting – actors already known, others seen before. He or she will browse through *Spotlight* for inspiration (half-remembered names and faces) and/or do searches in *Spotlight* for very specific requirements – French-speaking gymnasts, for example. Perhaps a 'casting breakdown' has been sent to selected agents or that job has been delegated to Script Breakdown Services (SBS), which lists much of what is being cast and is only available to agents. Perhaps there's a casting director with whom to hold discussions. Apart from the director's own ideas there will be many more suggestions to go through, from which lists for serious consideration are drawn up.

Within all this, it's important to understand the processes involved between the decision to go ahead with a project and the start of rehearsals. *Note:* This summary does not include all the other processes (designs, marketing, etc.) that a management also has to go through during the same period. Problems in these 'processes' can disrupt smooth running – and create delays – in the casting of actors.

Note: I will use the term 'director' throughout to cover both them and casting directors.

The casting process Once a list of 'possibles' has been drawn up, somebody has to check whether people are available for the dates – this can be a time-consuming and tedious process. It may not start until several weeks after the suggestions came in and some actors may have become unavailable and new names come into the frame.

Availability checks A lot of actors seem to take these too much to heart. Directors, when thinking about casting, like to check a string of people for a part to help gain a perspective on how they might cast it. That's all. It's a private process. There is no point in dashing off letters/emails if you hear you've been checked to say how wonderful you'd be in the part. You are in the running and are at least of some interest.

On some casting directory websites you can find out who's been viewing your entry. Invariably, agents, casting directors, etc. flick through many more entries than those they finally shortlist. These viewings are not availability checks and it's best to ignore them.

The actor without an agent Doing an availability check on an actor without an agent can be embarrassing, even for a secretary, if the actor treats it as all but an offer. Too many actors jump in and start asking what the money is, the domestic arrangements they'll have to make, and so on. Don't jump the gun; there's a way to go yet. (This can be even more embarrassing with an actor already known to the director. It's so much easier when there's an agent in between.)

An interview At the same time as an availability check is done there may be a request to come for interview (sometimes done via video and including a reading and/or audition speech), or perhaps that will come in a later contact – the director may want to rethink who he or she wants to see now that the list of who is actually available is clear.

If you're known to the director you might get an offer without interview. Whether or not you know him or her, there could simply be a deafening silence – you didn't make the interview list for reasons you will probably never know.

Then the interviews are held and the agonising decision-making starts. (However, you, the actor, mustn't wait around agonising – best to forget about it.) Crystallising decisions can take several days' thought and research, sometimes significantly longer. This can sometimes involve recalls – making the process even more long-winded.

Some directors like to phone actors directly about doing a part – sometimes even before the formal offer is made. This usually happens between friends and is really to establish interest, or not, before spending time on the money side.

Slowly, slowly . . . Any responsible director will cast gradually: offer the lead first and when that actor accepts go on to offer the other parts in whatever way is appropriate. The director wants to build a company of actors who individually feel right and will work well together. This is comparatively simple if it's a small cast of two or three, but becomes complicated when it's above about six and requires an enormous amount of work for above a dozen. For example, X may seem perfect to play the husband of A, but if she turns down the offer and B accepts, the director may feel that Y would be better than X. If the process of A and/or B thinking about whether or not to accept has taken too much time, Y may no longer be available; the same may be the case for X. The director may well have other options; if not, more interviews will have to be held and there still may be other smaller parts to cast. Each stage of this process can take days, which grow into weeks, and it can all become very complicated. In practice there is rarely time to cast in this slow methodical way, so several offers will usually go out at once – but rarely all of them at the same time.

Getting 'pencilled' This is a term often used in casting commercials and sometimes elsewhere. It simply means that you are definitely being considered. A 'heavy pencil' means that you're probably among the final handful to be chosen from.

The offer When you do get offered a job don't just blindly say 'yes' – without any thought. If it's your first one, of course you'll probably take it. But just take a moment to think twice, because once you've said 'yes' you have made a verbal contract which is morally (and possibly legally) binding. If you turn round a few days later, when, say, you suddenly realise the holiday you've booked coincides with the middle of rehearsals, you will throw the organisation into turmoil. Directors don't just make offers willy-nilly. They give a lot of thought to each one they make. If you've got a legitimate problem, which it might be possible to work around, discuss it with the director (via your agent, if you have one) at this stage rather than at the beginning of rehearsals when there's so much else going on.

If you have an agent, it is important to take seriously any opinion he or she may express about the job – it might be that he or she feels it better for you to wait for other possible (more lucrative) work.

The late offer The effort put into 'building a company' can mean that some offers go through a long time after meeting the actors. At other times a whole string of successive offers for the same part get turned down, or the director just needs time to think. It may be that you are the second choice, but there is absolutely no point in feeling miffed. Directors do try to keep this kind of fact confidential, but sometimes that's impossible. You have to get on with the job as usual and forget there was ever any other choice but yourself.

Thinking about an offer It is usually perfectly acceptable to ask for a few days to think about an offer, and you are well within your rights to ask the organisation to send you a copy of the script to read. Don't feel pressured! The ball is very firmly in your court, and you can take reasonable time to read the script and weigh up the pros and cons. I've only once heard of a part being 'gazumped', so think about whether you like the part, can sort out any domestic arrangements, and so on – usually a day or two from receipt of the script is reasonable. There are numerous circumstances in which you may need longer – another offer in the wind, for instance. You should negotiate that extra time with the management, via your agent if you have one. Just because the work doesn't start for a while it doesn't mean that the director can wait for your decision for too long. If you do take too long – without good reason – you (and your agent) are asking to be put down in his or her black book. Unless otherwise negotiated, a few days is generally regarded as a reasonable time to take.

Turning down an offer You don't have to give reasons for doing this, but it is a good idea to have some up your sleeve. After all the thought that's gone into choosing to make that offer to you, it is the least you can do. Make sure your reasons are good and don't appear petty or arrogant or in any way insulting. Follow up your decision with a brief letter/email.

The decision-making involved in making offers can be an emotional one for a director – like watching a football match with your heart very much on one team. Everything should be fine but sometimes the full cast won't be known until the last moment before rehearsals start.

It is as nerve-racking as it can be for you, the actor, waiting to hear whether you've got the job. Casting is probably half of the creative work involved in a production.

Changing your mind A director generally expects anywhere between 10 and 50 per cent of offers to be turned down – for all kinds of good reasons. That is respected, but if someone says 'no' after at first saying 'yes' it upsets carefully thought-out plans, throws the whole process out of joint and wastes several people's time. All the organisation's departments – wardrobe, wages, publicity, and so on – have then to be told of your change of heart, which takes up more administrative time. If a significantly better offer does come up, or some kind of personal difficulty arises, and there is decent time to recast, most directors will release you from your contract, but the reasons have got to be good. Be sure before you say 'yes'. Actually signing the contract is almost a formality.

Other issues

The money Thank God this is usually not the director's (or casting director's) job. Most organisations have their well-established scales of payment, and in many cases there is no room for manoeuvre. Most organisations are keenly aware that actors talk to each other and any apparent unfairness must be avoided at the outset. Generally, the actor who can negotiate more than an extra 10 per cent either has a lot of publicity clout or is in some way indispensable to the production. Agents will know the going rates and should do their best to get you more than the offer, depending on what arguments can be presented (you may have to help with this). If you haven't got an agent, check with Equity; it has been known for unscrupulous managements to try to offer under their normal rates to actors without agents.

It is almost always counterproductive to say 'no' because you want more money. You will be marked down as someone not worth bothering to ask in future.

Nudity and simulated sex Think very carefully before accepting a part that demands anything like this. Under Equity agreements a management is supposed to warn you even if it's only a possibility, at the contractual stage; but I have known several actors, when faced with actually revealing themselves, try to bottle out after initially going along with the idea. Some directors will be sympathetic, but it is yet another example of potential time-wasting. Consider it properly before you say 'yes'.

Silence It is quite normal not to be formally told that you haven't got a job for which you've been seen. If you've heard nothing within a week, you almost certainly haven't got it. In my view, it's much better to put the possibility to the back of your mind immediately after the meeting and occupy yourself with other matters.

If you are told without asking, that means that you came very, very close.

Agents

Some people do survive quite well without an agent – especially in those specialist areas like children's theatre where properly paid jobs are often openly advertised – but getting work without one is harder in theatre and extremely difficult in the recorded media. Actors without agents tend to lack credibility in the eyes of potential employers. It's not fair, but it's a fact. However hard you work at getting to know potential employers, most agents have their fingers closer to the pulse, know what's coming up, and simply have far more contacts than you can ever have. That's their job. Directors and casting directors rely on agents they trust to help in the filtering process of whom to interview. A good agent also understands contracts, knows the 'going rates' and has more clout to get money that's owing.

Individual agents vary in the ways that they like to operate. There are those who like to maintain reasonably close personal relationships with their clients; others prefer to be more businesslike. There are those who actively discourage clients from doing lower-paid theatre, preferring it if they wait around for a more lucrative television opportunity – even to the extent of not passing on an offer. (I discovered such an agent when my offer was turned down for someone who I knew (through a mutual friend) was available and wanted to do my production. I broke the rules and phoned her directly, and she sorted her agent out.) There are also those who are 'here today and gone tomorrow' – it's a very mobile population.

The important thing is that a good agent works hard at making contacts and makes sure that they are respected by those contacts. Just as the agent represents you, you represent your agent.

Being an agent is, most of the time, as disheartening as being an actor – and it's hard work, easily running into sixty or seventy hours a week. Agents putting clients up for things are putting themselves on the line. All directors and casting directors have blacklists of agents whose clients have messed them around too often, so good agents are very careful about how they select those they are going to represent. They have to feel that they can work with you at selling you effectively, just as directors have to feel that they can work with, and benefit from, you in a company.

Notes: There is huge confusion in the use of the terms 'personal manager' and 'agent' – this is compounded by the fact that many people whom I would call 'agents' are members of The Personal Managers' Association (PMA). (NB The Agents' Association largely consists of those who represent Light Entertainment Artistes.) To me, a 'personal manager' is someone who sorts out all the nitty-gritty details like travel arrangements and press interviews, while an 'agent' promotes their clients to potential employers and negotiates contracts. To add to the confusion, some agencies have the phrase 'Personal Management' in their titles.

Also, you'll hear the term 'Casting Agent/Agency' bandied around. These serve a different function. They are usually walk-on/supporting artists' agents who are employed to supply crowds in television and film. They have client bases of lots of different types and on request can supply a suitable crowd for any occasion. Thus they fulfil the roles of both agent and casting director for non-speaking parts that don't need to be auditioned.

Types of agencies There are all kinds of agency and agent listed in the 'Agents & Personal Managers' section of *Contacts* – around 600 (of which around a quarter don't represent adult actors) the last time that I counted. (All those listed in *Actors' Yearbook* do represent adult actors.) Roughly, the ones who primarily represent adult actors break down into the following types:

- The large and prestigious (several hundred clients) with lots of 'names'. These agencies are staffed by a number of individual agents (often with assistants), and the focus can tend to be on their stars – sometimes ignoring their less well-known clients.

- The large (a few of whom are prestigious) who also represent models, presenters, etc. Once again, their focus can meander through their various specialisms.
- The large and less prestigious with smaller staffs, who rely on sheer numbers to keep them financially afloat – client promotion seems to be effected by sending out great wodges of CVs and photographs randomly in the hope that a few will land on the right desks.
- The medium-sized (around a hundred clients) who are often staffed by a couple of agents with minimal assistance – a few are very prestigious.
- The small (around a few dozen clients) who are usually run by a single person often working from home with a part-time assistant – I don't know how some of these manage to make a living.
- The co-operatives (see pages 102–3), who usually consist of around twenty members and are run by those members, sometimes with a full-time manager.

Think carefully about which kind of agency might suit you in order to sort out who to target for representation.

Finding an agent

Targeting With so many to choose from, it is wise to spend time on researching which ones to target. Of course, you'll get ideas from teachers and friends, but you should also spend time looking at websites – unless you're prepared to spend a small fortune on postage and other costs.

Notes: A significant proportion of agencies require approach via the postal system. Some don't have publicly available websites and, of those who have, some only provide limited information. Some very good ones don't want their client list published for all to see. Such agencies are wary of other agencies knowing too much. So although a client list is useful it's not the be-all and end-all.

I suggest that a credible actors' agency should have:

- a good range of clients – covering the age spectrum;
- a credible male/female ratio of clients – across that age spectrum;
- professional-quality photographs;
- a reasonable client to individual agent ratio – I suggest around 40:1.

I am suspicious of agencies that:

- offer other services – photos, showreels, workshops, etc. – especially if these are conditions of representation;
- represent models and/or children *and* actors – generally, the work they broker is for photo-shoots and extra work;
- ask for up-front fees of any kind – however small, even if 'refundable' – apart from co-operative agencies;
- list their clients by first name only – a convention usually used only by models' and extras' agencies;
- list clients on their websites whom they no longer represent. I think it reasonable to allow a week for removal of such an entry (you can check who an actor is currently being represented by via Spotlight's website);
- have spelling mistakes and grammatical errors on their websites and other published material;
- go over the top in promoting themselves;
- are new and don't give any kind of pedigree – i.e. background – to their owner(s). There are no formal training courses for agents. The good ones learn through working for other credible actors' agencies.

After doing your research, you will still be left with quite a long list. If they don't make it clear on their website, it can be a good idea to phone round (using your best telephone manner) to enquire whether they are taking on new clients at the moment. (You'll probably get a lower response rate if you use email.) Be prepared to receive short shrift from some, as agents (and their assistants) get very fed up with such phone calls. However, you might strike lucky if an agent has lost a few clients recently, for instance.

Contacting agents Write to your target list; never email unless specifically requested as many will only accept postal submissions, let alone turn up unannounced on an agent's doorstep. Send your CV and photograph and tell them when and where they can see your work. It doesn't have to be a leading role; agents are not necessarily blinded by who had the most lines. A few agents will accept showreels, but check before you send one.

Don't expect an agent to come to see you in a production if you've tried to invite them at the last minute. They are very busy people, out on business seeing clients in productions and so on almost every night of the week, and will be booked up well in advance.

When writing, use all the parameters that are set out in chapter 6 – except that it is better to send an agent a 10 x 8 inch (20 x 25cm) photograph. Don't forget to enclose a suitably-sized s.a.e. if you'd like your photograph returned.

Note: Many agents won't take you on unless you are in *Spotlight* – if you're not it makes it much harder for them to market you.

Meeting an agent If an agent invites you to come and see them, approach the interview in exactly the same way you would an interview with a casting director or director (see chapter 7). Dress comfortably and well, and don't be late. The major differences will be that (a) you almost certainly won't have to do a speech or reading (but I have known agents ask for a speech, so be prepared), (b) you could be constantly interrupted by the phone and (c) you could find as much attention paid to a laptop, iPhone, iPad, etc. as to you.

What to ask? When meeting a potential agent, don't be afraid to ask questions. You are hoping to be 'represented'; you're not suing for work. Ask how long they've been in operation (unless they're obviously established), the fields of work they operate in, number of clients, rates of commission, their attitude to low-pay/no-pay work, and so on. In short, try to build an overall working picture of the agency and their professional clout.

Not quite Unless you are a well-established actor, an agent won't take you on until they see you in a production. I know of several instances where agents have said they are interested in an individual but haven't formally taken them on until the required showcase. This can take time, so be patient. And, of course, they have to like what they see before making the commitment. Being invited to go and meet agents who have seen your work doesn't mean that they are certain to take you on. It often happens that they will say: 'Not at the moment, but keep in touch.' It could be they have someone very like you on their books, that one more person will just tip the agency into being too big to handle, or some other good reason that is finally not your fault. You just have to go along with this decision. Don't get frustrated, and do 'keep in touch'. If you are in this position, you can always consult them about the suitability of a particular job offer. You might also be able to ask them to negotiate an offer for you; they'll normally take commission on it, even if you don't finally get taken on.

An offer Don't feel rushed into signing up at the first offer of representation. Get advice from other actors and directors who have current experience of particular agencies. Advice from others will be offered very freely but can be coloured by past experiences which may well have nothing to do with that agency's current situation.

If it's a newly established agency, it's wise to check on the owner's experience – which previous agents they've worked for. You can also check with Equity and Spotlight for any history of previous difficulties. Try to get a sense of how well organised they are. This can be difficult, but a disorganised agent won't last for long.

Also, can you work well with that agent/agency? I don't mean is there a good shoulder to cry on (see 'The actor-agent personal relationship', page 101), but do you feel that they would be good at working well with you – a bit like the ideal director-actor relationship? Don't sign up unless you feel at least fairly sure.

There are bigger, prestigious agencies who have access to more casting information than others, but although you may acquire some of their prestige, will you get sufficient attention?

Don't be beguiled by special offers like 'no commission for the first year'. It'll probably take at least a year before you start earning enough money to make the commission worth having.

Be warned that no legitimate agency charges a registration, or other up-front fee (for inclusion on their website, for instance); back off quickly if that is part of an offer of representation. The exception to this is the co-operative agencies who have joining fees which are perfectly legitimate – see pages 102–3 for more details.

Selecting an agent If you are one of the lucky few who suddenly gets an offer of representation from more than one agent, take time to think and carefully weigh up the pros and cons of each one and get further up-to-date opinion if you can. It is possible to change if you choose wrongly, but it can be quite a hassle and the others may not be interested any longer.

Signing up So, you've selected the agent you would like to represent you; what next? The agreement may simply be sealed with a handshake – or you may be offered a contract to sign. If the former, ensure that the details are clear to you (ask for them in writing); if the latter, read it carefully! It may simply consist of the rates of commission, but it may contain a period of notice clause – that is, the length of time, after you've given notice, that you will continue to have to pay commission on the work you do. (Not just to any new agent, but also to your old one – double commission.) Three months is common, but I've known it to be a year, which can be extremely awkward. Check any contract offered very carefully before signing – check it with Equity if in any doubt as they have a Code of Conduct for Agents and a standard contract.

Note: Most agents will insist that you agree to 'sole representation' for all your acting work. An exception to this is in the world of voice-overs, which has its own specialist agents.

Working with an agent

You can't relax just yet When you have an agent to represent you, don't expect them to do all the work of selling you. (There are occasional exceptions, when an agent feels so confident in a client's saleability that they say: 'Leave it all to me.') You will still have to send out lots of submissions on your own behalf, especially in the first few years of your career. Keep up your own contacts and make sure that your agent knows who you are writing to so that recipients don't get the impression that there's no communication between you.

The complete you Tell your new agent everything that might help to sell you. Be prepared to give them a very full biography – you never know what might be useful. Go through your CV together so that all the possibilities and pitfalls are clear. If you claim horse-riding, for instance, your agent needs to know how good you actually are at it. It can be as damaging for an agent to make a false or exaggerated claim as for an actor (see 'Exaggerated claims', page 120).

Also let your agent have all those little details that don't go on your CV (measurements, for example) for the files – just in case. You never know what peculiarity or apparently unrelated physical quirk or skill some production might need all of a sudden – including smoking. Make sure that your agent is clear about any kind of work you really don't want to do: it will be embarrassing and time-wasting if they get you an interview for such a job and subsequently have to phone back to cancel on those grounds.

The keeper of your CV It's quite common for agents to get details on CVs wrong – play titles, parts, writers, and so on. It's not necessarily their fault; after all, it was you who played the part. Did you give them the correct details? Errors can creep in very easily, especially when there are unfamiliar names. Periodically check up on the CV your agent has on file. I once came across a CV sent by an agent on which it was claimed that the client concerned had played a part in a particular production which in fact my own wife had played. I don't know whose fault it was, but agents do deal with lots of CVs.

It is common in interview for actors to complain in some way about the CV the agent has sent to the director – it omits recent and/ or important work, for instance. A periodic check should avoid this potentially downbeat moment in an interview.

Your availability You must keep your agency in touch with your availability for interviews as well as for work. For instance, if you have a regular non-acting job, how much notice do you need to give to get time off? Make sure that anything that could affect arrangements for interviews is clear; it'll save a lot of extra phone calls/emails/texts and hassle. Some interviews – for commercials, for example – tend to be arranged at very short notice and only take place through a single morning or afternoon. It will not always be possible to fit in with your requirements.

Make sure your agent knows your holiday plans as far in advance as possible, and if you are going to be unavailable for any other reason.

Stay in touch Don't use the requirements of the preceding paragraphs as an excuse to keep phoning or emailing with new fiddly little details. You should keep in regular but not persistent contact with your agent. Agents vary as to how often they like you to contact them; ask yours. Don't keep asking 'What am I up for?' – that can be extremely irritating as it takes precious time to comb through all the various lists. (Agents deal with an enormous amount of information.) Sometimes your agent will volunteer this information. Leave it at that. Often the office will be frantic when you phone – other lines humming, emails flying, even (in some offices) faxes whirring. Be quick to recognise the fevered voice and don't take offence at an apparently brusque manner. Make your point and ring off with decent speed. Remember all the time they spend on the phone already; don't add to that burden. However, don't become too remote.

Your general aim should be to keep your presence felt. You should do this subtly but consistently, especially if you are part of a large client list and/or are in a long period of employment or unemployment. An agent's life is an extremely busy one, and there are never enough hours in the day or days in the week. Even if it's a slack time for interviews there are always general promotions to be done, charities phoning up asking for the services of the agency's stars, and so on. It can be easy for your presence to get lost among everything else that needs doing. To earn a living an agency has to neglect some of its clients some of the time.

Times and means of contact Most agencies don't start until 10.00 or 10.30 a.m. (because they're often out on professional business during evenings), and work through until about 6.00 p.m. It's best to avoid phoning on a Monday or a Friday except on pressing business; especially don't phone at 5.55 p.m. on a Friday unless it's mega-important, and don't try to phone outside normal hours. Many agents work from home. Others are in their offices early, but this is their quiet time in which to sort out their desks and their minds. I know they could switch their voicemail on, but there could be an urgent call from a casting director that just fits you. Emailing or texting may seem less intrusive, but they are less personal. It's a good idea to check with your agent about their preferred 'times and means of contact'.

Note: Don't forget that agents have lunch hours too.

Social calls You should go and see your agent periodically. Phone calls are not as good as meeting in the flesh. Suggest buying him/her a drink or lunch every so often – perhaps every couple of months.

Your new image If you are radically changing your hairstyle or hair colour, or growing a beard, let everybody in the agency know immediately. They will be made to look very silly if you turn up at an interview having been advertised as having long hair and you are now a skinhead. I know time can reverse such changes, but your agent will have lost some credibility points with whoever is casting, and it could sour future relations – for the agency and for you.

Your agent seeing your work Hopefully your agent will come and see you in productions, but don't feel let down if you are so far away that he or she simply cannot make it. In these circumstances send copies of the good reviews you have received. You may not be able to get complimentary tickets – perhaps you have used up your allocation or your agent can only come on a 'no comp.' night. Unless your agent offers, you should pay for the ticket(s) yourself, without comment. However much agents may enjoy a production it is still work as far as they are concerned. It is therefore common courtesy not to add to that burden.

Also, don't feel let down if they miss television performances even with the opportunities to view things online afterwards; they may simply not have time to watch.

Note: Be tactful in finding out what your agent thought of a production.

Always be contactable Make sure your agent knows how to contact you quickly all the time. A young, broke and phoneless actor didn't phone in on the day an interview came through for a filming job for which he was perfect. The interview was the next day but, by the time he did phone, it was too late to get there; several hundred pounds and a few precious ounces of goodwill went down the drain. The same applies to checking emails, texts and voicemails.

Get to know everybody in the agency Get to know all the staff in the office and what jobs they do. Don't dismiss a secretary because you think they are in a lowly position.

Commission You will have to pay your agent commission (usually between 10 and 20 per cent) even if it was you who made the contact that led to your getting the job. You will often hear other actors complain that they get all their own work so why should they pay commission? The reasons are because your agent negotiated the contract for you and even if it is no better than anybody else's in the production your agency is also spending its time making phone calls, writing letters and emails and generally looking for work for you all the time. They don't give up because you've got six weeks' work coming up. Don't even think of querying it! If you do, it could well sour relations with them and make it more difficult for you to work together in the future.

There are some variations in commission charges, for example different rates for the different media. There is no statutory set of rates, but generally you'll pay a higher rate the better the work is paid. You should also establish clearly when your commission is due: weekly or at the end of a contract. Make sure it is all clear at the start of your relationship, so that there are no grounds for destructive disagreement later on. It is also very important to pay your commission promptly.

Sometimes an employer will pay your money directly to your agent and he or she will deduct the commission before sending the remainder on to you – which they should do within ten days.

If you change agents then the commission due on any residual payments (a repeated television appearance, for instance) is owing to the agent who negotiated the original contract.

Most agents' turnovers are high enough for them to have to register for VAT. This means that they will have to add the appropriate percentage to your commission charge.

The direct approach Sometimes a director will approach an actor directly about an interview or even an offer. This usually happens when the director knows you or perhaps doesn't realise you've got an agent. Ask the director to do all the business through your agent. This might seem like taking the long way round, but it may be that your agent has you up for another job, for instance.

Even if it's a Fringe production or student film, where there are no financial negotiations to go through, check with your agent first – too many actors don't. If your agent doesn't know your real availability you could put him or her in an embarrassing situation.

Reporting back Report back to your agent on how an interview went. This helps him or her to get to know you better at that vital nerve-point of the whole profession. However, if you are lucky enough to be doing a lot of interviews then it's not necessary to phone about all of them.

If one goes badly, work out what was your fault and discuss it with your agent with assurances that you can put it right next time. This maintains their confidence in you. If it was a difficult interviewer do mention it as the information can be useful for other clients.

'You're up for . . .' Your agent may well tell you that you've been put up for a particular part or that there has been an availability check on you – and then nothing happens. You don't even get an interview! Don't immediately blame your agent. It could easily have been down to the fickle nature of this profession.

'My agent cocked it up' In fact you shouldn't take your insecurities out on your agent at all. Yes, agents can make mistakes, but in my experience any 'cock-up' is much more likely to have been the actor's fault. You have to work together; it should be a professional relationship based on mutual trust. Inefficient agents don't survive for very long.

If you do discover that a serious error has been committed – you weren't even put up for a well-advertised part you were perfect for, for instance – check it out with your agent. The same applies if he or she hasn't seen your work for a significant amount of time. If you have a legitimate complaint, express it directly. Don't let it fester as gossip among other actors.

'My agent's doing nothing for me' Another common cry. Don't immediately blame your agent if nothing is happening. Inevitably, a few agents are lazy and/or inefficient, but remember that they only earn money from you if you are working and therefore it is in their interests to promote you for work opportunities. The only thing to do if you genuinely believe this is to put it, simply and positively, to your agent. I have heard of several incidents of people doing this, and their luck changed.

Your responsibility towards your agent It is important never to put your agent or agency into an embarrassing situation – not only will it reflect on them, it could also reflect on other clients. A recent example was an actor who phoned his agent to say that he couldn't go to an interview because he had a hangover. Not only was all the work the agent had put into getting the appointment wasted, it also made me sceptical about that particular agency – and its other clients.

Clarity If your agent is discussing an offer made to you, make sure your feelings about the matter are made absolutely clear; agents have been known to accept offers when the actors have said that they 'think' they'll do the job, when what they meant was that they would probably accept but they weren't sure yet.

The actor-agent working relationship Your agent is not your slave, but not your master either. Ultimately, you employ your agent – not vice versa. Ideally, your relationship is that of a partnership with each side having different but overlapping responsibilities. Your agent probably works harder for you than you ever realise, just as he or she may not fully understand what you go through in rehearsing a play, for instance. Trust and respect are essential, and a little appreciation from you in the form of home-made jam, shelves erected (these are real examples) or a simple 'Thank You' card can only enhance that relationship and ultimately make it more profitable.

The actor-agent personal relationship If this becomes too close, the working relationship can often go wrong. If you have personal problems, find someone else to help you. Your agent should only know about your problems if they affect your ability to work, and even then you only need to give the essential facts and not the nitty-gritty detail.

Your depressions about rejections and bouts of unemployment are common to all actors and are therefore tacitly understood. It is positively destructive to take those depressions out on your agent as it takes up valuable time and will almost certainly reduce their ability to work well for you. It could all become a vicious downward spiral.

Your other half Most agents won't take on both halves of a couple because of possible knock-on effects if there are problems and/or the couple splits up. However secure your domestic relationship seems to you both, don't even suggest the idea of your other half coming on to your agent's books. Nevertheless, your other half should get to know your agent; after all, he or she could be taking messages for you, and the agent wants to feel sure that they will be safely delivered.

Leaving your agent Like any relationship the actor-agent one can get tired. If this is the case, make a clean break. I have heard of too many messy 'divorces' which harmed the actor more than the agent: it's a small world and agents do talk to each other; some are even related to each other. Be especially careful if you are looking for a new agent while still with another one. The agents you talk to will be discreet; you should be too.

Your agent asking you to leave This happens occasionally when an agency feels that the relationship has gone sour in some way or other. I've never known it to be done indiscreetly, so don't create waves that might reach other agents' ears. There is no point in asking for a reprieve. Try to find out why it happened and make sure it doesn't happen with your next agent.

Co-operative agencies

This idea started in the 1970s and there are now about forty co-operative agencies each representing about twenty clients ('members') – many more than this makes the important internal communications a nightmare. It is vital to understand how they work before approaching them.

Essentially these are run by the actors on their books, everybody representing everybody else. Often there are no salaried staff and all the work is done on a voluntary basis as and when individuals are available. The only costs are administrative (rent of offices, phones, photocopying, and so on), with no profit going to any individual. It's a great idea that's hard to put into practice, as the pioneers discovered – in fact, some are taking on administrators to co-ordinate everything. The best are as efficient as the very best of conventional agents, a few as unprofessional as the very worst. In general, they probably don't have as much status as the more well-established conventional agencies but are certainly not to be dismissed.

The crucial thing a co-operative has to do is to ensure excellent communications between its individual members as they take turns in the office. It is essential that each member has a good working knowledge of every other member. Smooth running of a co-op takes a great deal of detailed organisation, and precise passing-on of information between the members is vital. For example, an offer will often take several days to discuss, and the employer won't want to have to go back over the previously discussed details when someone else takes over the manning of the phone. Indeed, some managements will have nothing to do with co-operatives because they feel they never know to whom they are talking. It has also been known for managements to approach individual co-operative members direct – mistakenly thinking that an agency staffed by actors cannot 'know what it's doing'. (Some managements feel uncomfortable about discussing money with a third party who also happens to be an actor.) However, co-operatives have learned these lessons the hard way and have adapted their democratic working processes to surmount these and other communication problems. Their credibility with managements continues to grow.

Commission is often lower than a conventional agency, but there is generally a joining fee and/or regular monthly or annual payments which are used to meet the costs of running the agency in which the member is a partner.

Before you are asked to join a co-operative the members will want to be sure that you will fit well into their team and are willing to and capable of learning the necessary office skills. Therefore there is usually a probationary period of membership after which you and the agency can decide whether or not to continue the partnership. You will also have to be sure that you'll be happy to commit time to taking your turn in manning the office and attending the regular meetings that are necessary to the efficient running of these agencies – democracy can be a very slow form of management.

A friend who joined a co-operative found a new lease of life and a lot more work and said, 'It's a wonderful family atmosphere.' Another who works a fair amount and had been with a co-operative for a long time finally left and found a conventional agent. She said: 'I'm right with "All for one and one for all", but you must remember the dark side of human nature. What actually happens is "All for me".' You have to decide if 'co-operative' life is really for you if offered the chance to join one. It can be a very good way for a newcomer to learn about the insides of the mechanics of casting. *Note:* Some co-ops are wary of taking on newcomers as they don't feel they have time to train them properly.

Finally, a comment from a friend with long experience of co-ops: 'In my experience the people who flourish in co-ops are independent-minded and experienced (although not starry) actors who have grown dissatisfied with the performance of their undistinguished conventional agent. The bane of their lives is omniscient and over-confident recent-graduate members!'

You can find out more about co-ops on the Co-operative Personal Management Association (CPMA) website <www.cpma.coop>.

Final thought

Agents come a close second to casting directors in actors' complaints sessions. I have several times been privy to agents' complaints sessions and some of their clients figure quite highly, although the problems are certainly more discreetly aired. There have to be faults on both sides – that's human nature. In the majority of cases I suspect that a lack of professional understanding is the root cause of most disenchantment.

6: *Your promotional material*

In spite of the incredible growth of the internet and the increasing facility to access it from almost anywhere, letters, CVs and photographs remain at the heart of actor-promotional material. Often you'll be asked to digitise these, but there is still a significant proportion of casting-brokers who insist on paper versions – especially when they don't know you.

Letters, CVs and photographs

Writing a letter, with CV and photograph, is the first step towards getting work (or an agent) for your first few years unless you are very, very lucky. Even if you are fortunate enough to have a good agent you will probably need to do some writing yourself. When you have some experience under your belt as well as a good agent it is amazing how a well-timed and well-presented sales package (submission) can open up new directions for you. Considering how crucial these are, the lack of care and attention the majority of actors seem to put into them is amazing.

A friend of mine estimates that she wrote 500 letters when she was first starting out and ended up with three agents wanting to represent her and a small part in a production that eventually went into the West End. She kept up this letter writing for two years and then decided that she couldn't be bothered any more, and her work rate went down. Especially in your early years, you will probably have to keep this subtle pressure up – even if you have got a good agent. You might be lucky, but until you are known in at least some circles the only way to get work is to keep up the publicity campaign. Even then you should keep plugging away, but perhaps not so often and not in such volume.

Each director, casting director and agent receives thousands of submissions per year – I received about a thousand for a recent production with a cast of four, for which I hadn't even circulated agents for suggestions. It takes time to read each letter and CV and absorb the photograph, and even more to select the roughly 5 per cent one has time to meet.

So what do you do in your letter (and CV and photograph) to attract attention if a recipient doesn't know you? There is no single answer to this fundamental question, and the best submission in the world can pass in front of blind eyes if the recipient has weightier matters immediately to the fore at the moment your carefully thought-out piece of advertising lands on the desk. On a bad day there can be a real sense that this is just more junk mail to be thrown straight in the bin – physical or the computer version. All look for ways of reducing the fast-growing pile as it threatens to overwhelm them. Some of this rejection will be done on the basis of appropriateness, some will occur for more trivial reasons – minor details which consciously or unconsciously irritate the reader – and some because of the crude attention-seeking nature of the contents. Remember, we in the UK react strongly against the obvious advert which bludgeons. Study an evening's commercial breaks for marvellous examples of the subtle sell.

Don't get the impression that receiving submissions is tedious in itself. It only becomes a chore when so many have contents churned out with the same old formulae, make the usual mistakes and/or rely on blatant gimmickry. Also, many of us would privately admit to feeling guilty at not being able to see everyone – and guilt can make people irrational.

The crucial thing to remember is that your letter, CV and photograph is your first point of contact with the recipient and will be flipped through along with a pile of others. The amount of time spent scanning your particular 'sales package' will probably be between ten and twenty seconds at the initial sort-through to decide who appears interesting and who doesn't.

Note: All that follows pertains when writing to directors, agents, casting directors and other managements. Also, my focus will be on paper versions with only a mention of the digital forms where necessary.

Some pitfalls to watch out for in your letters

Fundamentals Bad spelling and a disregard for accepted grammar and punctuation are immediately alienating to a literate reader. Remember, a lot of those you're trying to reach are language graduates and, even if not, they are used to working with – and care about – the written word.

Exclamation marks! Some people go overboard with exclamation marks and other visual emphases. The eye is instantly drawn to these, and they can easily undermine the impact of the actual words. The sense should be in those words – without any props.

Strictly, an exclamation mark should only be used after an order, warning or sudden expression of feeling – an exclamation.

Alan who? Equally off-putting are misspelt character names or play titles, playwrights' names – especially when they happen to be personal friends. (You'd have thought Alan Ayckbourn was so famous that people would know how to spell his name, but a significant minority of correspondents add an 'e' at the end.)

The look of your letter There is no doubt about how much the initial impact of the letter – before a word is read – counts. Unless your handwriting (see page 115) is pleasing to the eye and legible, use a computer and make sure that the printout looks crisp and clear. Cramped line spacing, splodgy or faded print and extraneous 'crud' (often added by poorly maintained printers) are common faults and make your letter – and consequently you – look amateur.

Note: The same applies to emails. Although not necessarily printed out, the look – if cluttered – will be instantly off-putting.

'Dear Sir/Madam' Over-formal letters which could just as well be requesting a consignment of bananas won't get you far. (Does this actor have any imagination?) Never write to 'Sir/Madam' and end with 'Yours faithfully'. Get a name and end with a warm greeting. However, don't get too familiar and address somebody only by their first name unless you know them.

It is accepted convention to use the recipient's full name rather than addressing him or her as Mr/Miss/Ms So-and-So. But be careful about using common abbreviations of first names – not everybody likes them and some prefer to reserve them for close friends.

Also, get their title right. As an Associate Director I used to get quite irritated if a letter was addressed to me as 'Simon Dunmore, Assistant Director'. Don't write to the Administrator/General Manager, either. They may have power but they won't have much, if any, influence over casting. They will usually pass your letter on to the director (or casting director), but he or she could be slightly alienated by its second-hand nature.

'I'd like to introduce myself . . .' Letters starting with this or 'My name is . . .' come over as being completely banal – the former is at the heart of the purpose behind your letter and the latter should be in your letterhead.

Other banalities A phrase like 'In my capacity as an actor' is also obvious, as are facts like 'I am an actor' or 'I would like to audition' or even 'I am writing'. Yet an amazing number of people use these phrases (and similar ones) in order to start their letters, bridge gaps or as a method of building up to a particular point. Don't do it!

Childhood dreams You are trying to convey something of yourself, but it's a big mistake to resort to childhood dreams of being an actor ('I was the typical little girl in pink ballet practice clothes spinning round the kitchen') or the 'buzz' you get from acting. It is important that you come over as a grounded grown-up with the imagination and skills of an actor.

Being too clever Quoting from obscure literature, being intellectually provocative ('*Hamlet* is a dreadful play'), and so on, are ways of easily alienating unknown readers.

Attention-seeking gambits It is a big mistake to resort to attention-seeking gambits like silly jokes, phrases like 'Gissa job' and vulgarity in general. Another popular but puerile trick is to send out spoof questionnaires for the recipient to fill in: for example, a list of potential reasons for not being seen, with boxes to put appropriate ticks in. This kind of stunt is incredibly annoying. I've known people resort to writing indifferent poems, appealing for the charity of an interview on the basis that it's their birthday or it's near Christmas. A friend once went so far as to dress himself as a motorcycle messenger and deliver an oar to an impresario with a letter saying: 'I just wanted to get my oar in.' He got no reply whatsoever.

What follows is possibly the most graphic piece of attention-seeking I've ever come across:

Hi Simon!

Here's something that might interest you:

WHAT THE ACTRESS REALLY SAID TO THE BISHOP

MARIA, 24, Fresh out of [*Name of drama school*]. Young, confident and bursting with enthusiasm.

BISHOP, 93, Wise beyond his years.

Maria enters open confessional box centre stage:

BISHOP: How long is it since you have been to confession, my child?

MARIA: About eight years, your grace, but I do have an excuse. I ran away to Hong Kong to pursue a life on the stage.

BISHOP: A life on the stage? But they don't have any stages out there, only stock markets and refugees. I'm afraid you'll have to do better than that.

MARIA: But it's true! I worked in television there for six years; writing, directing and performing in my own series of children's dramas.

BISHOP: Ah, television, that's not quite the thing is it? No, no. One must appear in, ah, the flesh. Although one must not be tempted by the flesh, indeed no. (*Coughs*) Tell me, my dear, have you had temptation put in, ah, your way?

MARIA: Yes it has, your grace, many, many times.

BISHOP: Good lord, my dear, can you, ah, describe them?

MARIA: Well, I started off with groups, you know, five or six of us – just for fun – and then it started getting quite serious . . .

BISHOP: (*Pause*) Yes, yes go on my dear go on.

MARIA: Recently it's been on my own . . .

BISHOP: (*Splutter*)

MARIA: Although I still really enjoy doing it in schools . . .

BISHOP: (*Suffers massive coronary from overdose of double entendres*)

Get the whole story on the attached CV. I'd be happy to audition for any forthcoming productions or simply come in for a chat.

> Yours devotedly,
> [*signature*]

However, a neat and clever gambit at the right moment, particularly if it's for film or television, can help. Mike Newall (director of *An Awfully Big Adventure*) told the story of how he met the girl who eventually played the lead in the film. She initially hand-wrote a letter on lined paper that was 'very characterful'. She went on to appear at the interview in knee-socks and clothes akin to the period – and 'all but played the part' in the interview. I suspect this kind of strategy is only applicable to film, where it is sometimes the case that directors want the real thing plonked under their noses.

The appeal Frustration with your lot is a fundamental part of almost every actor's working life. Don't let it creep into your letters. Too many people try to use it as grounds for appeal to the recipient's better nature. An approach like 'I've done my stint in children's theatre, so give me a chance' is not only condescending towards a fundamental part of the profession but also reads like 'whinge'. Logic goes out of the window. The attack is based on those notes in the audio spectrum calculated to go right through me.

'Brevity is the soul of wit' As for letters that go on for several pages, nobody has the time. Especially those that go on about your whole philosophy of 'life, acting and the universe'. Believe it or not, people do it. Two or three hundred words – at most – is perfectly sufficient, and fewer is better. That's not much – the next two sections combined contain just over two hundred words.

However, don't take brevity too far. 'I'm writing to you with regard to your auditions for [*name of production*], and I would like to be considered for an audition.' This tells me nothing about you.

Flattery Don't resort to base flattery about a recipient's productions. Compliments are good to receive, but some correspondents seem to think that going a little further can help their cause, and that is not necessarily true. People often try the more general gambit of 'I've heard about the good work you are doing' or variations on this theme; this comes over as ingratiating and patronising. The other popular tack is the double flattery approach: 'The wonderful work of your company would suit my talents precisely.' This is incredibly alienating. Your letter should be about you, not about me, but don't overly flatter yourself by making statements like 'I am brilliant; you cannot do without me.' That just comes over as arrogance, let alone writing about how 'dedicated' and 'committed' you are.

Undermining yourself The more modest correspondents go for statements like 'I'm a hard worker', 'I'd fit in well with your company' or 'I'll do anything, even work backstage'. Acting is hard work, so the ability to shoulder it is a prerequisite for the job and therefore doesn't need mentioning. Likewise the ability to work well with other people. As for implying that working backstage is the lowliest job – you are insulting very important people.

'But' and other qualifying words 'But' is a very useful little word, but it can tend to bring a negative feel to your prose. Try to avoid using it and similar qualifying words. 'I have been working on the Fringe; my main aim now is to work in regional theatre' reads more positively than 'I have been working on the Fringe, but my main aim now is to work in regional theatre.'

'I'd be so right for . . .' Don't start going over the top about how right you'd be for a specific part. You may well be perfect but you don't know the approach to the play and, anyway, it's hardly up to you to make the decision. And don't suggest yourself for a part for which you're blatantly unsuitable – that is incredibly annoying and very alienating. Such abuse of casting breakdowns is one of the chief reasons many employers restrict access to such information.

The first person singular Overuse of 'I' can make you appear arrogant. For instance: 'I went to a small community in Korea to teach English. I discovered I could use drama to teach English to students. I decided to pursue a career as an actor. I rehearsed my drama-school audition speeches above a paddy field.' Not only does this (real) example fail to convey the warmth of this particular actor, it also seems abrupt and somewhat disdainful. Simply joining sentences together not only removes excess 'I's, it also more strongly evokes the events: 'I taught English in a Korean village and through the process discovered the incredible value of drama. Rehearsing my drama-school audition speeches above a paddy field filled me full of excitement.'

'Who are all these people?' If you write as a group, the recipient will get no real impression of each separate individual. This is not to say you shouldn't write as a group to invite someone to a production, but by not writing an individual letter you are missing out an important part of the communication.

Couples often write jointly. This is a big mistake (a) for the reason above and (b) because most directors are extremely wary of casting couples in the same production for fear of domestic disputes colouring things in the wrong way. I know that in writing together you are not necessarily expecting to be cast together, but the fear will be that if only one is seen there will be a barrage of complaints from the other half. It happens. If your basic purpose is to save on postage, then put the two submissions into separate envelopes and put them into a larger one. But don't use exactly the same or even similar letters and CV formats (see 'I've read this before', page 119); you may be together in spirit but you still have your own individual personalities.

'How about your place?' A way of sticking pins under people's fingernails is to suggest that you could 'come and see them in their office'. This does not make life simpler. An office is a sanctuary in which to concentrate on other matters.

However, I have known several actors successfully using the tactic of travelling the country staying with friends and writing to all the theatres within range of their ports of call saying, 'I will be staying in your area on —. Could I come and see you?' This can sound like a more legitimate reason for inviting an actor into the 'sanctuary'. After all, if the actor knows someone in the area, that 'someone' is a potential member of the theatre's audience. But this is an expensive way of getting to meet directors and there are much greater priorities for your meagre funds.

Pretty paper Rainbows, teddy bears and pretty flowers are just some of the items I have encountered adorning actors' notepaper (from men as well as women). These decorations tend to suggest that you haven't quite grown up yet. Of course in some ways not having 'quite grown up yet' is part of the essence of being an actor, but you have also got to appear as a responsible professional.

The same applies to 'smileys' and/or other wacky decorations fun to use in emails.

Colours Various ink and paper colour combinations are adopted by some to add extra impact. Yes, silver ink on black paper will make your letter stand out in the pile of conventional black on white, but what does this, or any other striking combination, say about you? More important, the effect of such a visual impact can be so great that the all-important contents may not be properly digested. Also, if your choice of notepaper is of a particularly strong colour, be careful. All children have their favourite colour; most adults have their colour prejudices – in the legitimate sense. If you are going for colour, be subtle about it. (This also applies to CVs.)

Once again, the potential for coloured backgrounds, wacky fonts, etc. in emails should be resisted. It is also important to remember that such decorative effects may look good on your computer screen, but will it look the same on the recipient's screen? In spite of advances, computers still cannot communicate seamlessly with each other and many people don't know how to use them properly and/or are using outdated systems.

'You must remember me' Too many people write in follow-up presuming that the recipient remembers the details of the original communication. Yes, the original can be dug out of the files (physical or computer), but be warned that most organisations gut those files periodically because of the sheer volume of paper (or the mounting number of megabytes).

Also, direct statements like 'You will remember I wrote . . .' can easily embarrass because you are one of hundreds who write each month and it is impossible to remember each and every one. Changing the word 'will' to 'may' takes the curse off this approach, and you should reiterate the salient facts of your previous communication. Don't use exactly the same format and phraseology; if your original does come to light, your lack of imagination could count against you.

'I look forward to hearing from you' This may seem polite but it is another inadvisable example of conscience pricking. As one director said to me: 'It's nice when someone gives you permission not to reply.' However, don't end with 'Please don't bother to reply' as this has a negative feel. It is probably best to omit the subject of replying entirely.

Theatre-in-Education and children's theatre Too many young actors write to such companies talking about work for children being an apprenticeship – or similar word or phrase – for them. Various glowing adjectives may precede this crucial word but they cannot detract from the essential calumny. Working with and for children is a special skill in its own right. The legitimate companies have considerable expertise and cannot carry an apprentice.

Dull letters The following letter (a very typical example) does nothing specifically wrong, but gave me no idea of the writer as a person and did not inspire me to see her, when there are so many to choose from.

[*Name, address and date*]

Dear Simon Dunmore,

I am writing to introduce myself. I am, at present, in my final year at [*name of drama school*]. As I will be graduating in July, I am enclosing my CV and photograph for your reference.

I would like to take this opportunity to invite you to the 'Audition Show', which the students are organising on April 18th at the DONMAR WAREHOUSE in London or on April 20th at [*drama school address*]. This would give you a chance to view my work.

In the 'Summer Season' at college, I am appearing in *Danton's Death* from 24th to 27th May. I am also playing Mrs Temptwell in *The Grace of Mary Traverse* which runs from June 21st to the 24th. I would be more than happy to arrange tickets for you. However, if it is not possible for you to attend, but you are interested in seeing my work, I would, of course, be very pleased to audition for you personally.

I look forward very much to meeting you in the future.

Yours sincerely,
[*signature*]

Writing good letters

The preceding litany of what not to do may have left you feeling, 'But what can I do to attract attention in among all this intense competition?' An actor's job is to communicate another's personality through the spoken word. In order to help get that job you have to work hard at communicating your own personality through the written word. If you find this difficult (and most people do) then take time to experiment and evolve a good basic format. Try out drafts of your letters on other people – preferably someone who is used to reading such letters. As to content, more detailed suggestions follow, but basically you should use your actor's imagination to evoke the best of yourself to the unseen and unknown recipient. Aim to surprise: to make the task of reading all those letters suddenly enjoyable with a delicious piece of humour, for instance. You can use the fact that the recipient doesn't know you to develop or colour the truth, provided that you are sure you won't have to backtrack later.

You should write a brief introductory letter that puts over your personality with, maybe, the odd witty remark or brief personal anecdote thrown in. For instance, mention briefly the 'mad' sales job you've just done or the curious phrasing in the local paper's review of your last production. (Be careful about using up your best stories too soon – you should also have something that might be useful in the hoped-for interview.) You should imply a confidence in your abilities without in any way actually saying 'I am brilliant'.

Every letter from an actor is making the same statement: 'I want work!' We know this, so you don't need specifically to say so. However, don't go too far the other way and be so bland as almost to deny that fact.

Headed paper It is a good idea to get your own headed paper; it makes you look organised and professional. (*Note:* A good bonded paper can add a bit of class.)

You can create your own, using computer typefaces of your choice. Don't be tempted, however, to create a letterhead that is so wacky that it's semi-legible. Beatrice Warde, the passionate typography expert, said, 'Typefaces are the clothes words wear.' Find a typeface that dresses your professional name well.

Tip 1: Study advertising, newspapers, book covers, and so forth, for typeface ideas that could suit your name.

Tip 2: A name typed in upper and lower case usually looks more human than one all in capitals – the exception seems to be with very short names.

Contact details In this digital age it's possible to list a number of different ways of contacting you (or your agent) quickly. Alternatives can be useful – they can also be confusing. The important thing is to have a primary contact number, clearly listed. If you have an agent, then that 'primary contact' should be them. Also, think about how many other contact points you should list: it might look impressive to have a landline, a mobile, an email address and a website, but don't overload the letter with too many contact options. This applies to letters, CVs, photographs and labels fixed to anything else that you send.

Tip: Type in mobile numbers broken up into groups – say, two groups of four and one of three (0XXX-XXXX-XXX) or one group of five and two of three (0XXXX-XXX-XXX). This makes it much easier when being keyed in.

Important note: It is essential to have a professional-sounding email address – not one that makes you sound naïve or unprofessional, like 'starofthefuture@ . . .'. This is also true of your website address.

Handwriting Very few people have handwriting that is sufficiently good, stylish and even. However, if you are blessed with good readable handwriting, it can be worth exploiting. It can help convey more of yourself and can be a pleasure for the recipient to read among all the typed letters. (I have met one director who actively prefers handwritten letters.) I know an actor whose handwriting is not only beautiful to behold but also seems totally to contradict what he looks like (he's built like a heavyweight boxer). This kind of apparent contradiction is a very simple and effective way to gain attention. Contrasts like this are always intriguing.

Layout The overall look of your letter should be pleasing on the eye and easy to read. A page that is laid out with a reasonable line spacing and sufficient margins is much easier to read than one which has the minimum line spacing and is crammed nearly to the edges of the page. This can tend to look like a black splodge of words which will need some concentration, and extra time, to read properly. (Think of how difficult those tightly printed classic playscripts are to work from.)

Given that your letter is simply a brief introduction, you should be able to fit it neatly on to a piece of A5 paper.

Tip: If you are using email, put an extra return between paragraphs – thus preventing that 'black splodge of words'.

The English language The incredible variety of words that our language contains is a valuable resource for subtly enriching your prose. Check your dictionary and Thesaurus for possible improvements for your phraseology, but don't be tempted to become too flowery.

Your personality This has been growing ever since you leapt out of the womb (and possibly from conception) – it would take another lifetime to explain it. You can, however, evoke it – briefly – through things that you've done. These don't necessarily need to be acting things; they can be events that are now commonplace to you, but cause gasps when you mention them to someone new. Or, if you really don't think you've got anything that fits within this category, they could be the very ordinary jobs you've done before going to drama school, to help fund your training, for instance.

For example:

Dear –,

My first job was as a waitress in a cocktail bar. This proved to be a little more tricky than I had anticipated, so I moved on from spilling things over tablecloths to manufacturing them. I spent four years working for a textile company during which I began saving money to go to drama school.

I have nearly completed my training at [*School, then details of current production and how to organise tickets.*]

I am enclosing a copy of my photo and CV and a s.a.e.

This letter got a 75 per cent reply rate (from agents); contemporaries writing less characterful letters received less than 10 per cent response. Don't be tempted to copy it! It's the spirit of it that you should seek to emulate, not the form.

Tip: Start out by writing a simple list of things that you could incorporate. Then set about putting some (or all) of them into a brief, readable piece of prose.

Personalising each individual letter/email Early in your career especially you'll be writing to a lot of people. At the heart of the contents should be your personality. However, look for any way you can personalise each letter/email (through referring to someone the recipient knows well, for instance) in order to disguise the fact that it is just one of a mass mail-out. Of course it is difficult and time-consuming to find connections with each and every individual, but it is well worth it. Remember that if you do mention someone you must make sure they are happy to act as an unofficial referee for you – and that they really are known to the recipient. Work out a basic format within which you can vary details for somebody you have that 'connection' with and/or your particular suitability for a specific part.

Invite influential people to the production you are in at the moment – they probably won't come, but the fact that you are working will add energy to your letter. In fact, it's best to do your letter writing when you are working for this very reason. Even if you feel you've got no spare time at all because you are working, make some to organise those vital letters.

Strong skills Actors with strong skills in other areas are becoming more and more sought after. So if you play an instrument well, for example, it is well worth stating that in your letter as well as on your CV.

Clarity What is clear to you may not necessarily be clear to the recipient. Look at your letter again before sending it. Is it clear and does it make sense? For instance, if an incident is worth describing in your letter/email, can you be both brief and clear about it without having to explain too much about the context? Ask yourself at every stage: 'What am I really trying to say and to whom am I saying it?'

Your signature Of course you will put your signature at the bottom. (Some people stupidly forget this – I presume in the panic of mass-producing all those letters.) If your handwriting is really awful, it is well worth practising your signature to get it into a good strong shape. It is curious how so many signatures look tight and resentful as though the writer is signing a cheque for the rent. Always use your full professional name, not an initial and surname. And use black or blue ink – red or green or other bright colours look childish.

Finally Don't feel you have to cram too much information in. Let your CV take on the bulk of that load. Your letter should be the 'come on', your CV and photograph the details of the 'product'. Look at your letter and ask yourself if it's clear and expresses you and the best of your personality.

Some pitfalls to watch out for in your CV

All the comments above about spelling, layout, and so on, apply to CVs (or résumés). There are numerous other common faults.

Padding CVs padded out with amateur productions and exam results, for instance, don't communicate anything except a desire to make your CV look longer. If you are just leaving drama school, I know that they are probably a significant part of your life to date; but there is a general prejudice against amateur work and a recognition that the intellectual prowess implicit in passing exams contributes very little towards good acting. (I know that you may have sweated blood to get your degree, for instance, but you are an actor now – not an academic.) Youth theatre work is probably viewed more sympathetically but, even if you have played leads with the National Youth Theatre, put them in their place on your CV. Don't get paranoid because it seems too short. A good layout can solve that problem.

Note: 'Non-professional' reads better than 'Amateur'.

The obvious Don't put 'Curriculum Vitae' (or 'CV') or put 'Description' before 'Eyes', 'Height', and so on. Similarly, don't put in subheadings like 'Character', 'Play', 'Director' – or any other term that is inherently obvious.

Damaging information Some information can be positively damaging. For instance, giving your date of birth (or your age) can tie you down too much. If you have also directed, consider carefully the place of this information on your CV. You are trying to sell yourself as an actor – to directors, and some don't relish the potential of being upstaged. Put any directing credits in their place – that may mean omitting them altogether.

Irrelevant information CVs cluttered with irrelevancies like 'Equity number', 'Weight', 'Hair length', and so on, are boring. You are not attending a school medical. Your photograph will give sufficient information in these areas, and if you are extreme (in the useful sense) in any area you can put it in the letter: for example, 'I am a big actress.' (I once received a letter that started with this . . .) The only important personal statistics that cannot be gleaned properly from a black and white photograph are eye and hair colour, and height. If you are using a colour photograph, it is still wise to include eye and hair colour.

Playing range This is one of the most vexed questions in the actor-information arena. I maintain that (perceived) age is in the 'eye of the beholder' and can be gleaned from your photograph. But Spotlight insist that this is the question they are most frequently asked (they use the term 'Age band normally cast') – I suspect that this query generally comes from some blinkered media people. My suggestion is that you don't put it on your CV, but do fill it in (without compromising credibility – get a body of opinion) on your *Spotlight* web page. (A friend, although twenty-five, looked much younger and claimed that she was fourteen in a commercial casting and got the part. When filming was completed, glasses of wine were handed out. She was given an orange squash.)

Abbreviations Another common phenomenon is for people to use a sort of telephone directory style with initials for first names: 'M. Ellis in *Touched* by S. Lowe, dir. by S. Dunmore'. This so depersonalises the facts that it almost feels that the part, the play and director were all extremely boring (let alone the act of 'dir.'-*ing*).

Messy layouts Inconsistent spacing around slashes and dashes, left and right margins that aren't equal, spaces before commas and lines too closely crammed together are signs of laziness and liable to put you out of the running before a word is read. Technical details like these are time-consuming to resolve, but so important to ensure your CV is inviting to the eye.

'I've read this before' Similar CV formats coming from a number of different people can get very wearing. Once again, find your own way of expressing yourself. This may seem impossible as your CV is a series of facts, but they are facts about you and nobody else – find your own way of expressing them. It would seem that some drama schools preach their own particular layout; these range from the very formal to the very jazzy. I know that not everybody is good at layouts, and it is important that the information is clearly laid out. But stylistic repetition when going through a whole pile of submissions can become very tedious. A sudden piece of innovation – like your name in a different typeface – can break the monotony and draw attention to yourself in a strong, simple way. You have shown individuality and imagination – both very important qualities for the actor behind that CV. Especially early in your career, when you've done very little professional work, you'll seem very similar to several thousand others, but you are different, so find a way of expressing this.

More scrap paper CVs spread out over several pages make me wonder what the actor is trying to prove. You only need one side of one page – that's all the recipient has time to take in; and when you've done enough to fill that page you can start cutting out your less prestigious productions.

Brochure-style CVs These can look very good, and attract attention, but can also increase irritation. The fact is that we want to be able to turn over as few pages as possible – it all saves precious time. (If you only knew how much paper – and how much of its digitised equivalent

– we have to deal with.) There is also a sense that such presentations are almost too glossy, almost 'over the top'.

'Is this actor on drugs?' Some CVs are so jazzy that they are difficult to read. A CV decorated with artistically arranged extracts from favourable reviews, or one utilising all a computer's type-manipulation potential, might feel very clever – but is the important information it contains easily discernible? Remember that we only have time to give it a quick skim in the initial selection process.

There is a designer's rule that suggests you should use no more than two different typefaces on a page. I am not saying don't put play titles in capitals or don't use the 'bold' or 'italic' forms of a typeface, but use these forms sparingly. Avoid using 'underline' – that used to be the only way typewriters could emphasise and now seems very crude, as does the computer's facility for putting boxes round things.

Exaggerated claims Of course you want to present yourself in the best possible light, but bear in mind the actual level of your individual skills. Don't make vain attempts to pull the wool over people's eyes about your piano-playing abilities, for instance, listing Piano under 'Special skills' (or whatever) when the summit of your achievements is *Chopsticks* . . . I know an actor who claimed to 'play the flute very well'. She was somewhat taken aback when a director produced one from his bag and asked for a demonstration. She had reached Grade 8 in her youth but hadn't practised it for years. Your Geordie accent (for instance) may be reasonable, so mention it, but don't claim that it is 'excellent' unless it really is. You may get an interview on that basis, but you could easily be asked to demonstrate it there and then – to a Geordie.

Referees Unlike most professions, actors don't need referees and putting them on your CV can make you look as though you know nothing about how the profession works. Directors, casting directors and agents do talk to each other about individual actors, and reference is often sought between us. If necessary, we can always find someone to refer to from your credits.

Creating a good CV

Curriculum Vitae means 'the course of one's life', which, to me, evokes a rather more personal image than the bald lists of facts that I usually receive. (Incidentally, résumé means 'summary', which implies something less personal than Curriculum Vitae. It is also too often written without its accents, which turns it into an entirely different word.)

Your *Spotlight* web page is in a fixed format. Your CV is your chance to express your individuality. It should be personalised; it should reflect your life, your personality, your very soul even. It is not a shopping list. Someone once included 'Created the part of Chantale in *A Bridge Too Far*' to upgrade her CV. I fell for it; I hadn't seen the film at that point. Strictly speaking she wasn't lying as there is no such character in that film; Chantale was indeed her creation. I found this very witty. I'm not sure whether everybody would agree.

There is no template you should follow when writing your CV and no set list of headings (or sections). Individuality is the key and you should use your imagination and judgement to make it wholly yours.

The essentials Apart from good layout, the most important things to include in your CV are the 'names': those of the parts you have played and the people who have directed you. (Teachers, if well known, can also count.) The former are your achievements; the latter, the reader's reference points. A familiar name can be a point of contact with your reader and could be a good discussion point in an interview. However, don't go into tedious and pedantic detail – you are being patronising if you list 'Macbeth in *Macbeth* by William Shakespeare'. A taste of your work to date is all that's necessary – well laid out on one side of an A4 paper. The other important elements are what else you have done and can do.

Your CV should also contain your name (numerous people omit this detail from their CVs) and your primary contact details. Apart from your height and eye and hair colours, you should also list your current *Spotlight* (book) number and 'view-only' PIN. Don't include your 'update' PIN!

Your acting credits It's convention to put these in reverse chronological order, but it can sometimes be worth straying from this to improve the overall appearance. What else should you list apart from character, production and director (also MD [musical director] and choreographer, where appropriate)? The playwright is only important if they and/or the play are obscure. How do you know what is 'obscure'? This is almost impossible to answer absolutely, as playwrights come in and out of fashion – apart from a few 'ever fixéd marks', like Shakespeare, Chekhov, Ibsen, and so on. The only thing to do is to ask those with more experience. And when it's an obscure play by a famous writer, you only really need to use that writer's surname. (For instance, Noël Coward wrote numerous plays that have sunk into obscurity and John Galsworthy is now only really known as a novelist although he wrote some wonderful plays.) Translators are generally irrelevant in this context, but do remember who they are – for instance, some people are deeply interested in the relative merits of the Magarshack and Frayn translations of *The Seagull*. *Note:* There are over thirty other translations/adaptations of this play.

Tip: If you're listing several productions with the same director, don't list them successively, list others in between – it looks better.

The layout of your credits It's usual to lay your credits out in columns ('Part', 'Production', 'Director' – without those headings). However, I have seen them look good in prose form. *Note:* I suggest putting the character first. It's a curious fact that if you put the production first then the character is somehow 'dehumanised'.

If you've got a title that's uncomfortably long (like *The Effect of Gamma Rays on Man-In-The-Moon Marigolds*), put it on to two closely spaced lines and make sure there's a bigger space between that title and the ones above and below. Or you can simply abbreviate it thus: *The Effect of Gamma Rays . . .*

In order to accommodate those writers' names that are necessary, put them in brackets after the production's title – it'll save having an extra column. Similarly, venues and/or production company (only really useful if established) can be put in brackets after the director's name. The problem is, if you only put venues against certain productions it could seem odd and make a mess of your layout. There are several solutions to this. You could have a separate list of venues and if you've done several plays in one worth mentioning then list them under that venue's name.

In general, it's better to omit dates of productions on your CV as not only do they tend to clutter up the whole layout, but they also might start the reader wondering why there's nothing recent there (if that's the case).

If you played more than one part in a production think whether you need to list both (or all) of them. It's not the amount you did – it's the quality that matters. By putting in too many character names there's a sense that you're spreading yourself too thinly and potentially undermining yourself.

It is particularly important that your performance credits are well spaced – there needs to be sufficient space for each one to breathe out from the page. Think of each one as a 'little island of information'.

Note: When adding new credits, make sure that you don't mess up your carefully crafted (and well-spaced) layout. It is sometimes better to delete an older credit.

Media and film credits The problem with these is that there is so much attached information that could be promotionally useful that laying them out neatly is difficult. Obviously 'Part', 'Production', 'Director' are important, but mentions of the producer(s), the star(s), the channel it was screened on, the production company (if different) and even the writer could also be useful. You have to assess what will catch the eye – crudely, who and what are well known/famous? Then work out how to lay it out neatly so that it's easy to read – you'll probably have to go on to two lines.

If you have useful credits (with a prestigious director, for instance) where the character wasn't given a name in the script (you were in the chorus line, a one-line messenger, for instance), then make one up. If you were doing this no-name part properly you will have created a character history including a name for him or her. Use it! That's not lying.

Professional credits as a child Think carefully before you include these. As I've said before, it's very different acting as a child and most people recognise this. It might be worth including just the most prestigious of such credits.

Accents What to put under this heading is another of those eternally vexed questions. It is definitely worth putting in a good, strong native accent and any others that you are sure you can do well. It is better to avoid generalisations like American or Scottish – be specific to an area like The Bronx (New York) or Kelvinside (Glasgow). In theory all those voice lessons should have given you an infinitely flexible voice that could cope with any accent. In practice I've only ever met one actor who could do this – he had taken a degree in phonetics before going on to drama school. So it is probably best to list (a) native accent(s) and (b) those you've actually used in productions – provided the results were good. I'm afraid that expressions like 'Good ear for accents' just don't sound convincing; better to list specific ones.

Skills You need to list every practical skill that you've ever mastered that could be used in a production. For instance, horse-riding, keyboard skills, bar skills, swimming and driving are often required in television.

Note: If you list singing then you should include your vocal range.

Skill levels You need to find the right level for a skill to qualify it for CV status – that is, could you convince an audience (containing someone with that skill) that your character can really do it? There is rarely time to train someone up.

Note: Keep any skill that you do claim up to the mark.

Interests, experiences and other work These may not seem strictly relevant but do serve to give a more complete picture of you. Use this information judiciously to add life to either or both your letter and CV, and not as another piece of pedantic detail. 'Other occupational experience includes mortuary attendant, market research, grave-digging and helping to build the M25' attracted my attention at the end of one actor's CV. A friend has 'inventor' tucked in at the end; this is not invention on his part, it's absolutely true.

Many people say to me that they've got nothing interesting in this area. If this is so, then look for something different to do that would enhance this section of your CV. You don't need to be an expert for it to qualify for CV status, but make sure you can discuss it in interview and carry it through in the 'field'.

Photographs on CVs Inserting a small copy of your photo to your CV might seem like a good way of saving paper. However, what happens is that even if the combination is well designed, you can defuse the individual impacts of both CV and photo. Also, many people like to look at photos (and CVs) separately. However, not everybody agrees with me about this.

Digital CVs It is important that your carefully crafted CV looks the same on all computers. The only reliable way to ensure this is to convert it to Portable Document Format (PDF).

Some pitfalls to watch out for in your photographs

After talent, good photographs are probably the most important part of an actor's professional armoury. Given their importance it is vital not to make mistakes.

'Everyone's got a camera' While cameras seem now to be built into almost anything electronic, this does not make everyone a photographer. A photograph that might impress friends and family – even get you off a parking fine – will probably not impress professionally. Indifferent and amateur photographs are another excuse to put someone in that bin. You'd be amazed at how many holiday snaps I've been sent over the decades – often with the actor blinking into a strong sun or starry-eyed from the 'in-your-face' flash. The age of digital photography has not removed the necessity of using a photographer with professional skills. Make sure of your results before sending them. An amateur photograph makes you look like an amateur actor.

'Are you an actor or a model?' The other extreme – the glamour shot – is equally off-putting. Is this a dummy or is it a living, breathing actor? Don't ask for bags under your eyes, moles, and so on, to be edited out. These phenomena are an essential part of you and cannot be removed for the hoped-for interview.

'My head's falling off' Before training, one of your major concerns may well have been with where to put your hands. You can laugh now, but why do so many of you pose for photographs with one or both at the side or back of your head or underneath your chin? I know that this kind of pose is often used for models, but they are often in full-length shots. Hands appearing in a head and neck shot can look peculiar because we cannot see the connecting links. More importantly, such photographs tend to look much more posed, unnatural and unconfident.

Attitude Too many people think that they should have an 'attitude' in their photograph – broadly, either strong or submissive. A shot staring hard at the camera might be appropriate for a 'strong' part, but you are tending to restrict yourself. A shot looking too far down, or to the side (or both), can make you look like a frightened rabbit who would never be able to face an audience. As an actor you have to connect with them – not try to stare them out or have your eyes darting towards the nearest exit.

Funny photos Don't try to be funny in your photograph either. John Cleese may once have had a *Spotlight* photograph of himself dressed as Elizabeth I, but he can get away with it – you can't!

Mimicry There is absolutely no point in mimicking the photo of a famous actor; it will simply demonstrate lack of imagination on your part. I once came across two photographs on the same page of *Spotlight* which not only had the same first name and similar surnames, but also were in exactly the same pose. The same unimaginative photographer had taken both.

The last-minuter Don't try to get your photograph done at the last minute. Like performing, you need to be in the proper state of mind to have a good photograph taken. It's not something that can be slotted into the odd spare moment – like going to the loo – either by you or by the photographer. Bear in mind that as the deadline for *Spotlight* gets nearer, photographers become increasingly busy and it becomes more difficult to book a session. And make sure you've had enough sleep the night before or the results will add years to your face.

Pornography I have never received an overtly pornographic photograph. I have, however, come across several examples of highly suggestive photos that have made me blink. My feeling is that, if you choose to advertise yourself in this way, you are going to such an extreme that I suspect you have very little else to offer.

Getting good photographs

Your photograph is a silent, static, two-dimensional representation of vocal, mobile, three-dimensional you – and can be the most important part of your publicity package. ('A picture is worth a thousand words.') It is also important that it convey that vital 'you' when converted to black and white, which remains popular and is still (as of 2012) used in the important *Spotlight* book.

Your photograph should be of your head down to your shoulders, reasonably stylish and well produced without necessarily being too glamorous. It should look natural and have life, energy and personality – especially in the eyes, the most important part of your face. Your photo should say, 'Here I am; I know who I am; I'm OK with who I am.' Also, it is very important that your photograph really looks like you when you arrive for interview.

Note: The term headshot is becoming more commonly used. I am not alone in disliking this term as it seems somehow demeaning . . .

Choosing a photographer Not every photographer suits every actor. The actor-photographer relationship – much like the actor-director one – must be good and positive if it is to produce good results. Like acting, photography is a highly skilled art which cannot be measured by the complexity and virtuosity of the camera. Of course in going to an experienced professional you will probably be faced (currently) with a bill of around £250, if not more – and that's before you've had all the copies done. (*Note:* Many photographers will charge reduced rates for students.) Even if you feel you cannot afford such an investment, you have to find a way. Good photographs are essential for anyone who is at all serious about being a professional actor. It is probably the most important single investment you can make, especially at the outset of your career.

Look through *Spotlight* and talk to other actors (and other experienced professionals) to help pick out people whose work might suit you. (*Note:* Some agents will suggest individual photographers, but back off if an agent insists that you go to their recommended photographer as a condition of representation.) Many photographers advertise with samples of their work in *Contacts* and most have websites. *Actors' Yearbook* contains details of many photographers' charges and services – with some offering advice. However, it is important not simply to select the cheapest. You have to try to assess which one you feel could be best for you – that is, work with you to produce the best results. Once you have put together a shortlist of possible photographers, look at their websites – not just at their portfolios, but for any advice they give. Is it clear? Do you get a good 'buzz' from it? This is another highly subjective judgement, so it's important to spend good time in detailed research.

If you still find it hard to make a final decision, phone each of your final shortlist to see how you get on with them in conversation. You could check details of what they offer and/or simply enquire about their availability. In my experience the best photographs come from photographer and actor getting to know each other, at least a little, before the first picture is even taken.

Note: It is important to be clear exactly what you're getting for the agreed fee (how many shots, how long the session, how many prints, copies on CD, etc.) and what will cost extra.

The photo session Think carefully about what to wear, arrive on time and take a positive attitude.

Clothes The photographer may well tell you to 'wear what you like'. That's right, as it is important to feel comfortable, but be careful that your clothes – and especially the top – help to emphasise your face and doesn't distract or blend in with it. Excessive patterns on a shirt or blouse, which look fine while you are mobile, can easily detract in the static photograph. Similarly, a floppy jumper with an unpredictable neckline or a collar that sticks out at strange angles can make you look most peculiar, and polo necks tend to disconnect your head from your body. Take several alternative tops with you if you are not sure. I like V-necks as they provide classic perspective lines that lead up to the face, but not everybody agrees with this.

Make-up Wear as much (or little) as you would for an interview. It's important that the 'natural' you shines through the photograph so it's probably better to wear little. *Note:* Don't wear deep red lipstick or your lips will come out nearly black in the black and white version.

Hair If yours is of a length that can easily move around, try to ensure that it doesn't mask too much of your face or cast too much shadow. *Note:* It's a mistake to get a new hairstyle immediately before a session as it tends to take about a week to settle in.

Colour Your publicity photographs will probably be the only non-colour ones you've seen of yourself if you were born after about 1970. A black and white photograph is mostly made up of shades of grey – it should really be called 'black to white'. What really counts is how well the tone and texture of the top you are wearing sets off your face and hair, so wear a top the tone of which contrasts well with your skin tones and hair colour, and which won't blend too much into any background the photographer chooses to use. If you have light blonde hair, pale skin tones and wear a pale top, everything will tend to blend together. If you happen to have such Aryan looks, then go for a darker, rougher top which will highlight them. Think 'black to white'; it's positive textures and colour tones that read well, not subtle shade variations on the same colour. *Note:* If you have red hair, remember it will come out looking either brunette or blonde on a black and white photograph depending on its tone.

Glasses If you normally wear these, it is a good idea to remove them about an hour beforehand, otherwise the pinch marks could show up in the final results.

Attitude You will need to bring energy and commitment, to feel happy and confident and totally relaxed for the photo session. You need to be able to treat the camera and the photographer as friends, just as you would an audience – and aim to show the positive aspects of yourself. Aim to play to the camera rather than lean away from it. This doesn't mean leaning towards the camera; your head could end up out of proportion to your neck in the two-dimensional photograph – something akin to the classic stick man.

Exterior or studio This is a much-debated topic and is largely up to the photographer. I prefer natural light to create a more honest look, but you may run the risk of a sudden breeze blowing your hair into a strange shape on an otherwise perfect shot. It's a good idea to discuss location with your photographer before the session.

If, like so many people, you are 'camera-conscious' and find being natural difficult, take along your iPod or wear your favourite perfume or just remember good times in order to make you feel good. I believe the best photographs are often caught when the subject is doing something positive rather than stuck in a static pose. The word 'snap' is a very accurate one as it expresses that capturing of a real moment which can be so expressive in the final photograph. However, you will have to avoid excessive movement or the final result could be blurred or out of focus.

Choosing your photographs You can easily end up with a hundred or more images of yourself to choose from and it's often difficult to get a professional perspective on which one(s) will promote you best. You are never the best person to select the photographs of yourself that will do this. You have become so used to your face and its tiny faults that you cannot see the wood for the trees.

I think that it's best to start by eliminating the obvious no-hopers and then examine the details of each of the remainder. If you can enlarge them; so much the better.

- Start with the eyes: make sure they look reasonably even, that is, one is not half-closed or focused in not quite the same direction as the other. This often happens; the sixtieth of a second (or less) in which the photograph was taken can often be just slightly the wrong sixtieth. (The normal human eye cannot capture a moment faster than about a tenth of a second.)
- Next look at the mouth. It should have strength and not be too open, revealing too many teeth – not everybody has sufficiently regular teeth to survive the close scrutiny of a photograph. Also, a really broad smile might be giving off a lot of warmth, but how many extra creases has it added to your face?
- Consider carefully any photos which cut off part of your head (especially the top). A scalped head can look odd when blown up.
- Be wary of any where the background takes attention too much away from your face.
- Eliminate any where parts of your head are out of focus – however good they look otherwise. A blurred nose-tip or earlobe will severely detract from the overall impact – especially when blown up to 10 x 8 inches (25 x 20 cm).

Looking carefully at these vital areas can eliminate a further number of frames and focus your concentration on a smaller selection. The next stage is to ask the opinion of other people and get a consensus from these. There will probably be disagreements between those you consult – so keep a score. If possible, get a director, casting director, agent or someone used to looking at photos to help you choose a shortlist from these. A (female) friend grudgingly suggested that it is probably better for a male of one of these species to help you as the majority of directors are male. I am not convinced of this, but I mention it for consideration. Never ask parents and/or lovers to choose, as they will select the 'pretty' photo that probably won't show your important strengths.

So far, you'll have been looking at them on a computer screen. Ever noticed how things (pictures and text) look somehow different when printed out? As hard copies of your photos are important, you should get your shortlist printed in 10 x 8 inches (25 x 20cm) – in black and white. Then get a variety of opinion – as with your smaller selection – in order to make your final choice.

Note: Creating a good black and white photograph isn't just a matter of simply switching off the colour channels. It usually needs adjustments (brightness and contrast, for instant) to ensure a good range from 'black to white' – and not just a range of in-between, muddy greys.

Subsequent copies These can be cheaply mass-produced by one of the Repro companies listed in *Actors' Yearbook* and advertising in *Contacts* and *The Stage*. It is worth checking other people's recent results to select the best, as standards seem to vary from time to time. It really isn't worth attempting to save money by getting indifferent reproductions from a good original.

How many? Most people tend to underestimate their needs, allowing only for their initial mailing list and not for follow-up letters and new contacts that suddenly emerge. Adding a postscript to your letter like 'I'll send a copy of my photograph when I've had some more done' sounds pathetic and disorganised.

What size? In general you should send 10 x 8 inches (25 x 20 cm) prints. However, one casting director told me he 'feels guilty' about the extra money spent on the prints of this size that he receives, and is happy with postcard-sized ones.

A new photograph probably has a life of at least two years, so try to be realistic in your estimation of quantity and then add about 50 per cent. The more you order the less the unit cost.

Copyright Under the Copyright, Designs and Patents Act 1988 the photographer owns the copyright on any new photograph, even though you've already paid for the original. That means that you have to obtain his or her permission to have new photographs reproduced in *Spotlight* or anywhere else. Your photographer may be happy for such reproduction, but may not be so happy about any cropping or other alterations – you must get permission if you intend to do this. The other important legal requirement is that your photographer must be credited on any reproduction of the original. Some of the repro companies will do this as a matter of course.

Other things to think about before sealing the envelope/pressing the send button

Contacting you Always make sure that your 'primary contact' details (see 'Contact details', page 114) are not only contained in your letter and CV, but also on your photograph. It's very cheap to have personal sticky labels printed for this purpose.

If emailing is acceptable, make sure that each attachment is clearly labelled with your name. 'Photo.jpg' (for instance) could apply to anyone. It is better to keep the number of attachments to a minimum and include links to your *Spotlight* page and independent showreel, voicereel, website, etc. in the body of your email.

Note: Some repro companies will add your name below your photograph, but I much prefer all the details to be on the back.

Sticking your CV to the back of your photograph I know that this ensures their continued companionship but it can be irritating to have to keep turning the sheet over. The ability to survey letter, CV and photograph all at the same time is very useful. In North America affixing your CV to the back of your photograph is the usual convention – it isn't in the UK.

Enclosing reviews I often wonder about the value of these – unless they are very good and written by a very reputable national reviewer. An extra sheet of paper (or attachment) with your mention(s) highlighted may make you feel good, but can feel like yet another piece of paper to a recipient. I suggest that it can be much more effective to put a quote into your letter or in your CV.

'My photograph is in *Spotlight*' If it is, it could be unnecessary to enclose a photograph with your letter and CV. However, with so many submissions to peruse it can be annoying (and time-consuming) to have to refer elsewhere. If you can afford to send one with your letter and CV, then you are saving the recipient time and trouble. If economies are necessary, referring to *Spotlight* is legitimate.

Other contents Showreels are another extra expense, and a lot of people won't look at them because it takes up too much valuable time. Before sending out one of these check whether it will be received with interest.

If you do go for one of these, it is essential – as with photographs and voicereels – to label them clearly.

All those bits of paper Paper-clip everything together – it saves the envelope-opener a little bit of time and trouble. It's possible that everything will be stapled together to ensure the continued companionship of your bits of paper when they are placed into the filing system. This will damage your photograph – yet another argument for not asking for it to be returned. Also, filing systems are generally designed to accommodate standard A4 paper. If your entire sales package is significantly smaller it could get lost. It is very annoying to open a letter and find each item separately folded and inserted. All this means is that precious time is wasted in putting them together in order to be impaled by the staple.

Postage Ever since the 'Letter', 'Large Letter' and 'Packet' rates were introduced there has been a great deal of confusion – with too many applying an ordinary 'Letter' stamp to a 'Large Letter'. The recipient has to pay the extra when such a letter arrives. All the details are on the Royal Mail's website <www.royalmail.com> and in post offices.

Facts: An envelope containing a 10 x 8 in photograph is a 'Large Letter' and a hardbacked envelope containing a letter, CV and photograph – plus another hardbacked sae – will almost certainly make the whole package weigh over 100 g. This takes the postage cost up into the next price bracket.

Marking the envelope 'Personal' Essentially this is another attention-seeking gambit to avoid. Even if your request is acceded to, you'll just get thrown into the pile of actor-letters anyway.

The same is true of using one of those email urgent/priority flags.

Email etiquette When using this form of communication – especially if you have no previous contact with the recipient – it is important to go through the checks above before clicking 'Send'. The problem is that it is too easy to send an email accidentally – which can be embarrassing. (Recall buttons rarely seem to work.) Also, the informality of email makes too many lazy in attention to detail.

I suggest the following:

- Approach the content just as you would a letter. In particular, use 'Dear . . .', not, 'Hi' or 'Hey', etc. Only resort to the less formal when you feel confident that it's appropriate.
- Treble-check (at least) the copy before sending. It seems to me that because you don't get a chance to read it again in hard copy (paper), people are more prone to make silly errors.
- Double-check (at least) that you've included the correct attachment(s) and ensure that your photograph doesn't exceed any maximum size specified by the recipient.
- Ensure that there's a suitable something in the subject line. It is frustrating and annoying to receive an email from someone unknown to you with this left blank. Remember how cluttered our inboxes are already.

Tip: To ensure that you don't actually send before you've sufficiently checked everything, make adding the recipient's email address your final action before sending.

Final check When doing a big mail-out, make doubly sure that you put the right letters into their corresponding envelopes. You'd be amazed at how many people make these basic mistakes. This is even more true with big 'email-outs' . . .

Now forget about it Once you've posted your letter (or sent your email), forget about it. However confident you feel about its contents, the ball is out of your court now and there is nothing you can do. So why waste time and energy worrying about it?

Targeting your submissions

The late Barbara Cartland managed to write about ten novels a year – that is equivalent to several thousand letters. She was rich enough to employ three secretaries to transcribe all those words. In theory there are as many agents, directors, casting directors and other potential employers for you to write to just as much, but it is an impossible task unless you spend all your waking hours doing it. You have to be selective.

A hit list The only way to sort out a suitable 'hit list' is through research: asking other people, checking websites, using casting-information services, and so on. Time spent sorting out potentially sympathetic ears will save a considerable amount of time and money later on. It isn't always necessary to write to the top dog: an assistant or associate, for instance, may well have more time. If there's a casting director in place, he or she should be your first port of call. However, check the relevant names as they tend to move around.

Joint letters It is always a mistake to write to two or more people in the same letter – unless you know that they work in close harmony. Working in the same organisation doesn't mean that they share philosophies.

Short-term memory syndrome This is a profession-wide complaint. You've worked for someone and know that you've gone down well, but they haven't employed you since. It is almost certain that they would like to work with you again, but the other incredible pressures have squeezed you out of their memory banks. Don't be too shy to write. Evoke the glow of your joint success and write with the energy of what you've been doing since.

The following correspondence or lack of it

'I wrote to/emailed you months ago' If you want a reply to a letter (and/ or return of your photograph), you should enclose a sae. One second-class stamp doesn't cost much, but several hundred will add considerably to your budget, let alone the stationery and time costs. Even if you have enclosed a sae, the recipient may well have been frantically busy ever since you wrote and only just found a little bit of time to go through the accumulating letters from actors. You can easily wait several months, and some people don't reply at all despite your sae. Unfair, but it happens – even when an advertisement has requested one.

In fact, I don't think the traditional sae is really worth it. All this really does is elicit confirmation that your letter/email actually arrived. If someone is interested in you, they will get back to you anyway – via phone or email. Many organisations have standard responses for those who send one: these are almost always quite pleasant but finally noncommittal. Some actors take sentences like 'We will consider you when we are next casting' too much at face value. In general that means 'No, not for at least the next six months', but I have known people use it to blitz me with letters (and emails) saying that I had promised to see them when all I have said is that I would 'consider them'. The problem is that, at heart, most people are too soft in this area and cannot write an outright 'no' to an actor.

If you want your photograph back, you must enclose an envelope that's big enough. A surprising number of people don't.

Replying to replies There is no point in replying immediately to a 'standard' response. All it means is that your details have been filed and that file might be looked at and even referred to at some time in the future. You have done all you can for now. Write again, with a fresh CV and photograph, in about six months. The exception to this rule is when your research turns up an opportunity for you to suggest yourself for specific casting.

'How often should I write?' If you've had some kind of positive response you think worth following up, never hassle but do gently remind. Always write to follow up; never phone (or email) unless specifically requested to do so. And don't keep on writing every month as some people do – you are only adding to the recipient's guilt complex, and you are even less likely to be seen. A gentle hint in about six months is probably the best approach, unless you feel that you can genuinely suggest yourself for a specific piece of casting.

The reminder postcard It can be a good idea to send out reminder cards – especially to people you know. A simple postcard with basic details (of your current production, for instance) is perfectly sufficient, and is quick and simple to read. You can get these made up with your photograph and contact details incorporated.

Keep records It is important to keep records of what you've said to whom and any responses (written or verbal) for at least two years so that you don't get caught repeating yourself.

Timing The success or failure of your letter-writing can also depend on when you write. Of course you'll write when you discover there's a particular part you'd be right for, but it can also be worth writing in general terms. For instance, directors of theatres seem to be at their most receptive when they first take over, that is, in that honeymoon period when they are optimistic that the inherent financial problems can be solved. The same tends to be true after a well-earned holiday.

There are also times when you can reduce your chances, like just before Christmas and at other especially busy times of year in that particular company's calendar. You should try to keep in touch with each organisation's pattern of work via *Actors' Yearbook*, *The Stage*, websites, etc. to work out optimum times for contact – if any.

A fundamental note Always write with something positive to say and with a strong sense of purpose. Never write in desperation as in the following. This was a handwritten letter from someone I did not know. (You can find the original on my website.) I haven't corrected any grammar, punctuation or spelling, and there was no CV or photograph:

> [*Address and date semi-legible*]
>
> Dear Simon,
> I have written to you a few times in the past this time I hope I will be successful in my application for a job. I am 24 on 19 of this month 23 at the moment so it would be a very nice birthday surprise. I have been singing and touring with cabaret and show band, you have most of my details of file. I really want to be an actress but how can I when I get letters saying no vacancies at the moment try later without even chance of an audition if there are no vacancies as an actress then perhaps you could offer me some backstage work. Im a hard worker easy going and really like working in theatre so come on Simon spread a bit of Christmas Spirit.
>
> yours sincerely
> [*Name almost illegible*]

Warning Many people have found this, and the other letter on pages 107–8, very funny. However, bear in mind that they are the sort of thing you might write either when feeling lonely and desperate, or when feeling extremely cocky.

Other promotional material

The main things to remember about promotional material such as showreels, voicereels, business cards and personal websites are:

1) Although they're becoming more popular, they're still not absolute requirements although showreels are becoming more requested for screen work.

2) They're further drains on your bank account – unless you have the computer skills to create them for yourself.
3) They should be simple, straightforward and effective.
4) They should be of professional quality – just like letters, CVs and photographs.

There are now companies specialising in one or more of these areas. A few of these offer their own excellent advice on their websites and/ or in *Actors' Yearbook*. As with photographers it is wise to research before further contributing to your debt mountain.

Business cards and postcards

If you do decide to go for these make sure that not only are they as professional looking as your letters and CVs, but they are printed on quality card. There are plenty of very cheap design and print services available, however the cheapest incorporate their own logo, have a limited range of designs and use very thin card. If you present yourself cheaply, you won't be taken seriously.

Showreels

A casting director told me recently that she was thinking of tiling her bathroom with all 'those discs'. Bear in mind the time it takes to watch each one is limited – and most are too long, possibly because Spotlight allow up to five minutes. It's long been established that an actor's paper CV should be no longer than a single page. I'm waiting for an industry-wide acceptable length for a showreel. I'd like to suggest one-and-a-half to two minutes. A friend suggested that 'A showreel is not an archive of one's work and is not about telling a story – it's about your casting brackets. As soon as that colour, that casting bracket has been established, cut away to the next.'

Contents Ideally, these should consist of short, varied and evocative extracts from actual broadcast work – a bit like trailers for films or TV programmes. If you don't have suitable material it is possible to make one up from scratch. In either case, it is essential to use the services of a specialist company who can produce a professional-looking, broadcast-quality result – don't be beguiled by a friend's spanking new digital video camera and 'whiz-bang' software. It is much, much better when your showreel contains snippets of actual broadcast work – preferably showing a range of performances. If you don't have sufficient broadcast work some specialist companies will offer scripts and the facilities to record fresh material from scratch; you could also write your own. However, I've never seen one of these 'from scratch' pieces that showed the actor(s) in a good enough light – although I have been told of the occasional good example. The other problem is that it can take a long time to rehearse and record a 'from scratch' piece properly, and studio time is expensive.

Getting a showreel made There are numerous companies listed in *Actors' Yearbook* and *Contacts* who will not only put a showreel together for you, but also advise on content. Some have websites where you can view samples and some seem to cover the gamut of recording possibilities from weddings to corporate events. To find the right company for your needs, you should use many of the same parameters I suggest in the 'Getting good photographs' section (pages 126–31).

These might be summarised thus: ask around for recommendations, check how well they understand actors and their requirements, ask to see samples of a company's previous work and check the pricing details. It is essential the finished product is professional-looking and of broadcast quality, which takes a lot of expertise.

Copyright It is likely that some (or all) of the material that you are using is somebody else's copyright. Although the fees involved will probably be quite small, or sometimes waived, it is essential that you have the appropriate permissions before you start creating your showreel. This can take some time. Some showreel companies will help with this, and it's worth going to one which does as copyright can be a highly complex issue.

Guidelines for putting together a showreel Because studio and editing time is so expensive, it is a good idea to go in with some ideas of your own.

1) Your showreel should be no more than three or four minutes long (preferably less) with a good range of performances, each of which shows you off at your marketable best.
2) No extract should last more than about thirty seconds and each should be sufficient to establish the character.

3) Make sure it's clear that it is you whom a recipient is supposed to be watching – start with a shot in which you are prominent in the frame, for instance, and make sure that all the scenes favour you.

4) Consider carefully whether each extract needs a title – these can sometimes distract too much.

5) Don't try to convey a storyline in an extract – it'll take too long.

6) Be wary of using extracts from stage productions or audition speeches – they rarely work on screen without significant editing.

7) Don't try to write your own material unless you are very sure of your dramatic writing skills.

8) If you are going to include some material about yourself, treat it like a real interview.

9) Make sure that your name (with your 'primary contact details') appears at the beginning and the end.

10) Do as much preparation as you can before recording in order to save on expensive studio time.

   i) If you are recording from scratch: organise your props, costumes, etc. and rehearse as much as possible before the day(s) of recording.

   ii) If you are using existing material: work out exactly which extracts you'd like to use (and in what order) before taking your recordings into the studio.

11) It's a good idea to have thoughts on running order, any linking music that you'd like to use, and so forth. Also ensure that your editor doesn't clutter up the final result with too much music and/ or too many flashy effects.

12) If you are providing your own script, make sure that it is clearly typed, widely spaced and with wide margins – and take sufficient copies for everyone involved.

13) Have a professional-looking label (with your 'primary contact details') printed on the disc and on its packaging. It's also a good idea to add the running time.

'Do I actually need a showreel?' You can easily spend several hundred pounds (much more if it's from scratch) on getting one made, and even more for extra copies. There's no question that a good showreel can tip the balance in your favour, but an indifferent (or worse) one can be deeply damaging. Effectively, you are doing an audition without actually meeting the auditioners. Ask yourself (and others) if you really are exposing yourself in the best light. A showreel might show how you appear on screen, but a good letter, CV and photograph, and actually seeing you in the flesh, are far more important.

Unlike CVs and photographs, showreels are not yet the norm – in spite of the fact that you can include one in your online *Spotlight* entry. They take more time to view and can be an expensive way to market yourself. It is essential to feel absolutely sure that you've got the best material to sell yourself and can afford the expertise before embarking on such a venture.

Voicereels

You must get this right first time. If you don't, the listeners will not be inclined to bother with the next one you send, unless enough time has elapsed for your failure to be erased from their memories.

The quality of a voicereel is just as important as the quality of a showreel – the only difference being that it is much more viable to create a professional sounding voicereel 'from scratch'. It is no good doing one on domestic equipment – however good the material, the product will sound at best adequate. You will have to get it done in a proper studio with a good sound engineer who really knows what he or she is doing. All the flash gear in the world is useless if the voicereel is not recorded, mixed and edited properly. Acoustics has always been an inexact science and has taken on the status of an art form; that is because each set of equipment has to be specially tuned to each individual voice – no domestic audio system is equipped to do this. Such professional equipment takes great skill to operate to bring out the best from you. A recording session – let alone the copies of your final voicereel – could cost several hundred pounds.

Note: Voicereels are also known as 'voice-demos' 'voiceover demos', 'demos' and, sometimes confusingly, 'showreels'. Spotlight use the term 'voice-clips' and the BBC 'voice CD'.

Shop around You'll find listings in *Actors' Yearbook* and *Contacts* of companies specialising in making voicereels, many of whom will offer help with selecting scripts suitable for your voice, background jingles, copyright, and so on. Many have websites where you can hear samples and get details of costs and services offered and other advice on creating your voicereel – there seems to be a wide variety of opinion, but it's free. Don't be tempted to use a music studio as these use different equipment which is usually not sympathetic to recording the spoken voice.

Don't think it will only take a few minutes to record a three-minute voicereel. Even if you are completely rehearsed and prepared, it could easily take an hour or two to record properly.

Your voice Before you go to a studio it can be a good idea to analyse your voice. (Some companies offer such analysis over the phone.) What are its strong points and what can it promote? I'm not just talking about a facility with accents, for instance. Think about all the aspects that make it special to you, the actor – such as its timbre. You should listen for those special strengths that you can bring to a character expressed only through the voice with no visual support. Find your own voice 'presence' and find what characters and moods it suits. Look on voice-agents' websites for some evocative descriptions and listen to the clips behind them to help focus on your own strengths. (Don't try to copy them, however! The world of voice-overs is a very small one, and virtually everybody knows [or knows of] virtually everybody else.) You should also think about your vocal age range and the types of product that someone really in that 'age range' would use and you can sell.

Also, listen carefully to voice-overs on commercial radio and television to get ideas of how to approach yours. Listen to the style and the attack (or lack of it) of each professional voice, and find aspects that are useful to you. Don't go to the studio with fixed ideas, however – be open to whatever else the experts may suggest.

It's a good idea to practise sight-reading a lot – not just from dramatic texts, but also from newspapers, advertising copy and the like – even the telephone directory.

A kaleidoscope and some commentary Part of your voicereel should contain a variety of snippets of material – a kaleidoscope of about half a dozen voice images (generally radio commercials) rather than a detailed picture. A voice agent won't really listen to the details of the actual words, more to the quality of your voice and what it is capable of. However, don't make it so kaleidoscopic that it becomes confusing. Also, don't go mad and try to do lots of different accents and funny voices unless you are really very good at them. Keep the whole thing simple and within your vocal range.

Your voicereel should also contain a couple of short commentaries that paint pictures for a listener – a passage from a novel or some other descriptive piece from a newspaper, for instance.

As with audition speeches it is generally better to use material that is not well-known – taken from a short-running campaign, for instance. Some companies can supply such material (check if there's an extra charge for this) or you might try to write your own. However, copywriting is a not inconsiderable skill; you have to find a way of assessing whether you can really do it well. You could pay somebody to write your script for you, although obviously that will add further to the cost, and it will be hard to find somebody good and understanding enough to fulfil your particular needs.

Try out your ideas at home and, as with a photograph, get other people's opinions. It is worth working at the contents of your voicereel as well as at the performance of it for a considerable time before you commit yourself to the recording studio, where time is money.

Note: If you have a genuine (and saleable) native accent, it is important to include an example of this – perhaps one with your accent strong, and others with varying degrees of dilution.

Guidelines for putting together a voicereel Although a good specialist company might help you as part of a package deal, it can be well worth going in with some ideas of your own:

1) It should be no more than three or four minutes long.
2) No commercial should last more than about 30 seconds and the commentaries should be no longer than a minute each.
3) Start with something that is especially evocative of your personality.
4) Consider carefully how to link the material together (with music, for instance) – a good studio should be able to help with this. For example, in his voicereel a friend preceded his name with 'Prince of pronunciation. The acme of accents. Mr Voice-Over Himself!' and similar slogans. (Don't be tempted to copy that!) It is not essential to incorporate links and/or have a storyline, but it might make that final difference if you can do it – the cherry on the cake.
5) If you are going to include some material about yourself (an introduction, for instance), keep it brief.
6) Don't try to mimic anyone – make each interpretation your own. (A friend was nearly sued by a Hollywood megastar for his very accurate impersonation of that star's voice on a television commercial.)

7) Don't be cheap by telling a series of jokes or mocking familiar advertising. The key to any piece of advertising is its apparent integrity. Overall, the more original the material (and your delivery of it) without being downright quirky, the better your chances.

8) If you are providing your own script, make sure that it is clearly typed, widely spaced and with wide margins – and take sufficient copies for everyone involved. (*Note:* Don't use all caps for what you're actually going to say.) If you go in professionally organised, you will save time and money, and you may get some good suggestions – at no extra charge.

9) It is a good idea to aim to make the contents, and their presentation, appear like excerpts from material you could have already broadcast, so that the listener might believe that you are already experienced in this field.

10) Stick a professional-looking label (with your 'primary contact details') on the CD and on its packaging. It's also a good idea to add the overall running time and those of the individual pieces.

Note: For guidelines on putting together a voicereel for radio drama see <www.bbc.co.uk/soundstart/faqs.shtml>.

Recording your voicereel

Recording is a highly technical world, and knowledge of simple techniques and technical terms can save valuable time when making it.

A few basics Always take a pencil and a highlighter. These simple tools will enable you to mark your script as the session develops and you'll save expensive studio time. Don't wear clothes and/or jewellery that will make any kind of extraneous noise – microphones pick up every sound. And don't wear strong perfume – the smell can be overwhelming in a small studio.

Where to stand A good microphone will have a diagram indicating its directional characteristics marked on it: the areas where it can pick you up properly and those where you are dead to it. Usually you should stand within a metre of the microphone but this can vary if there is any shouting or whispering involved. There are several different types of microphone with different directional characteristics, so look out for those diagrams.

A voice-for-level The equipment needs to be adjusted to your voice and its level before doing anything else. People waste time when asked to do this by not using their performance level. This may only be marginally different from your speaking voice, but that small difference could make a considerable one to the settings on the sensitive equipment. This is not something that can be done automatically; it requires skill, a good ear and patience from the engineer. The important thing is that you give the person behind the glass what you will be giving in performance. It can be a good idea to offer a piece which contains the loudest and quietest moments.

When to start You might get a simple visual or verbal cue from the engineer or there might be red and green lights. The red light means 'recording'; the green light turning on means 'go'. Don't wait until the latter turns off or you'll be there forever.

Page-turning Find your own way of turning the pages silently without disturbing your flow. Many people like to gesticulate while reading. If you are one of these, then ensure that a gesture doesn't collide with the script.

Fluffing Even the most experienced people fluff (listen to news-readers), and of course, a simple edit will solve the problem. After a brief pause go back to a convenient point, such as the beginning of the sentence you were on (the engineer may well advise you), and start again. Don't try to go back further than suggested in order to get back into character. It takes longer to find the edit-point – more expensive time-wasting.

Finally Before recording your voicereel do a good vocal warm-up so that your articulation is tight and your range is free and easy in order to bring fully to life the words on the page.

Personal websites

In theory you could email an invitation for someone to look at your details on your website. In fact, if you are in *Spotlight*, they can already check out your details on that site; however, it can be useful to evolve your own website to help you stand out from the crowd. Overall, it must look professional, and be easily accessible and navigable to the first-time eye – just like a good letter, CV and photograph. There are plenty of people willing to design and maintain a website for you. As when looking for a photographer, check the quality of any potential designer's work and compare prices. (It's also important to check the cost of making changes. In fact, it's probably better to ask for a copy of the site – with the appropriate access codes – because the website-design business seems to be very volatile.) It's also not too difficult to build a basic one for yourself.

Before you start on your own design, look at other actors' sites to see what you like and what you don't.

. Here are some basics to consider:

- As with letters and CVs, don't go overboard with jazzy graphics and colours, let alone background music, quirky animations and advertising banners.
- Don't be tempted to fill your site with items that are irrelevant to your professional life. Photographs of your dog, you at a wild party or you surfing may amuse your friends but don't promote your professionalism.
- Avoid interactive elements such as guestbooks, as anyone can leave an inappropriate message that will mar your professionalism.
- Ensure that your site can easily be updated as you gain more credits and/or want to make any other changes and additions.
- Make sure that your photographer is credited (see 'Copyright' on page 131).
- Check that you have permission to use anybody else's copyright material – for a showreel, for instance.
- Make sure that your professional name appears in the title-bar. If this just has 'Home Page', for instance, your site could get lost among the many others that are similarly labelled.
- Make sure that you include an email address and/or your 'primary contact' number. And make sure that that email address is hyper-linked so that the viewer can just click on it to respond.
- Make sure that the pages load quickly – especially the first one.
- Ensure that links to other pages on your site (a) work and (b) are clearly labelled.
- If you include external links make sure that they work.
- Check regularly that your email inbox doesn't get full up so that professional approaches embarrassingly bounce back to their senders.

- Look at your site on lots of other people's computers. The content may survive but the layout could well acquire some odd quirks on arrival on the recipient's screen, and photographs can lose some of their lustre.

Once you've created your professional-looking site, make sure that (a) the address is on all your printed material, and (b) you register that address with as many search engines and free listings sites as possible.

A few actors' experiences and observations An actor-friend has had a website since 1993 and has never got a job through it. A few other observations:

> 'A website is just like a telephone. Unless someone is motivated to dial your number then your telephone won't ring. The trick is to get people to know and use your website address. Reliance on random events does not have a good chance of success.'
> 'Can you imagine a casting director sitting down and typing "great actor play Hamlet" into a search engine?'
> 'Hopefully in the future things will change, and a website might be a good place to give an expanded showcase of yourself, but I think it would still only be used by someone you'd already made contact with.'
> 'I think of my site as an electronic business card.'

Additional internet promotional opportunities

The likes of Facebook and Twitter have proved extremely effective for publicising productions. However, instances of actors making useful new work contacts via these means are extremely rare. It is essential that if you are using your professional name you should always appear professional. The same applies to YouTube!

Final note

The incredible developments in means of communication (and recording) have changed things radically since the millennium. These have opened up opportunities for a rapid increase for the untrained to advertise themselves as actors. As a consequence, an increasing number with casting clout are insisting that those they don't already know use the postal system for initial contact. (It is also a fact that reading from paper is easier and less tiring than reading from a screen.) To many, a personal computer is private space and a submission arriving in it is almost equivalent to the actor arriving on the doorstep in person without an invitation.

It's also important to understand that while communication systems have become more widespread and much faster, people don't think, read and absorb any more quickly. Microchips become exponentially faster every year, but science hasn't yet created versions that can be implanted to get our eyes, ears and minds to speed up any further.

7: *The casting point: interviewing and auditioning*

So, your promotional material has attracted someone's attention and you're asked to a 'meeting', 'interview', 'audition', 'casting' . . . There are a number of ways in which this could work. The main possible elements are an interview, a sight-reading and an audition speech, an audition song – in any combination.

Notes: The words 'interview' and 'audition' are commonly intermingled. Strictly speaking, an audition (from the Latin *audire*, 'to hear') is the speech or sight-reading and the interview is the chat between you; but, apart from musicals and commercials, generally the word 'interview' is used to cover everything in theatre and radio. For television, commercials and film, the term 'casting' is often used and usually means an interview and a sight-reading – although it has been known for an audition speech to be added into the mix. Some companies (those specialising in work for children, for instance) go in for forms of workshop auditions in order assess how well you would work with their team.

Interviews

Ideally an interview should be an informal mutual testing in the best possible sense. It should really be an equal assessment session of whether you'd both like to work together – an informal mutual testing. After all, rehearsing a production is probably one of the most intimate of shared human activities. (Good working relations between agent and client are also essential.) Unfortunately for you, the actor, there are almost always too many people after the same job (agent), and the privilege of deciding whether you'd like to work with a particular individual or not is afforded to very few actors. You are in the position of having to sell yourself subtly but effectively to him or her, and not vice versa. Perhaps if all actors decided to make interviews an 'informal mutual testing' the more obdurate interviewers would have to respond and the whole system might become more satisfactory. However, while things remain as they are, here are some preparatory observations.

Note: Much of what applies to directors also applies to meeting agents, casting directors, and so on, unless otherwise stated.

Your interviewers Although I have outlined the work of directors, casting directors and agents in chapter 5, I think that it's important to stress that there is no one particular type of personality that fits any one of these labels. They are as varied as any random sample of people. Some can seem super-confident; others can be just as shy and/or nervous as those they are interviewing. Crucially, virtually none have been trained in the art of interviewing. Some have evolved good techniques that aim to put you at ease and allow you room to give of your best; others hide behind glasses, laptops, assistants, etc. Among the former, you'll meet those who go so far as to say 'I know I could work with you' to everybody – perhaps because they cannot bear to be resented. Among the latter, you'll meet those who communicate very little – and when they do sound terse, even aggressive. If it is a good atmosphere, then it will be easy to give all you've got; if it is a difficult one, you cannot let it get you down. You have to be stoical and give the best you can. Treat interviewers well without being obsequious or grovelling, or you'll come out feeling badly compromised. Would you want to spend time working with such an appalling individual anyway? Save your feelings about the session and your interviewer until afterwards.

Most interviewers do recognise the potential dangers of casting purely on the basis of an audition speech or reading. Talking to the actor, discussing and/or working on the audition piece or reading are useful. In fact the chat can be more than 50 per cent of the session and in some cases more influential on the final decision than anything else. It can be useful to think of the interview as a chance to promote yourself. Even if you find yourself in a situation where the chatting time is minimal, you must focus just as much on that 'promotion' as you do on the product: your speech or reading.

Personally, I find interview days even more exhausting than technical rehearsals. Lunch hours usually end up being twenty minutes, and there is absolutely no time to relax when you have to bring fresh concentration to bear on each new person every ten or fifteen minutes.

Everybody's different Elaine White, an actress, received sponsorship for a research project on Auditions, Interviews and Casting. She circulated numerous directors with a questionnaire asking what each felt about interviews and auditions, what they expected from actors and what general advice they could offer. She received over 200 responses from directors, including a few very well known ones. Not only was there a wide range but there were even contradictory responses from four pairs of directors working in the same theatres. Her statistical analysis came to no definite conclusion and as she commented, 'At the end of the day it seems that auditionees must suit their presentation to that particular director, working with that particular company on that day.' However, 'It does seem that an actor's personality could be as important a factor as his technical ability.' Her full report is available for download from my website.

I hate interviews I'm told that the very words 'interview' and 'audition' are to the actor synonymous with the word exam. You have to go in with the idea of giving all that you can offer. Be vulnerable but don't display your insecurities. In a sense you need to drop a little emotional blood, but be able to recover easily. Don't get so wound up that the whole thing becomes a great blur and you cannot respond properly to anything that's asked of you. Be relaxed, assured and open to anything and everything. Treat the interview like a joyous improvisation, but make your interviewer feel as though he or she is just one step ahead of you.

Through everything, don't let your actor's instinct desert you, and remember that your interviewer may well be ill-prepared, suffering from a hangover, worried about an unfinished report, and – crucially – has probably just done another interview concentrating on somebody completely different.

Preparations for an interview

You will never finally know what you will walk into – even when you are a seasoned interviewee. However, there are certain ways in which you can prepare and certain mistakes that you can plan to avoid making.

A call is a call is a call You must never be late. This is the cardinal rule of the whole profession, and it doesn't just apply to a working call; it also applies to an interview. Interviews may start on time but almost always run later and later as the day progresses. You, however, must still be on time. There will be a carefully calculated schedule with each actor slotted in at ten- or fifteen-minute intervals (longer is a luxury). There may be contingency times, that is, deliberate gaps to allow for the almost inevitable overrunning. However, you cannot rely on this. Some actors on the schedule might find they cannot attend at the last minute, thus creating spare time, so you could go in early. Your job is to make sure you're ready and willing in good time for your appointment. I'd suggest aiming to be at least fifteen minutes early – if not more. This will give you time (a) to relax and acclimatise and (b) to absorb any extra material (a script, for instance) that's waiting for you.

You should have been given precise details of the location. However, these details may only go as far as the entrance – and that may not be clearly labelled. Especially in city centres, there are a remarkable number of buildings whose identifications have been ravaged (if not removed) by time. I'd suggest allowing extra time whenever this is a possibility. It's also possible that finding the appropriate entrance is only the first navigational hurdle. You might find yourself in a vast building with a veritable Minotaur's labyrinth of corridors. Allow time to find the appropriate room. Of course there might be a receptionist and/or signs to guide you, but you can never be quite sure. It is essential to estimate not only your travelling time but also the time you will need to complete the initiation test of finding the interview room. Finally, allow time for transport problems – my rule is to double the optimum travel time. Of course, an interviewer will be sympathetic if a bomb scare means everything has suddenly ground to a halt, but try to help by setting out extra early and beating the chaos. It doesn't matter if the schedule goes out of order; at least they will have fewer people left at the end of the day to interview in the café down the road because the hired room has been booked by someone else. It is wise to have a note of a suitable contact number, so that if something unforeseen occurs to delay you, you can get a message to your interviewer.

Note: I suggest that it's a mistake to be completely reliant on a Sat Nav or Google Street View – the former are currently not accurate enough in crowded areas (like central London) and the photographs in the latter were taken several years ago and things change.

What to wear? Dress comfortably and not over the top or very scruffily, unless you can carry it off with style. Extremes of dress can totally dominate your interviewer's perception of you. Don't wear:

- brand new clothes (or shoes) that you haven't yet broken in;
- extremes of dress that can stereotype you too much – find a good balance for the visual recorded media (see below);
- clothes that strongly distort your body shape;
- strong colours or patterns that can be distracting – or clothes that have provocative slogans emblazoned across them;
- attachments (large earrings, nose rings, badges, etc.) that could catch the eye too much;
- clothes that rustle too much;
- clothes that restrict your movement too much – especially when you might be asked to demonstrate some physical skill (also wear outer garments that are easily removable);
- footwear (from flip-flops to high heels) that will make too much noise on hard surfaces – their sound could upstage you. (*Note:* Be wary of trainers as their thick soles can make you bounce – it is important to have a firm connection with the floor);
- clothes (or shoes) that obviously require maintenance – I have been riveted by several pairs of shoes that looked as though they were auditioning for a remake of Charlie Chaplin's *The Gold Rush*.

For television, commercials and film You need to dress as close to the part as possible, while still being yourself. Several experienced actors have said to me that you need to go in 'looking successful'; you need to look as though you'd be at one with the stars who will be playing the leads. That doesn't mean dressed as though you are going to a society wedding. If it's a dowdy part, then go designer dowdy; scruffy, then designer scruffy, and so on. Don't wear clothes that will upstage that most important part of you – your face.

Be aware of the details. It is no good looking right to play a business person but walking through the door with a carrier bag full of the trainers, jeans and T-shirt you've just changed out of.

For the theatre You will get more of the benefit of the doubt in what you wear – provided you don't go to extremes. In general, avoid excessive make-up and formal suits. Go feeling comfortable in what you wear and looking as though you'd be prepared to work there and then. I once turned somebody down for a part and subsequently realised that I should not have done. I met her and then recalled her to read again after she'd read the entire script (along with five others). She was very keen to play the part, but on both occasions she appeared very sloppily dressed – in the same shapeless jumper – with no energy in her appearance. From her television work I felt she'd be right, but in taking the final knife-edge decision against her I subsequently realised that I was deeply influenced by that sloppy jumper. Your visual impact can easily upstage what you say because human beings take in far more information through their eyes than through their ears. You are your own shop window; you should dress it well.

Women and trousers A subtitle for this paragraph could have been, 'Trousers can hide a multitude of sins'. If you are going for a part that specifically requires skirt length above the ankle, then it's probably better to wear a skirt. Sexist but true. If your legs are excessively thin or fat, then you'll be used to finding a length that disguises as much as possible; this is probably your best option as trousers worn for an obvious legs part could make the interviewer suspicious. For instance, good legs are important for the traditional pantomime principal boy, for Louise Page's *Golden Girls* (a play about female sprinters) and for some other parts.

Hair, perfume and aftershave You may have long and beautiful hair, but can we see your face properly? It can be irritating if you're constantly having to push it away from your face.

Strong perfume and aftershave (just like strong colour) provokes strong reactions – positive and negative – so be wary of using it.

Sex appeal Don't be sexually provocative in your dress. One woman semi-exposed her bosom to me by the surreptitious undoing of an extra blouse-button – I have no memory of the rest of her. The same is true of the man in tight, revealing trousers pointing his crotch at whoever might be interested. Don't – as someone once did to me – take all your clothes off as part of an audition speech. The striptease may have been justifiable for the speech, but I – a broad-minded, red-blooded, heterosexual male – did not know where to put myself and could hardly continue. I don't remember anything else about that session beyond mumbling, 'Perhaps you'd better get dressed' and my hurried exit. A strip can be effectively mimed or not be nearly so extensive.

Forewarned is forearmed You should get as much information about the job, the interviewer(s) and what will be expected of you as you reasonably can. You should have been given essential information beforehand, but you should do whatever extra research you can. Indeed, 'extra research' is expected with so much information freely available on the internet. Check productions previously cast or directed by your interviewer(s), and so forth. However, never entirely trust all the information you unearth – use it judiciously. It could be that you discover that an interviewer likes cats, for instance. You may also discover, after you've spent several precious minutes extolling the virtues of your ginger tom, that your interviewer is only interested in pedigree Siamese and despises common or garden moggies. This is a real example.

State of mind It is crucial that you focus on the fact that you are a skilled and accomplished professional, not a hapless beggar desperate for work. And, if it is necessary for you, find that positive interview 'state of mind' and be prepared to sell – but not oversell – yourself. A friend does workouts to get himself up to that positivity level before he goes to an interview, and another sings along with her favourite grand opera arias. Prepare well and then be prepared for anything and everything.

I used to do a lot of hitch-hiking. I learned that I stood a better chance of a lift if I didn't look too scruffy and didn't overplay my hand – in both the physical and the presentational sense. Just make your point – 'I would like a lift, please' – and that's it. At the same time, don't just sit there looking bored and fed up, limply waving your thumb. There has to be energy behind each request. The same ideas apply to your general presentation in an interview.

Portfolios These are collections of production photographs, reviews and press-cuttings neatly displayed in a portfolio. They can be useful to show a range of your work, but too many people try to hide behind them and use them as a substitute for talking about themselves. An actor once handed me his in answer to my 'Tell me a bit about yourself' without saying a word. It contained some riveting photographs of him and a rather elegant naked woman. I asked what the play was – he couldn't remember. Others have had modelling shots, badly photocopied reviews, even holiday snaps. If you go for this extra encumbrance, make sure that all the material is quality, that it emphasises your acting work (neatly labelled) and that it's not too long. In an interview the stress should be on you, in the flesh. It is probably better to reveal your portfolio later on in an interview – if it feels appropriate – and it can be briefly skimmed through. *Be warned*: some people do not like them at all.

'What have you been doing recently?' Most interviewers open with this question (or variants). It is the most popular way of getting the conversation going. Don't think less of interviewers for being so unimaginative and don't have your response so well rehearsed that it trots out without any passion. It's your life you are talking about. Don't respond with 'It's on my CV' – that will kill the conversation stone dead, and it's difficult to get it going again. Get together a mental checklist of about half a dozen activities with which you could respond – including non-acting ones that could serve to enhance the overall impression of you. Don't write a script, however! The specific question could be marginally different.

Don't presume everybody will start with this question either. 'What's been your favourite part so far?' is another popular starter, and 'How do you see yourself as an actor?' and 'What do you want to be doing?' are all opening gambits I have come across. You have to be prepared for anything.

Periodically, I get bored with these standard opening tacks. I'm not saying they are wrong, but they are almost equivalent to the standard social greeting of 'How are you?', and the sincerity can wear thin with too much repetition. Beginning one interview, I suddenly found myself saying: 'Well, how shall we start?' My interviewee responded with 'Well, why don't you tell me something about yourself?' So I did. We eventually worked together, and during a rehearsal break we talked about the interview and she volunteered that she had not done anything like that before in her fifteen years' experience and would never dream of doing it again. 'It simply felt fine there and then.' And so it was.

CV and photograph Always take spare copies of these to any interview. You never know.

Some things to consider on the day

Every interview is different – as is every audience. There can be all kinds of unknown factors that determine the course of events. Treat each interview afresh and anticipate nothing specific. Essentially, you should aim to be as relaxed and real as possible within the confines of what is essentially an unreal situation. You can exploit the fact that you've only got a short time just to put over your good points. That is not lying, it is being economical with the truth, which may not be legitimate in a courtroom but certainly is in a brief interview. It is also not the modern political practice of spinning ('setting out to cloud the truth'); more the ancient art of diplomacy ('tactful skill in dealing with other people').

You should present yourself as a confident human being who has the sensitivities and skills of an actor. Stay centred and honest, and sustain yourself through all the doubts and fears that are an actor's lot with that life force of humour. Don't find yourself driven into a corner where your soul starts lying. 'It's your job to enjoy talking with people' sums up the general attitude necessary.

Pre-interview checklist

1) Is your mobile phone switched off?
2) If you wear glasses, have you got them in a convenient place for easy access?
3) Will you need a notepad and pen/pencil? And are they easily accessible?
4) If you've been sent a script, have you got it with you?
5) Is your clothing secure against any accident or embarrassment?

I mention these obvious precautions because failures in the above areas are all too common. I can only presume that the incidents happen through nerves and concentration on getting that job.

Aim to arrive early Apart from the possibilities of finding the audition room and finding useful information, there's a more fundamental reason to aim for this. Most people need a period of adjustment to settle into new circumstances. Even if you've been there before, there could easily be something different – not the usual room, for instance.

Signage So you've found the building. Next you have to find the interview room. It might be easy and there is an obvious gaggle of actors crowded into a small, scruffy waiting room. Wait a moment. Are they waiting to see the same person as you are? There may be a notice on the door indicating the organisation concerned. There may be a friendly caretaker to tell you – or, even better, a receptionist who knows the difference between the Belgrade Theatre, Coventry, and the Library Theatre, Manchester. But be warned: there are several popular (and cheap) places to rent that can house several companies at one time in their rabbit warren of rooms.

Essentially, look for the signs and arrive early enough to find them. They may be badly scribbled and taped on to walls, pinned up next to the Alcoholics Anonymous notice. The crucial thing is that they will rarely be larger than A4, and in a vast Victorian building they may not be obvious and will probably be easy to miss in a panic. You may suddenly come across a door marked with the obscure name – probably one of the founding fathers of the institution – that you were given in your instructions. Think before you knock, let alone barge in. You may be late, and silence seems to reign; but if there is no sign beyond that faded nameplate – wait, relax and think. Look around the vicinity more carefully. There could be two doors to the interview room. Look for a waiting room or area (it might be a corridor). Only in the last resort should you knock. It is always better to be in a situation where you can wait to be called.

Waiting and listening in Once you've arrived at the appointed place you will usually have to wait. Some actors need to be quiet, some need to talk, but natural curiosity insists that everybody will be after clues as to what's going on in the interview room. Of course hints might be useful, but they might also be misleading as no two human interactions are exactly alike. A glimpse through a door, loud laughter permeating the walls, a snatch of conversation as somebody is ushered out might generate presumptions on your part. You may be right – the interviewer is friendly; but it could be that he or she was very jolly with the last person because they already knew each other well and just wanted to chat about a part or simply that two strangers suddenly clicked. You will never be able to get anything like a complete picture of a previously unknown interviewer, and a strong presumption on your part could easily lead you up the garden path.

I was once having a very good and jolly chat with someone after having done the business side and ran late because I was enjoying myself. That session over, I admitted the next person, with apologies for the delay, and suddenly she came out with a barrage of chat and jokes in the manner of the previous interviewee. I had, quite firmly, to call a halt because it was getting me nowhere and by then I was running significantly late. She protested: 'But I thought you were such a nice man from what I could hear.' I am – usually – but not when I'm informed that I have been monitored for the previous ten minutes through a private conversation. It was very difficult to establish any kind of relationship after that.

However, a friend was once waiting peacefully when he suddenly heard the sounds of a terrible row emanating from the interview room. After a few minutes, somebody came flying out and passed rapidly through to the outside world. Then my friend was aware of a red-faced and shaking presence standing at the door of the interview room. 'You're next, I presume,' it said and stalked back inside. My friend decided that he would have to work subtly at calming his interviewer down. He succeeded, the session ended very happily and he was offered the job. You may be able to capitalise on your perceived assessment of the atmosphere inside the interview room or you may be catastrophically wrong.

The waiting room full of beautiful people Sometimes you'll walk into the waiting room to find it full of people who look perfect for the part. It is true that the 'look' of someone (which can include their looks) can count – especially for commercials and often in television and film – but generally not as much as you might think. Anyway, the first thing is not to let it get you down. If your spirit flies out of the window at this early stage, you are doomed. If their presence really starts to bug you, look for things that might be wrong with individuals. How someone gets up from a chair is a good test of their cool. There are others – watch out for them. As a friend pointed out: 'You have to work on convincing people that you're glamorous.' She also observed that 'Great British actresses aren't known for their looks.' Another said, 'You're as glamorous as you feel.'

A friend in the waiting room It's often a relief to find people you know in the waiting room – you can help each other ease the pain of waiting. However, don't let the fun of the renewed contact detract from your focus for being there. I'm not suggesting that you ignore them and sit in stoical silence – that's an even worse preparation for what's to follow. Look to helping each other to prepare and arrange to meet up and compare notes afterwards.

Similarly, don't let casual waiting room conversations get out of hand. On several occasions I've had to quell persistent, loud conversation that was disrupting my interviewing.

The earliest impressions While waiting outside the interview room, don't try to draw attention to yourself by attempting to make eye contact with the director/assistant each time he or she comes to collect the next person. This kind of attention-seeking is terribly alienating and typifies the bad, but generally unfair, public image that actors have. An actor is an adult with special skills, not an attention-seeking child.

The long walk The interview area is often on the opposite side of the room from the door; this is to cut down the chances of being overheard. If you are nervous, it can seem miles to your chair. Not only should you use this time to assess the ambience, you should also use it to begin to establish yourself – just as you would when making your first entrance on to a stage.

First impressions As you walk confidently into the interview room, take the time (it doesn't take long) to assess the ambience of the room in which it's all taking place and the people it contains. Try to measure the energy of the space and aim not to go above or below it. That walk from the door to the table, however long or short, can be an invaluable time to acclimatise and make yourself feel at home. Also, take the opportunity to check the whereabouts of the important pieces of furniture and the acoustic that you're going to be speaking within. Your interviewers will also be assessing you – unconsciously perhaps – in those first vital seconds. I know one director who claims to do most of his casting on that first impact: 'After all, that's how the audience will react.'

Baggage Be wary of any baggage you are carrying in these first few moments. Don't let depositing your belongings take away from the vital beginnings of getting to know your interviewer(s). It can often be a good idea to leave anything inessential by the door of the interview room as you enter or (even better) with someone remaining in the waiting room or (probably best) by your chair – partially tucked under it to lessen the chances of tripping over it. It is probably better to minimise all external encumbrances in order to reduce the chances of one (or more) taking on a life of its (or their) own in these potentially nervous circumstances – a bag strap getting caught by a door handle, for instance.

Introductions Listen carefully to introductions, especially if there's an army of people there. Make sure you remember those names, even if it's only first names, and try to take in what each one does. It doesn't matter if you have to ask for a name to be repeated – it's easy to miss one through nerves or individuals slurring them. (It is curious how many people seem to do this.) Anyway, you should aim to get all the names when contacted about the interview – you can help yourself if you learn them beforehand.

Sometimes the odd person may be left out of introductions. This can be an oversight or it might be deliberate. If this happens, don't exclude them from what follows. Everybody is there for a purpose.

When you have finally settled after the introductions, your interviewers' opening smiles will probably turn to what look like frowns: it is strange what concentration does to many people's faces. Don't let that throw you. After everybody's seated there could be a horrid pause before the first question is asked – don't feel that you have to fill that aching silence while your CV (for instance) is surveyed once again.

Handshakes If hand-shaking is in order, do it positively. There is nothing more off-putting at the very start of an interview than a limp handshake. (Nevertheless you mustn't be perturbed if you receive one.) The act of shaking hands is an act that suggests mutual trust; it is also your opportunity to say silently 'I am me!' But don't be too strong or hearty either – your interviewer has probably got to write with that hand. Know your own physical strength, or lack of it.

If there are several interviewers, don't try to shake hands with everybody unless offered: it can take forever. Don't just shake hands with the men either; I've seen that happen far too often.

Occasionally, no handshake will be offered. Don't worry about this – it can become very tedious going through this ritual umpteen times a day.

An illustrative story from an actor at an interview: 'One Director even refused to shake my hand, lurching it in the air and pontificating: "No Hands!" – like I was a Leper Extra from *Ben-Hur*.'

Your chair is not glued to the floor A surprising number of people will sit in a chair that is found slap bang up against the interviewer's table, threatening an eyeball-to-eyeball confrontation rather than a pleasant chat. A few cowardly souls will sit in one that's on the other side of the room. (How does the chair manage to get into such strange places? It was moved by the previous interviewee.)

You should move your chair to a place that suits you, from which you can talk easily with all of your interviewers – that is, you are not so close that you invade your interviewers' personal space, and not so distant that proper personal contact is difficult. You should do this without asking. It shows you have a personality of your own and are not a complete wimp who will do nothing beyond what you are actually told.

The position of your chair is especially important when you are facing a gang of interviewers. You have to place it so that you can take in as many of them as possible without finding yourself constantly watching tennis. Place it centrally so that everybody is within good contact range. However, don't spend hours fiddling with your chair's position. This should become an instinct as natural as breathing.

Note: Lift your chair into position – don't drag it!

Sitting down Sitting in a familiar chair needs little thought; in an unfamiliar one – in professional circumstances – it does.

- It can be good manners to sit after whoever ushered you into the room – unless this would cause you to hover for too long and you begin to appear creepy.
- Although many chairs are of a standard height, a significant minority are that little bit lower – and occasionally higher. It can throw you if you make contact with the seat that fraction later or earlier than you expected. Try putting a hand out discreetly to help anticipate your arrival in the sitting position.
- You'll appear more open and positive if you sit up reasonably (but not ramrod) straight.
- Try not to cross your arms and legs – you'll seem more open. If like me you find that the latter entwine almost without thinking, then aim to do it lightly. I know it can feel comforting to wrap one leg round the other, but what happens is that you start compressing the blood vessels in the upper leg and in a short time it will begin to go numb. Then the attached foot will take on a mind of its own and start jigging without you realising it – and when you try to stand

up the numbing effect will prevent you from walking properly until circulation is restored.

'Who's in charge?' Never act on the assumption that one person present is more important than all the others. You may well be right, but don't let this make you direct all your answers to that person to the exclusion of the others. I have known people direct all their answers to me, even when some questions were coming from the trainee at my side. The trainee was most put out and so was I. Everybody in the room will have at least some influence over the casting – even a secretary or assistant stage manager. Don't alienate one apparently lowly person for the sake of giving your all to whoever's in charge – even the person ticking off names outside. He or she may be an employee of the organisation that runs the building and nothing to do with the interviews, but even so, comments will be made – especially on intolerable behaviour.

Assistant stage managers and trainees might become influential in years to come, and memories are long for those who hurt us unnecessarily.

'You could be just what I'm after' Most interviewers start with the hope that you could be just what they are looking for. This is partly because they have very little reason to have anything against you as yet and they rarely know exactly what they are looking for. It is true that some do have a preconception of the type of actor they want – especially in television and films, but I don't believe that anybody has it completely worked out. You can show such people that you could come somewhere close to their preconception and bring your own special talents as well.

A few directors are downright cynics and start out with the idea of specifically looking out for what's wrong with you, but they seem to be in the minority and you simply have to work harder at proving yourself and not be put down.

Time passes more quickly when you're trying to sell yourself Sight-readings and/or audition speeches can easily take half, if not more, of your time. That doesn't leave very long – and can feel even less – for the interview part. So aim to be concise, but not so precise that you appear calculating and cold. Principally, you need to find a way of opening up as early as possible, and the rest should flow from there.

Listening and receiving Listen carefully to questions asked and be positive and concise in your responses. You may be nervous, and nerves tend to stop people listening properly. If this is the case, then try focusing on this 'listening' and it could help calm you.

And don't just listen – receive! That is, receive the message that is being sent to you. Think of this like catching a ball: hold on to it for a moment while deciding how to respond and return the metaphorical ball. It can also be useful to keep the original question in a corner of your mind for reference, in case you start deviating too far from it. Too many actors seem to concentrate so much on giving little nods and smiles that I know full well they are not taking on board fully what I am saying or asking.

The same old question Don't respond to 'What have you been doing recently?' with a basic telephone directory of facts which can be gleaned from your CV and letter anyway. Use it to show your wit, charm and personality. You will be asked this basic question frequently – never let your response get stale. (See 'What have you been doing recently?', page 156.)

Talking too much The majority of interviewees talk too much – a few talk far too much – and it is either a very rude or a desperate interviewer who will cut you off in mid-flow. Where is the dividing line between too much and too little? That varies enormously and depends on (a) your interviewer's willingness to listen, (b) how relevant to the question each element of your response is and (c) how much time is available overall. For many it is terribly easy to amplify too much on a basic answer. For instance, an actor was introduced to a director by a close friend who also happened to be the director's assistant. A natural opening question from the director was, 'So how do you two know each other?' The friend launched into the complex series of events that first acquainted them. The assistant, realising what was happening, cut in tactfully by saying: 'It's personal as opposed to professional.' Then they got down to the interview proper. If you are a talker, then work hard at sticking to the subject and resist any little deviations that 'won't take a moment'. Develop an end-of-subject awareness – the ability to recognise when a particular subject is covered sufficiently for now, and it is time to move on.

The truth – or one's perception of it – is infinitely complex. Theoretically, we could talk for ever on a single subject, and it is easily done if it is of great importance to you. You have to resist the temptation when those subjects come up. Think beforehand what your personal talking danger zones are, and think how you might paraphrase without losing the essence and passion for that subject.

Some directors talk too much. If this happens to you, then look for ways in which you can tactfully, but firmly, bring the subject round to yourself.

Talking too little A few actors talk too little. Monosyllabic answers do not help to give a good impression. Your response to even the most banal question should aim to convey something of the positive aspects of yourself.

Nerves can make some people tongue-tied. An unsympathetic interviewer or even a shy one can make it difficult for you to find words to express yourself. But 'find words' is what you have to do. Anticipate this possibility and work out a scenario of what you could talk about beforehand.

'What are they writing?' Your interviewer(s) will probably spend a lot of the time writing notes. Give him or her just enough time to do so; don't get paranoid about it and don't, under any circumstances, try to read what is being written. (Often it's simply your basic physical details – hair colour/style/length, clothes, and other distinctive marks – all very useful as memory joggers when going through the notes later.)

Some write very little, if anything. 'Does that imply a total lack of interest in me?' It might, but you have to ignore this and continue regardless. Some people like to write their notes immediately afterwards. There is absolutely no point in worrying about what they write or think. If you do, it could inhibit your efforts.

Mutual friends Try to find some kind of personal contact with the person(s) you are meeting and make sure your information is correct. On several occasions I have been told by an interviewee that A, B or C 'sends their love', when I may have met the 'friend' once but cannot remember them from X, Y or Z. Also be careful about how you phrase a greeting. 'Love' is a commonly used word in this profession, but you should be sure of yourself before using it. Perhaps something like 'sends their best wishes' might be better.

If it's the case, be wary of admitting that the third party concerned also happens to be your lover. This somehow opens up other connotations that are unnecessary and can cloud the central issue and/ or take the focus away from you. Marriage is different, but it still should only be a passing reference. The interview should be about you and not about some third party whom you both happen to know. In general it's better to keep intimate relationships out of the discussion altogether – you never know who might have known who.

'I want work!' Never be overtly desperate for a job; it can colour the whole session in totally the wrong way. A classic example of this was the actor I was seeing for the part of Mozart in *Amadeus*. He expressed his enthusiasm for the subject matter by saying: 'I've got all his records.' He was deadly serious. Acting requires objectivity as well as subjectivity, and dispassion as well as passion. A director must see that objectivity in you.

Several people have suggested that it is better to approach the session with the idea of not wanting the job: for some that can be the best way of coping. For others, that attitude can make you seem so casual it might well turn the interviewer right off. Somebody else suggested to me that it's probably best to go in thinking that the job is yours for the taking and, when you've left the room, get it into your head that you haven't got it and forget about it. Or 'Care when you're in there; forget it when you're out of the door.'

Acting confident Some people find it very easy just to go in and be totally relaxed and confident: they can enjoy the session and be totally open, and show easily that they care about their work. If you are the sort of person who needs to act 'confidence', be very careful because an acted confidence can come over as arrogance which is very alienating. It is essential not to overdo confidence and/or be too assertive. I'm afraid this is especially true for a woman being interviewed by a man. Some of my sex are too easily put off by the apparently assertive woman. Essentially, assert yourself but don't make it look as if you are doing so.

If you find that your mouth dries up with nerves, scrape your tongue hard along the back of your teeth surreptitiously; that soon gets the saliva circulating again.

Role-playing In spite of what you might feel about interviews, enjoy being there. Role-playing because you get nervous isn't necessarily wrong or insincere. It's not 'not being yourself'; it's your way of dealing with the interview situation. In taking on a role you will be showing at least part of yourself, which is all that can be expected in that short space of time.

A friend takes the role-playing even further. She will adapt an aspect of herself – where she lives, for example – to come closer in reality to the character she's up for. This may be a good idea – she works a lot – but you must be sure you can carry it through and don't get found out. There is also the danger that if you go too far, that particular interviewer will only think of you in that kind of part when considering future casting. (To some extent the clothes you wear will dictate the role you play: see 'What to wear', on pages 153–4.)

What is your face saying? Too many people seem to think that the best way to sell themselves is by sitting there with a forced, fixed and blasé theatrical smile on their faces: the 'eyes and teeth' approach. I've known others sit there looking totally vacant. Concentration does strange things to some people's faces (I'm told I can look angry), but nobody maintains a fixed expression if they are listening and receiving properly.

Don't start putting on faces. If you are connecting properly with what's going on, then simply use your actor's training and instinct to inform your face and your whole body.

The sin of being out of work Obviously you try to disguise those great grey patches of unemployment when talking about your recent career, but some interviewers are very sharp at reading between the lines and, if it's the case, will detect that you have in fact been out of work for too long. If they comment (which I'm told is unusual) to this effect, don't worry or be embarrassed; just be positive about the painting and decorating, the temping, and so on, you've been doing to keep the wolf from the door. Talk about the amazing characters you've met and what useful studies they've been. In fact, you should go into non-acting jobs (and about life as a whole) with your actor's antennae alert for such useful observations – after all it's those real people that you have to bring to your craft. Some interviewers seem to relish discussion about non-acting matters. For instance at the start of an interview a friend was told, 'That's an interesting T-shirt.'

Excuses and apologies Don't make excuses unless some kind of genuine apology is necessary: for example, if you are late. If something does require an apology, do it simply and straightforwardly. Over-apologising can easily waste precious time and can embarrass.

There is no excuse for being under par because of a hangover, for instance. That is your fault and, if it prevents you from interviewing properly, it is unprofessional.

Mumbling 'When in doubt, mumble' seems to be some actors' way of covering a hangover or other embarrassing fact. You are only undermining yourself further.

'Only connect' Do your damnedest to 'connect' with your inter-viewer(s). They should be trying to do the same with you, but in practice the onus tends to be on the actor.

Every interview is different. Even someone you have met before will – to at least some degree – seem different in a different context. You have to find a rapport with each individual in each case. You should try to interact with each interviewer, just as with all your fellow actors in rehearsal.

Status Apparently some directors are actually afraid of actors. This makes connecting difficult. Certainly I often feel, in the first interview of the day, that I don't know what the hell I'm talking about and can start thinking that the actor must think I'm stupid. I don't care about being thought stupid but I know that some interviewers do like to 'maintain their status'. Whatever communicates, never let them know that you know – unless it's obvious they don't sit on their status. They are your only route to the job. You can help your interviewer(s). They may get into a muddle about information they're trying to get over about the production – when one is repeating the same thing over and over again that's very easy to do. Listen carefully, and if something doesn't make sense to you, then ask.

'Power tends to corrupt' It is also true that for some the power inherent in being an employment broker can tend to corrupt. If you do meet this phenomenon, there's only one thing you can do. Be strong!

When there's someone in the room you know The strangest thing can be the interview between two people who already know each other reasonably well, which takes place with nobody else in the room. There can be all kinds of reasons for this to occur: a director who feels he or she doesn't know somebody quite well enough; a dangerous piece of potential casting; a casting that is outside the actor's perceived range. As a friend said, 'It felt extremely odd' when I asked to see him for the first of those reasons. Don't feel offended. Your director friend may also feel embarrassed, but you can help by aiming to treat the session as professionally as possible and put the relationship to date in perspective. Some (but not all) directors think even harder about employing friends than strangers. I know at least one director who won't employ his own wife as a matter of principle.

If there is more than one interviewer, and there is someone there whom you know very well, then you have to push that personal relationship to the back of your mind. That is not to say that you should ignore them, but you should treat them as another interviewer and not miss things out that they know well but the other interviewers do not.

Instant friendships Yes, one aims to make friends with one's interviewer, but don't be over-friendly. This can often happen when interviewer and interviewee have a close acquaintance in common. It can lead to the presumption on both director's and actor's part that they are therefore already close acquaintances and don't need to go through those essential early 'connecting' stages. They do. Don't, as I have known people do, dive in, in the first moments, treating your interviewers as long-lost friends when you don't know them from Adam (or Eve). It will crowd them, and they won't be able to start off as they want. At the beginning the field is your interviewers', so let them make the running and set the pace.

Diplomacy With some more open, friendly interviewers it's easy to feel very relaxed and open yourself, and you may well find yourself coming out with a minor piece of bitchery. This may be fine, but there's a chance that he or she might be friendly with the person you've just bitched about. I know of someone who was distinctly unkind about his drama school to a director. What the actor didn't know was that the director's wife had been one of his teachers. Be careful. Diplomacy rather than candour.

It's easy to be negative Don't give negative reasons for anything unless you can be positively negative. That is not a contradiction in terms. For example, if you didn't enjoy a particular job because of the laziness of some of the company, be positive in your criticism of such unprofessionalism. Beware: spreading doubt about others can create doubt about you.

Especially, don't complain about one director to another even if pushed. In fact don't run anybody down – ever. Even if your interviewer seems to be enjoying it hugely, it's not worth the risk.

Generosity If you know somebody who is perfect for the part you're up for – and you're patently not – then say so. This kind of generosity, in this fiercely competitive world, could reap rewards in time to come.

The natural rhythm of an interview Two people who are genuinely getting on find a natural rhythm to their dialogue – just like that natural rhythm that actors look for in a scene. This will partly come through trying to 'connect' with your interviewer and partly through being aware of natural hazards. For instance, you could be offered a cup of tea. That's probably a sign that things are going well. But however parched you may feel, you should usually politely decline. Why? Because this encumbrance can suddenly make the whole session take on another course. Consider the analogy of a scene from a play. You've rehearsed and rehearsed, and it's going well, then comes the moment when you stop miming and use real tea in a real cup. The whole scene suddenly falls apart because you find there is a great pause while you drink the hot liquid. You may have marked this moment in rehearsal, but virtually no one leaves long enough. Of course, a short amount of rehearsal time will sort this out, but in an interview there is no rehearsal time. The pause while drinking can strain, or even sever, the gossamer thread that is the connection you are building with your interviewer(s). You have interrupted the natural rhythm of the all-too-brief session. (Once a nervous actor missed his mouth completely – through concentration on the conversation – and poured orange squash all over himself.)

Eye contact Don't overdo eye contact. Be natural about it. A lot is made of eye contact in acting; that doesn't mean you try to do it throughout an interview. Of course you make eye contact in the first instance, but don't hold on to it like a limpet; that seems to be the prerogative of the newly in love. If you push it with the idea of making even better contact, the interviewer will probably feel that you are invading his or her space and may even feel threatened. Remember playing stare-you-out games as a child? Also bear in mind that the director will often be looking down at papers and writing notes.

Make 'em laugh Yes, a few laughs are a good way of 'connecting', but don't overdo humour and don't force it. Humour is not always the art of making jokes; it is that zest for life that made you become an actor in the first place and without which you'd have slit your wrists long ago. It is the way we get through the months while we're waiting for Godot to offer us a job.

The balance of humour Like the 'balance of power' you must be careful that it doesn't tip too far one way or the other. Early on you need to assess whether your interviewer has a sense of humour or not. If he or she has, then be careful that your combined humours don't take over the interview too much and detract from your other efforts.

Politeness Be pleasant, but don't go to the extreme of being over-polite, even formal, for example, by addressing your interviewer as 'Mr X' or 'Ms B', asking if you may take your coat off, and so on. You may have been well brought up, and there is nothing wrong with the basic rules of politeness, but you should use them to suit each occasion. Regard the situation as if you've been invited into a vague acquaintance's house for a social drink. Don't be too casual, however; it is also very important that you come over as someone who cares about their work.

Flattery is base Don't plead or flatter; both are more alienating than anything else I know. Essentially avoid extremes of behaviour (which can happen through nerves). Never get to the extremes of either subservience or plain bloody-minded cockiness. Never flirt with your interviewer. Even if you do suddenly find yourself fancying them, and you think you feel it reciprocated, concentrate on the job in hand, which is to get a job. The casting couch is an extremely rare phenomenon.

'You remember, we met . . .' Tolerate with good grace an interviewer who cannot remember meeting you before, even if the meeting was recent. Directors, agents and casting directors meet an amazing number of different people, in all kinds of different contexts, day in and day out. There is no way, even possessed of very good memories, we can immediately remember each and every person we have ever met. It can also be very confusing if you've changed your hairstyle, grown a beard or acquired glasses since our previous meeting, or are simply dressed completely differently.

The reverse can also happen, with interviewers saying they know you 'from somewhere' but you cannot for the life of you remember them. Don't worry about it; this profession is an ocean of ships passing in the night.

'You turned me down for . . .' If it's the case, don't bear a grudge because your interviewer previously rejected you. Most directors do feel a little bit guilty about those they liked but rejected in favour of people they liked even more. You probably wouldn't be in the interview at all if you hadn't come over well at the previous meeting.

Superstitions A lot of people would deny being at all superstitious, but in this profession that is generally not true. If you are asked about current job prospects and you don't want to discuss anything about possibilities in the pipeline, that should be respected.

Interruptions Anything might happen during an interview: a phone might ring, someone might interrupt with an urgent message. Don't let this throw you. Concentrate on where the session was interrupted to help your harassed interviewer pick up from where you left off. The interruption will have wasted precious time and has probably made the interviews run even later than they were. Don't feel rushed by this – that is the interviewer's problem, not yours. (I was once severely embarrassed by a director friend barging into an interview in order to arrange lunch. The actor in the middle coped extremely well – even ending up with a job with my [rude] friend.)

Irritations Occasionally, an interviewer might indulge in one of those activities which are downright irritating when you're trying to concentrate – eating crisps, persistent pen-tapping, and so on. These activities can be particularly counterproductive at times when you're trying to absorb a script you've just been given to read from or focusing before starting an audition speech. If you're being too distracted, don't be afraid to ask them – firmly, but politely – to stop. It is a fact that most people perpetrating such acts don't realise how distracting they are until it's pointed out.

Politics and religion Never discuss politics unless absolutely sure of your ground with your interviewer. A significant number of directors are at least moderately radical, but a significant silent few are not. You may think you will be on safe ground if you take a swipe at whichever politician or party is today's joke; in all probability you will be, but bear in mind that an awful lot of people voted for him/her/it and some of them do work in this profession.

Treat religion (or lack of it) in exactly the same way. The silent majority of directors are probably apathetic agnostics, but there are a few devout believers and some angry atheists among us.

I do know actors (and directors) who maintain that they could not work with somebody who held diametrically opposed political or religious beliefs. This may well be true, but unless you are prepared to sacrifice the chance to work for your beliefs there is no point in waving a flag of extreme colour. Even if the director does agree with you, your viewpoint usually has nothing to do with your acting ability.

Taking the initiative Don't try to go on the offensive too much by asking the interviewer about his or her company, the productions, artistic policy, and so on, too early on. You may want to glean some information, but it's not helping the interviewer to get to know you and you might inadvertently tread on some sore spot – for example, the production that went disastrously wrong.

Always let interviewers take the initiative to start with, even if it does not seem very imaginative. Ask your questions if invited, or if appropriate, when the main business is done with. (See 'Any questions?', pages 174–5.)

'I don't agree with you!' You may find an incautious interviewer commenting adversely on something or someone you hold dear. Some directors are prejudiced against some drama schools, for example. If you feel you need to disagree, do so! But do it well. I once had a very spirited discussion with an interviewee on the subject of her drama school and its methods. She was strong in its defence and I was strong in my attack. There was no resolving our disagreement, but it had nothing to do with whether or not I wanted to work with her. In fact, her spirit warmed me to her.

Hazardous furniture Accidentally walking into doors and chairs (for instance) might be ignored, but the director might wonder how you will cope with similar items on a set. Somebody once walked into an interview with me and bumped into a large and obvious piano near the door. 'Sorry,' she said, 'but I've only got one contact lens in, and that's not my own.' I don't remember her name, what she looked like, her interview or her speech – just the incident and that remark. If she had laughed at her stupidity, she would have put the incident in perspective and taken the first step in connecting with me. Inconvenient shafts of sunlight suddenly hitting you between the eyes, and so forth, are understandable natural hazards to be dealt with simply and acknowledged briefly before getting back to the main point.

Other potential hazards include door handles that don't turn the way you expect, and doors that open similarly. You can avoid minor embarrassment simply by taking a fraction longer over the process.

Don't let the cat out of the bag There will often be certain things it is tactful not to mention – for example, your acquaintance with an actor whom you know the director does not get on with. Or it might be something more prosaic as the following example illustrates.

A friend once went up for the part of Miranda in *The Collector*. 'Do you know the book?' she was asked.
'Oh, yes! I know I haven't got blonde hair, but I could always wear a wig.'
'Is she blonde? I missed that.'

It was a pleasant interview and a good reading, but the director then concentrated on the blondes.

I'm not saying that you shouldn't talk about the background knowledge you've acquired, but try to avoid something that might affect your suitability for the part. That's tact, not lying.

Singing This paragraph is here because you might be asked to sing unaccompanied if you claim singing as a strength. You need a song prepared whose first note you can hit accurately – and remember that when you are nervous your voice automatically rises.

'Any questions?' Many interviewers like to round off with this invitation. Usually it's fine to respond positively with the negative, but it has been suggested to me that it can be good idea to take a suitable question in with you. The important thing to remember is to keep your question simple and straightforward – there is not time for complicated discussion. And whatever you do, don't ask what the money is or when decisions will be made unless it is important – for example, you are considering another potential job.

Don't overstay your welcome Some people are very bad at ending interviews. Things are going well, you are prattling away and your interviewer seems to be having a good time. If all the usual processes have been gone through, then it's time for you to go. Develop an end-of-interview awareness. Remember that ancient theatrical cliché: 'Leave 'em wanting more!' And when you do go – go! Don't try to cram in more irrelevant information as you are leaving. It will be a waste of time; the interviewer is already thinking about the next person.

This is true even if your time has been very brief. Don't feel short-changed; it can be a good sign.

Leaving things behind Leaving things behind can be very irritating for your interviewer(s) as well as embarrassing for you. I have known people do this deliberately to draw attention to themselves. It does not work and it could well mark you down as potential chaos and not worth employing.

The final touch Do thank your interviewer at the end and if you've enjoyed the session say so. Or you can write a brief but not creepy letter afterwards.

A few final notes . . .

Recalls Sometimes a director will go in for what seem like endless recalls. You may think that he or she must know you, and your capabilities, sufficiently by now. What else can you do to prove yourself? But you go on being asked back. There can be any number of reasons for this. You have to go on exactly as you did in the first interview, doing whatever is asked of you. Don't let it frustrate you.

Casting and assistant directors (or the in-betweenies) You may meet one of these before going on to meet the director in a position actually to give you a job. Obviously you treat the first round with the casting/

assistant version as per usual, but meeting the top person can have some peculiarities. The director must have a fair degree of trust in the lesser mortals to employ them, but I have heard numerous stories of enthusiasm from the junior and virtually nothing from the senior partner. There are two fundamental problems:

1) The presumption on the actor's part is that the interview is going to be similar in mood to the one with the junior, and that there is very little more to prove.
2) The overenthusiasm of the junior alienating the senior, who consequently sets out to be sceptical.

The answer is to focus on the senior without excluding the junior. Don't keep giving the latter little familiar smiles, or looks for confirmation, or constant prefacing of remarks with 'As I told [*the junior's name*]'.

This phenomenon is much more common when assistants are involved, but I have heard of it happening when a casting director is the link.

Children I'm told that mothers with small children are advised not to admit this fact to potential employers on the grounds that if something serious happened to a child at a vital point in production, then her priority has to be with that child. However, doesn't the same apply to a father and also to the serious illness of a parent or spouse? Unfortunately there are directors who don't realise that a working parent will ensure that there is someone *in loco parentis* while she or he is away. Anybody who feels they have to run home at the slightest childish sneeze is acting unprofessionally whether they be male or female. I agree that children shouldn't be an issue, but discretion probably has to be the watchword.

Gatecrashing Most will see gatecrashers if there's time. But always have a copy of your CV and photo for them to keep and, as you wait patiently for a gap to appear, don't try to blackmail your way in with whoever appears to collect the next person.

Smoking Although this is illegal in all public buildings, a minority of interviews take place in private premises. If you are a committed smoker, try not to – even if your interviewer is and invites you to join in. In these nervous circumstances one cigarette can lead to another, and another – I know! The interviewer, even if a committed chain-smoker, could think, 'I have got a real neurotic here,' and you will go right down in the employment stakes.

If you're a committed anti-smoker, it's better to hide your feelings much as with politics and religion.

If you are a smoker, it's a good idea to conceal evidence of your habit for the duration of an interview held in a non-smoking location. And don't light up until you're well out of sight of the interview location.

60 per cent You will often come out of an interview thinking of ways you could have done better and cursing thoughts that didn't come out right, moments blown, and so on. There is nothing you can do now except learn for future reference. Anyway, if you've done 60 per cent of what you feel you are capable of, you've probably done as well as anybody else. This rule applies to audition speeches, sight-readings, musical auditions, and so on.

Consequences If you are not what they want, then that's fine. Don't feel cheated because you felt you'd done very well. You haven't failed if you are not right in their eyes, and a good session could lead to work at another time – you never know. By going to interviews you are initially looking to get that particular job, but you are also sowing seeds for the future. (My wife got a very good job nearly twenty years after first meeting a particular director.)

Unfortunately, too many directors wind actors up at the end of interviews by all but promising them the job. I think I've done it myself. If a director meets someone who feels dead right, there is a terrible temptation to say so – there and then – almost to ensure that they'll take the job. But then someone even more 'right' comes along, and the first disappears from view. You have to be sceptical after you leave the room, even if they've promised to 'get in touch' or 'let you know'. (Note to directors who do make such promises: Stop it! It is one of the worst cruelties you can inflict on an actor whom you don't subsequently employ.)

An unlikely, but true, story: At the end of an interview a director went as far as to say he 'really wanted' a friend of mine to play the part. Already quite experienced, she knew that she had to remain sceptical. But it hurt her deeply to read a few weeks later in *The Stage* someone else's name against that part. Several years and some success later she was having her new house decorated. One afternoon she returned from filming and went round to view the improvements. Upstairs she found that director at the top of a ladder painting her ceiling.

An illustration The following is an account, from a student I taught, of a successful meeting with an agent:

'I found at the very outset (after the firm but fair handshake) that a good way to establish a bit of confidence for myself was to simply be assertive when offered a drink. It was a tiny thing, but to be able to ask confidently for a glass of water rather than to ask if he minded if I had a glass of water gave me a confidence in myself and set me up for the rest of the interview. It may sound ridiculous, but I was tempted to say "no" just so it was easier for him, but the truth is that I needed a glass of water!

I totally forgot to check for the chair with my hand but thankfully stayed upright(!) but made a conscious effort to sit quite openly even though I really wanted to sit clutching my bag to my lap. I put my handbag down by the side of the chair and left it there, using the arm rests of the chair as a way of staying open – rather than have loose flailing arms, I tended to rest my elbows on the chair arms and use my lower arms to gesture when speaking.

I held eye contact with him for about half the time I was in there, perhaps a bit longer, but made sure that I didn't particularly look at anything else in the room, just took it all in. And I looked at him every time he was speaking, smiling only when it came naturally, but obviously not having a "screw" face on me the rest of the time! The main thing about that aspect of the interview for me was to make sure that I was listening but not being overly attentive the whole time. It was a general, quite informal chat but I made sure that I was taking in every part of every question or comment that he asked. Hopefully I answered everything right!

He asked me about the showcase and how I felt about it in general, and to stop him following that with "how did you feel personally about your own performance?", I answered the general question generally and a bit personally too so that I could avoid blowing my own trumpet or feeling awkward about talking about myself at all. He asked me quite a bit about the course and the way that the course and the showcase worked, and highly praised the fact that we presented live and recorded pieces. Of course, I replied with even higher praise of the whole process, emphasising that I was grateful that it enabled me to show myself off in two completely different lights vocally, visually and personality wise. He also asked me about my training and will I miss it etc. (of course, I said "Yes but I can't wait to get out and start putting everything into practice"), and which area of acting I would prefer to do, to which I replied eagerly that, basically I want to act and that each different medium gives me a different buzz, but that if I had to choose, I would choose film. I think that both of these answers did me well, one because obviously, I said I would be more than happy to do it all so anything he presented me with would be great, and two because they have quite a few big screen actors on their books and he'd said I came across naturally on screen. One of the hardest things to do was to accept praise graciously. He said a couple of times that I really stood out to him and that he was glad to be talking to me etc., and I tended to just say "Thank you". I think that was OK!

He also mentioned that I have a list of accents on my CV and quoted a couple, at which point I wasn't sure whether I should prove to him that I could do them, but I held off, and he was happy with the confirmation of me saying "Yes, I can do them!" I also joked that I couldn't drop out of my Nell Gwyn accent after the showcase and that I couldn't drop her bolshieness or accent all afternoon and he seemed to like that and take that as proof of my accent ability.

He also asked if I'd had any other interest and if anyone else from the group had had meetings and I told him the truth – that CVs had been taken from many piles and I hadn't had any other calls but wasn't sure if anyone else had.

When he told me about the company, the size etc. and what he wanted to do as the first step for me, I was genuinely pleased and told him that that was perfect for me because I didn't like the idea of being an anonymous face in a huge agency or one of a couple in a smaller agency, and that I liked the idea that I would get personal attention to a certain degree. To be honest, I'm very glad that I said that because he now knows that I expect that of him.

It was slightly difficult to know how to end once he had said he'd like to take me and that he hoped I'd call him soon, but as I knew that it was coming to a natural end, I thought it better to reach down for my bag rather than to stand up straight away and that gave him good time to stand up himself. Basically, we exchanged one more little joke and then I shook his hand again and said I'd be in touch soon and thanked him for his time.

And then I grinned and grinned and grinned!'

A postscript A piece of basic advice from someone I met at drama school and then invited to interview (her very first, but I didn't know that until later) and subsequently offered her a job. She wrote to me later:

> 'I am currently dipping into your book (ugh! what a creep I am), but it appears you missed out a vital piece of advice – "The A, B, C – X, Y, Z formula for auditioning: Always Be Clear and (more importantly) Examine Your Zip!"'

She'd done the complete interview, a song and a sight-reading with the zip in her jeans undone. Fortunately she didn't realise until after she'd left the room.

Sight-readings

While these are only a minor part of drama school auditions, sight-readings (usually known as 'readings' and sometimes 'cold-readings') are at the heart of the professional casting process and different people expect different things from them. Most will say they 'don't expect a performance'; this doesn't mean doing it without any 'life'. 'Performance', in this context, means one that appears fixed and final with no room for change. You should try to show as many as possible of the aspects you could bring to an eventual performance without that sense of 'a final coat of varnish' that can stultify it. A director worthy of that title will look for potential rather than for perfection, except, perhaps, in the case of commercials. Don't use the lack of rehearsal as an excuse to show virtually nothing and just read the words out loud with no inflection, as some people do. Approach the text with all your instincts humming and respond to notes given and clues discovered. Then make what sense you can and give a life to the piece.

Some people are not good at sight-reading. This is not necessarily through dyslexia or some other technical problem, it is simply a fact of their working lives. (I know an actor who feels he has to learn the entire play before the first read-through – something I would normally discourage as pre-learning tends to make most actors somewhat inflexible – he isn't.) A sympathetic director may let you do an audition speech instead or even be happy just to chat – but you are making it that much more difficult for him or her to assess you in comparison to those who have read. Others will insist that you read anyway, so you have to try. Work at reading out loud from unseen texts and find your consistent stumbling blocks (fading out at the ends of sentences, for instance). Record yourself reading and find tricks to overcome them. It is also well worth reading to a small child; you'll soon find out if you are communicating well. Nobody, except the chronically dyslexic, is incapable of reading out loud. Your big problem with doing it is almost certainly a combination of several minor ones that with perseverance can be ironed out. If necessary, seek advice. Don't use it as an excuse.

In advance

The script If you are invited to read for a part in a published script, you must get a copy and read it thoroughly; don't just concentrate on the scenes that the character you're being seen for is in. The same applies to any source material – the novel it's adapted from, for instance. This may seem obvious, but it is surprising how often actors don't even try. This is sheer laziness and no director wants to work with a lazy actor. (However, some people do seem to find it easier just to dive into a reading with no foreknowledge: see 'Or jumping straight in', page 187.) If you are not sure whether it's published or not, find out! If it isn't, try asking for a copy from the management. Sometimes you'll only get the small portion that you'll be asked to read from.

Note: The North American term 'sides' seems to be creeping over to the UK – it simply means selected pages from the full script that involve the character you are being seen for.

Character clues Obviously you'll dig out as many of these as possible, but don't start forming fixed ideas that you cannot change – your interviewer(s) may see the character differently. Look for sections which you could be asked to read from (more often, these will be early on). It can also be a good idea to invent some things about the character which aren't in the script, but could be a useful anchor to your emotional understanding of that character – his/her favourite colour as a child, for instance.

Do any background research that you can – even if you don't get the job, what you learn could well be beneficial in the future. Who played the part originally? This could give you another hefty clue. However, once again the director's interpretation could be different – and don't try to mimic how a well-known actor might have done it!

Rehearsal Don't just study and research the script: rehearse it with friends! There's a world of difference between reading to yourself and reading out loud. However, don't start forming fixed ideas – the director's may be different. Some people like to learn a script acquired in advance (especially a short commercial). Generally, I think that this is a mistake as most actors tend to over-concentrate on getting the lines right when they've only just learnt them – to the detriment of making everything real. You have to know whether pre-learning works for you.

Textual details

Whenever you get the script, it is important to take these on board.

Punctuation Commas, semi-colons and full stops all provide possible clues to shifts in thinking (often only slight). There is no definitive set of rules as to how spoken language should be punctuated on paper (virtually nobody observes the rules of written grammar closely as they speak). So think of punctuation marks (apart from the obvious question and exclamation marks) as possible pointers; not as specific orders to pause for a set amount of time.

Be wary of dots and dashes. I have not yet come across a writer who uses '. . .' or '–' consistently. It seems that both can mean either the speaker ending up in mid-air or being interrupted (by someone else, or if in the middle of a line by oneself). Be decisive about what you think each means and go for it.

Note: Some contemporary playwrights use little or no punctuation in their dialogue. The argument is that 'this is how some people speak'. However, there are still 'shifts in thinking'. Within the time available mark (lightly in pencil) where you think these are.

Stage directions Largely ignore stage directions unless they are crucial to the action ('She shoots him'). Some others might be useful, but be selective: concentrating your energies on 'moving upstage' (for instance) because a stage direction tells you to will demonstrate a singular lack of imagination on your part. Stage directions are not gospel, but possible pointers. Some of those (from a performed play) come from how it was done originally. (Those from a new play are how the playwright sees the action in his or her mind's eye.) Your reading (or production) will be different – maybe only subtly, but because you're different from the originating actor, inevitably it will not turn out in the same way. There is no one definitive way to play any part.

'Pause' and 'silence' Find these moments; don't feel you have to impose them – use them if they feel right there and then.

Italicised, **bold,** <u>underlined</u> *and* CAPITALISED *text* Do your damnedest to ignore these unsubtle instructions. You may end up stressing the particular word(s), but if you simply do so because that stress is signalled, you will find it harder to come to terms with the whole line.

Emotive stage directions These are very disruptive – especially for a first-time reader. It is impossible to react instantly with genuine 'happiness', 'despair', or whatever. The actual words you're fed and the words you say are much more important indicators towards how you say your lines. Again, 'find' these feelings; don't feel you have to impose them.

Pause-sounds and other vocalisations Try to find sounds like 'Er' and 'Um' naturally, and don't add more than there actually are in the text. A good writer will have found the right 'pause-sound' for each character and circumstance.

Scripted vocalisations like 'Arrrrgh', 'Gah' and 'Tch' are more difficult to vocalise. The most important thing is to focus on a motivation for such a sound – don't get bogged down in trying to vocalise it exactly as written.

Apparently unsayable words and names Again, an approximation will suffice. Don't find yourself tortuously trying to get them right to the detriment of the sense and your flow.

Abbreviated words It is the writer's job to abbreviate words appropriately for each character; it is the actor's job to respect the degree of abbreviation inherent in the script. Too many actors think that a sloppy speaking character can abbreviate even further – which can be to the detriment of communication. For instance, 'It is like . . .', 'It's like . . .', 'S'like . . .' and 'Like . . .' represent different degrees of sloppiness – it is important to adhere as accurately as you can to the writer's intentions. Aim to be neat and crisp, not all mumbly and 'Method'. Good acting is very precise and clear as well as containing a deep inner truth.

On the day

The script in the waiting room Sometimes complete scripts (or just a few scenes) will be left out in the waiting room. There may be even more information than you were given beforehand: a description of the play and a character breakdown, even a list of sections from which readings will be done. It is worth arriving especially early to take advantage of these possibilities.

If there is just a script then look for your character's first entrance for some kind of description and then for the first big scene or long speech; you will probably be reading either or both of these. (Take pen and paper to write down any character clues – it will help you remember them.) It is less likely you'll be asked to read from near the end as it is harder to assimilate the rest of the script's build-up. When you do light upon what seems to be an appropriate section, don't start forming fixed ideas; you don't know what extra brief (or alternative approach) you're going to be given.

If there's anything you feel is important to your understanding, but you can't glean it from the material you've been given, remember to ask when you get into the room.

Glasses If you need these to read, then don't forget them and ensure that they are easily accessible! I've a strong suspicion that a few actors deliberately forget these in order to avoid reading or excuse a poor reading. I'm afraid that even legitimate excuses will get you nowhere.

It is better to have glasses with light frames – thick ones tend to obscure the face too much and can put up a barrier between you and your interviewer(s).

Listening in It may happen that you can hear the previous person's reading and it's from the same character as yours. You can now feel fairly sure of what you are going to be asked to do and can learn from his or her mistakes and/or decide what you might do differently. Be careful, though; that person could be spot on in the director's eyes, and/or there may be another section to read from. Listen for clues, but don't rely on them. (See 'Waiting and listening in', page 158.)

In the room

'**What do you make of it?**' Some directors like to ask this question as part of the 'getting to know you' process. You may be one of those who can't answer in an intellectual way. Why should you? Acting is primarily about communicating, not discussing, a text. You are not sitting a literary exam. Give your head reaction if you have one and give your gut reaction without feeling pathetic about it. Then the interviewer may well start to open up and give you clues that you haven't so far been able to uncover. I'm not suggesting that such clues are necessarily being hidden from you; he or she has been living with this script for weeks, months or even years and ought to know it much better than you do. Things which are now as obvious as breathing to them are not so to you with only a short study period. Try to ask some well-judged questions – these could open the way to your being given insights from elsewhere in the script.

Guiding thoughts You will probably be given some of these, but in the short space of time available these are likely to be brief and superficial, and your interviewer could be fed up with repeating – yet again – the same information. (Also, it's very easy to miss out vital pieces of information when one is so familiar with it.) However, it can happen that you're given so much information that it's difficult to take it all in. If you find this beginning to happen, politely stop the flow and be selective about what you feel is most important for you (write notes, if possible). You mustn't find yourself drowning in information; you must feel sufficiently buoyant to lift the text off the page.

If you feel you're getting very little from the text through nerves or because it hasn't been explained well, open up a dialogue about it.

Note: Don't try to study the script while you're being briefed.

This is not an exam Don't ask endless questions about how to play this or that line or what the character is thinking at a particular point in the text. There isn't time for that kind of rehearsal discussion, and by concentrating on such detail you can lose your essential perspective on the whole piece.

The trauma part If discussing a 'trauma' part, don't indicate that you've recently been through a similar experience yourself. Even if you have, keep it to yourself, as many directors believe that recent direct experiences may kill a performance. However, it can be useful if there's something non-traumatic in your life that is (or could be) part of the character's life.

'I'm not right for this' You may feel this, but now is not the time to say it. Even if you are correct, you haven't yet shown off your skills and you don't know what they are casting next. If you do say it now, you'll be introducing a negative element that could easily cross you off that director's lists for a long time to come. If you feel you do need to say it, wait until afterwards and do it simply and positively with coherent reasons.

One of the problems when reading for a specific part for which you are obviously wrong – in that particular person's eyes – is the tendency for you to be dismissed entirely from future considerations. It's unfair but it happens; I've done it myself. I'm not sure what the solution is – it can be very hard to see beyond the part one is casting – but perhaps you should try to convey as much of yourself and your various qualities as possible so that I and my colleagues are not as blinkered as we might sometimes be.

Take your time! If your first sight of the dialogue is inside the interview room, then take reasonable time to study it calmly. It is natural to feel pressured and rushed in these circumstances, but stand your ground and take what time you can reasonably expect.

Don't just take in what your character is saying; also take in what the other characters are saying and doing. Don't feel pushed by that aching silence while you are studying: try to ignore scratching pens, heavy breathing and other distracting forms of human behaviour, and ask if there's something you don't understand. A friend suggested imagining that 'you've paid for the director's time – so exploit it'. Look through the text carefully and ask yourself questions as you would when rehearsing a part. Try to find keys to latch on to so that you can make something of what's there. Look for the central energy of the scene. Use aspects of your own life that fit the part – just as in a rehearsal. Make sure you've got some idea of the emotional as well as factual history that leads up to the section you are reading. Create in your imagination a location (possibly one you know) and immerse yourself in its ambience. Conjure up images of the other person/people involved, but don't rely on the person you are reading with having the same pictures in mind. Think about what your character could wear – different outfits make us move in different ways. In spite of the fact that you'll probably be sitting throughout, your whole body should still be involved – a pre-1920s woman would not cross her legs, for instance.

Or jumping straight in A minority find it easier to jump in blindly without considering it first and then, after discussion, read again. I see no harm in this; it is amazing what can happen by just diving in, antennae alert and instincts buzzing. Essentially, you need to know which method suits you best. In either case, don't let the circumstances make you rush the reading itself.

Respond! You'll get a lot more out of a reading if you look to 'respond' to what you're given. Too many actors seem to charge in with the next line immediately their cue comes – just because it's there. (The same happens – too much – in early rehearsals.) Don't do it! Imagine each line given to you, and your character's perception of its subtext, as a ball thrown (by the other reader) in your direction. Look to how you might catch it safely (that is, absorb the content – words and apparent subtext) and then respond (throw it back) with your scripted line combined with the subtext generated by the interaction. This will take a moment, but that silent moment – if you are properly connecting – can be very powerful. ('Good actors are good because of the things they can tell us without talking.' Cedric Hardwicke.) The overall reading will be slower than a performance, but you will be able to give much more substance to your part of it.

A character is gradually created through absorption, which is a slow process – a bit like eating a sumptuous meal. If you take your time and savour the food you'll feel much better than if you bolt it down quickly. Similarly, lines chewed over carefully will contribute far more to your evocation of the character. I believe that a writer's words and phrases should be treated like good food and savoured accordingly.

Note: Don't feel rushed if your reading partner is jumping in with his/her lines without going through this process.

Cliché performance Sometimes you will get what appears to be an obvious cliché character to read. There has to be more than just the superficial there (nobody is completely good or completely evil, for instance); look for the subtext – underneath, these stock characters have blood, hearts and feelings like everybody else. Even if the text is apparently superficial, you should aim to make it three-dimensional. It can be a good idea to look for the opposite to the obvious: for example, if the character is overtly strong, look for that inevitable Achilles heel of vulnerability. A good director will probably choose sections with a good variety of mood and emotion; look for those changes. Don't generalise because you haven't got enough time for study. Every script is a new journey.

A graphic example of this was Adolf Hitler. A (now dead) friend was translator to the British Ambassador to Germany in the 1930s. They would visit the German Chancellor every week – to them he was 'utterly charming'.

An accent If you are asked to read in an accent, don't make getting that right the dominating factor. (You should be told about it beforehand.) Get as close as you can, but don't worry about it. Good dialogue, written in an accent, will have the rhythm of that accent embedded in the lines – find that rhythm and you are halfway there with very little effort. If the director likes your reading, but the accent wasn't quite right, he or she should concentrate on that separately and may ask you to come back another time when you've had a chance to work on it. If you know an accent is required beforehand, then you must do some preparation. If you know that you really can't do that accent, consider carefully whether you should go at all.

In fact you really should know clearly what you can and can't do in terms of accents: too many people are too optimistic about their range. Of course new accents can be learnt, but each one takes time – and once you know it, can you act in it? I have worked with several actors who could demonstrate facility with an accent not their own, but couldn't give flesh and blood to it in performance. (Learning an accent is like learning to drive – it's one thing to learn the techniques, but it takes a lot of practical application to do it convincingly.)

Relax You need to feel as free and open as possible within the confines of your chair and script. Hold the script with one hand, away from your body and slightly to one side. It is important to be open to your reading partner – just like in a good rehearsal. If you find it useful, use a finger (or thumb) as a marker to follow the dialogue as you progress.

Don't hold the script right up in front of your face or slump over it as you cower in your chair. It's very off-putting not to be able to see your eyes at all. If you can't be seen properly, it is much more difficult to listen to you. As a general rule: script down, eyes up.

Scan ahead Scan ahead as you are reading. Try to have half an eye on the phrase or sentence following the one you are actually saying.

You don't have to be word perfect If you stumble over words, don't over-apologise and worry. Don't go back unless you really have made a mess of the sense. Just don't lose the essence of it.

Do go back over part of a reading if you realise that you have made a real mess of it. Don't ask permission: just do it – but not too often.

Silences are golden If you are properly connecting, the fractional moment(s) in which you are formulating your response(s) will be just as exciting as times when you are vocalising. Don't feel that you need to fill them with heavy breathing, 'er' sounds, and so forth. This also applies to a long speech – it is essential to try to find an impulse for each new thought without such extraneous vocalisations that are not in the script.

Also remember to stay in character when you're not speaking – with only that half an eye on your cue and next line. Your thought processes are just as important as your actual speaking.

Take risks A reading is another artificial situation. Try treating it like an improvisation. Take risks! Experiment as you would in a rehearsal. Feel free! Of course you will have to rely on past experiences, but aim to find that magic synthesis between what you know and what is suddenly a new experience.

Commitment Commit yourself to decisions that you take – even if you feel that they were wrong a fraction of a second later. Also, go with any new stimulus that suddenly appears – it doesn't matter if it later turns out to be wrong if you are committed to it in the moment. Don't let your intellect inhibit your gut reactions too much, and don't find yourself falling into the void between the two.

Doing a reading the right way is impossible. You have to use what you know and not worry about what you can't be expected to know yet. There is no definitive way of playing any part, no definitive interpretation. You have to listen, think and bring you, your skills, imagination, instinct and energy into what you are doing.

Eye contact Don't try to make eye contact with your reading partner at every possible moment. (See 'Eye contact', page 170.) A lot of people try to do this – perhaps in an attempt to connect better. It really isn't necessary and can appear intimidating. It is just as important that you use what space you have to look ahead.

However, don't avoid eye contact altogether as other people do. I know you are concentrating on unfamiliar words on the page, but there will be spare moments when you will be free to take in your reading partner as you would in rehearsal.

Your reading partner The people you read with may well not be very good at it. They will probably mistime things, put on silly voices, almost certainly won't interrupt on cue, certainly won't slap or kiss, and may even read some of your lines by mistake. Also they will probably read some lines with what seems like crass disregard for the sense. Occasionally I've known directors to read deliberately badly to test people; I don't see the point of that. More often than not, your interviewer's apparent lack of ability is because he or she is (a) not a good actor and (b) concentrating on watching and listening closely to assess you. You have to aim to do everything for yourself – all the interruptions, slaps, kisses, and so forth. I don't mean literally. Do them in your imagination, which is secure in your imaginary space. However, don't let this imaginary world cut you off from your reading partner; use it as a springboard from which you can fly and balance your acting with the acting you are given.

By contrast, some reading partners seem to fancy themselves as actors. I've even heard of some choosing pieces of dialogue which had far more for them to read than for the actor. You can exploit this absurdity by concentrating harder on working with them – however badly you may think they are performing. Acting with someone whose work you did not respect must have happened to you before; use the devices you employed then.

Reading with another actor Some directors like to do this in an attempt to find the best chemistry. It can also occur when you're up for a take-over in an established production – in this context you could well be reading with an understudy. Aim to work with your fellow actor – don't think of it as a competition.

Moves as well! Occasionally you'll be asked to 'move' a reading. Some actors like to move during readings; this is fine, but unnecessary. Moves come from a deeper understanding of the text that only comes with rehearsal time. To include them in a reading may take away from what you are able to do with it at this early stage. This is not true for everybody; some find that walking around enhances their immersion in the text. Know what's best for you and use your own instincts. It is not laziness just to sit while you read – providing that your face and the rest of your body is involved in what you're doing.

Under-reading I find that younger actors are often better at readings than the more experienced. I suspect that some of the more experienced among you can see far more of the possibilities to be gleaned from the text and try too hard to cram in as much as possible, ending up with a kind of blur. Others, I know, instinctively feel that they don't want to commit themselves yet, just like in early rehearsals. I am very sympathetic to this in principle, but in practice it doesn't help anyone decide whether you'd be right for that part in that production. Of course the interview should help, but there has to be at least a little bit more than that. You may have a 'track record', but if directors have never seen you in something similar, how are they to judge whether you'd be right for them and their way of working?

I sometimes get the feeling that some experienced actors are thinking: 'Well, you should realise what I'm doing.' Not true! Once again, most directors don't finally understand how acting works, and all actors have different ways of doing it. It is highly personal to each individual. You should regard directors as members of the general public who don't properly understand the need for sufficient rehearsal – so give them something. If it feels clumsy, that doesn't matter. That is where the director is not a member of the general public and knows that you will refine it. A child's first attempt at walking is inevitably clumsy but you know that with practice – and a few accidents – it'll come to fruition in time. If in doubt, do more rather than less; they can always pull you back.

Sight-readings for musical theatre All the same parameters hold that apply to reading for a straight play, but in reading for a musical bear in mind that the writing will probably be very thin and you almost always have to generate your own subtext. Don't just launch into some stock characterisation. Think about it.

Very often, the climax of a scene will be a song, so you will have to end in mid-air. Don't 'cop out' that fraction of a second before. Make your interviewers believe you are going to launch into the song there and then. Remember that in musicals the three skills of acting, singing and dancing are not separate; they interweave, and you should show that you can make the transition into a song with consummate ease.

A second try You may well be asked to read a second time. This doesn't necessarily mean the first reading was bad; rather, that the director wants to assess your flexibility as an actor or try out a different way of interpreting the script. If given direction, don't throw out everything you've done in the first reading by exclusively concentrating on the notes you've been given. Those notes may well have come from what you did in the first place.

No reading at all Assessing readings is another highly inexact science. Some may not ask you to read at all, fearing the 'good reading – bad performance' phenomenon (and vice versa). That is about as true as 'a bad dress rehearsal means a good first night'. (And vice versa.)

Providing all other factors are taken into account, I do believe it can help to assess an actor's suitability by including a reading. Everything helps. Each piece of the assessment has to be put in perspective with the others to form the whole opinion.

Finally If you write later to a director for whom you felt you did a bad reading (or speech), don't mention that poor performance. Too many people use such self-deprecating comments in order to highlight the memory of the previous meeting. This tack will only lessen your chances of being seen again. In all probability he or she won't remember the specific reading, so you just need to mention that you've met – and perhaps add something good that happened on that occasion.

Additional considerations for television, commercials and films

The fundamental difference between these and the theatre (and radio) is their far greater emphasis on the visuals – which are two-dimensional. The stress is often on making everything appear as realistic as possible. There are occasional courageous experiments that use non-naturalistic settings, but these are, regrettably, few and far between – so how you appear can play a large part in your chances. You have to be able not only to fit inside the appropriate screen but also to project from it. For the interview you must be aware of the production's specific requirements as many directors don't seem to be able to visualise very far beyond what they see in front of them. They tend not to understand that it's an actor's job to become someone completely different. (I think it's useful to remember that film is only a century old and television is even younger – both still have an awful lot to learn.) This is not to imply that they are unpleasant in interview – in fact the opposite seems to be generally the case – simply that many lack a basic understanding of acting. There are some notable exceptions, but they are generally those who started out in theatre.

Television interviews

Essentially you should follow what you need from the guidelines outlined earlier in this chapter. The crucial differences from a theatre (or radio) interview are the following.

A script Sometimes you will go to a television interview equipped with only the briefest of character descriptions because it's original material – and the script is yet to be completed. For others (for a soap, established series or sitcom, or an adaptation of a book or play), it is essential that you have a working knowledge of the existing material, but be prepared for a featured character in an adapted book or play to be reduced to two lines in the television script.

It is worth arriving reasonably early because there might be a script available for you to look through.

Your presentation How you present yourself – both visually and verbally – is crucial. Of course there are limits as to how far you can adapt yourself to suit each occasion, and you wouldn't be there if you didn't already appear to be similar to what they are looking for, but you will get less of the benefit of the doubt than you would in a theatre (or radio) interview.

However, the director may not be able to find the physiognomy that is in his or her head; you could be a compromise or might even fit another part. Your own personality may do the trick. A friend, with a naturally outgoing and bubbly personality, went for a small part of similar temperament in a major series. He dressed casually, the interview was funny and fine, and my friend left feeling reasonably optimistic. On the off-chance he sent a copy of his showreel to the director. This contained a range of performances from the classical-serious to the outrageously silly. A few days later he was offered a much better and more serious part. Eventually he discovered that the showreel had swung the better part his way. Pleased but curious, he gently asked the director: 'Why didn't you discuss the "serious" part at the interview?' 'I hadn't really got time,' came the limp reply. My friend was lucky that the director happened to have a few minutes to look at the showreel.

There is a distinction between 'dressing appropriately' for the part and 'dressing as' the part. Television directors, however much many of them lack the understanding of an actor's ability to play a whole range of parts, will be very annoyed if you do the latter because it will seem that you have no respect for their powers of judgement.

More than one interviewer There will probably be more than one interviewer. A director, producer and casting director (and, possibly, the writer) is quite a common line-up.

Not every interview is held in a private room – there could be a lot else going on in the background.

Level The tone of the interview will almost always be pleasant but low-key, probably because television requires low-key, intimate acting, but be careful that you don't get so low-key that you start to disappear. Television acting is larger than life in spite of being on a small screen. It needs to be contained, but not bottled up. It is smaller in scale than stage acting, more compact and economical physically – especially facially and obviously vocally – but you should still aim to shine through the small screen. (*Note:* In your containment, be careful that you don't drop too many consonants – an all-too frequent failing.)

The structure of the interview You may be asked something about yourself or the interviewer may simply rely on your CV and plough straight into telling you what the script is about – which can take time. Compose yourself and try to sit reasonably still without concentrating so hard on doing it you cannot listen and receive properly. (See 'Listening and receiving', page 164.) Then you might be asked to read, and that could well be that. What about the whole 'getting to know you' process? It often won't appear to happen – another consequence of that lack of understanding of acting.

A reading? The crucial thing to remember is that you may not even be asked to read, so your interview performance will be a large part of the judgement made on you. If you are asked to read, follow what's right for you earlier in this chapter but bear in mind that you should aim as far as possible for a performance and bear in mind the scale necessary. You need to demonstrate that you can be physically and vocally contained but still perform.

Commercial castings

Although mostly intended for television, the casting process for these is different from that described above. They're usually called 'castings' and are often akin to the cattle-market musical theatre audition in apparent insensitivity towards the craft of acting. In fact they're probably more like a sheep dip where each person is processed to see if they fit the interviewers' requirements, with no interest in acting ability.

If it seems as though your face might fit you could well have to go through hundreds of castings before getting a commercial. As time goes on and you get some 'pencils' (i.e. you come in for definite consideration but don't actually get it), casting directors will know better when to call you in and your strike rate could become higher – but not necessarily. However experienced you are, you will still have to go through this 'sheep dip' in order to get each one.

Most commercials shown on UK television are extremely clever and well made. They should be. Teams of creative people spend hours/weeks/months dreaming up ideas and developing the scenario, layout and visual ideas to be presented to the client company. When the script has been approved and finalised a production company will be given the job of filming it and they will look for actors to fill the very specific scenario.

Presentation 'If an advert was casting for Roy Rogers, then the person who came in fully dressed as a cowboy would stand much more chance of getting the job.' No, this remark is not from a cynical embittered actor, but from a realist who gets commercials periodically. There is a sense in which they are not looking for an actor to fill the role but hoping that the real person, as defined on paper, will walk in through the door. So make every effort to look right for the part. Don't go over the top – the 'Roy Rogers' analogy above is an exaggeration. Be subtle about it.

You should be told what the part is beforehand, but beware: details can get altered in the Chinese whisper chain of communication between director, casting director, your agent and you. A friend, who has a good strike rate, was told she was to appear as a dowdy character. She did so. The basics were gone through, and it emerged that the opposite was required. She explained that she'd been misinformed, but the director still asked: 'Have you got any other clothes?' That is a classic example of some directors' level of imagination as far as actors are concerned.

Note: Commercial castings are often carried out at short notice, so you need a good choice of outfits always readily available.

Arrive early It is definitely worth arriving early. At least you'll get a chance to look at the script (although you may be sent this beforehand), learn it reasonably well – taking in the stage directions – and begin to get ideas on how to tackle the reading. There won't be time for study once you are in there. That script will probably be no longer than two pages and could be entirely stage directions – occasionally with only one line that involves you.

The committee The room will usually be dark with a brightly lit acting area. There will usually be a 'committee' of people in there, most sitting in semi-darkness. The session might be run by the casting director (sometimes the director won't even be there) and there will probably be several other people sitting in the background, often from the client company. The latter won't speak, but don't ignore them. You probably won't be introduced to them, they will know virtually nothing about actors and acting, and they will appear catatonic. If you can make them laugh easily in what follows, it can enhance your chances.

Passport control You may well have to fill in a form (or forms) asking basic details like height, age and agent. They may well take a photograph of you 'just for the records'. Then you may be led to a chair and plonked in front of a camera.

Ident. You may be asked to 'Ident. for camera.' (Sometimes, simply 'ID'.) They want you to give your basic details (usually name and agent) to mark the beginning of your section of the recording. You may then go straight on to performing the reading.

The interview As someone put it to me, 'You go in there as though you had no CV at all.' What matters is how closely you fit the scenario. You might be asked a few questions about yourself. The interviewer might look at you, but often will be looking into the monitor connected to the camera to see how you are coming across on it. He or she is almost certainly not thinking: 'How well could we work together?'

You have to try to find out what they want and conform to it. Their imaginations are tied by what's on their pieces of paper. You should aim to be individual but don't go over the top. Be aware that you are probably being videoed from the moment you are plonked into that chair and possibly from when you walk through the door. Be happy about all this and be warm to this apparent wall of indifference.

Note: You may well be asked if you've done any other recent commercials in the same country (many foreign commercials are made in the UK) or area. The client might not be happy with the same person endorsing another product to the same audience – especially if it's a competitor.

The reading What you have to do will probably be over-explained to you. Take what you need and ignore the rest, and hold on to what you've worked out unless a new, unscripted factor is introduced.

Your main objective is to present the committee with a performance:

1) As far as is possible, avoid looking at the script – they'll want to see your eyes. It is useless to be constantly looking down at the page while on camera. You have to be a quick study.
2) You will be expected to perform there and then, conforming to all the stage directions and mime props when necessary. Be neat and clear with the mime; never do it tokenly as you might when in the early stages of rehearsing a play.
3) Sometimes you will be asked to do an accent. Make sure that you can do what you say you can do off the top of your head. It is a good idea to have key phrases for each accent that contain enough of the pertinent idiosyncratic sounds, inflection and rhythm to set you off on the right foot.

4) There may be another actor reading with you, or the casting director will fill in and you may have to react to badly given feedlines.
5) You might be asked to do it again with a simple note in mind – 'slower', 'faster', 'bigger', 'smaller' . . . Go with what you're asked to do; this is not the moment for discussion, whatever you feel about that note. Have an open mind about what they want.
6) Occasionally you might be told to 'Forget the script as it's being rewritten', and 'Just improvise'.

This is instant acting and it's very silly, but you shouldn't feel silly. In fact you should take it very seriously. Use all your instinct and experience and do whatever comes off the top of your head without resorting to caricature unless that is specifically required.

Your whole body It's not just how you bring the words off the page that's important – you should be aware of what each and every bit of your body is doing and incorporate it into your performance. That's what you have to do: perform with no rehearsal and no real direction. You may be given specific directions about how, when and where to move – all at precisely defined moments and to precisely defined positions. Don't let your performance be reduced to just a set of mechanics – there has to be a real person carrying out these otherwise robotic motions.

It is important that your hands are in good condition. They may be used in close-up, and they might be photographed.

Stanislavski In performing, don't dismiss the reality of character but do aim to concertina real reactions – a kind of subtle mugging.

Sometimes you'll feel that you're being asked to exaggerate badly, even be blatantly 'off the wall' – you should still bring that inner core of truth to your performance.

The camera Through all this you should make the technology your friend. Unlike most television drama you may have to look directly into the lens. As with a static photograph, it will show graphically if you are camera-shy or nervous. Treat the camera as another actor who could respond to anything you present to it. This simple device of the imagination can easily overcome any camera inhibitions you may have. You may be reading with someone else or concentrating on a prop and not talking directly to the camera. In this circumstance the camera is the fourth wall of a theatre, and you have to ensure that everything necessary can be seen by 'cheating out' in that direction and that you are 'thinking' everything out to the audience.

Finally Somebody once described commercial castings to me as 'in – grin – out'. Think fast and concentrate on the camera. It will probably all be over in a few minutes. A friend once described acting as 'committed pretending' – I think that's a very good concept to carry into a commercial casting.

Films

Most of the parameters that apply to television and commercials interviews apply to those for a film. The extra elements are that there may well be an American involved – and they find it peculiar that we don't hustle like our transatlantic counterparts, and that the film could be for both the big screen and the small one. As in television, you will find some directors who do know how to conduct an interview and have an understanding of actors' methodologies, and those who patently don't. Interviews for this medium seem to range over the whole spectrum.

If you are lucky enough to get an interview and reading for a film, remember that the acting required is on the most intimate scale because your image will be blown up on to a giant screen where the merest flick of an eyelid in close-up can create waves round an auditorium.

Processes It is becoming more and more common for film interviews and readings to be conducted via video – either via a direct link or for later viewing. It is also not unusual for there to be no reading at all. Here are some illustrative examples:

The meat market The late, great Alfred Hitchcock walked along a line of nervous actresses. He inspected each one closely, then grunted something at an assistant and walked off. The assistant did at least say, 'Thank you' before they were ushered off the set.

Be prepared for anything These film interviews were conducted by a famous actor/director/writer.

An actor was led in by a PA. The star was crouching down and holding the radiator and never looked at him. The actor was supposed to be reading; the accent was South African, which, in the circumstances, just would not come out right. So he stopped and started again and then finally gave up and said, 'I'm terribly sorry,' and the PA said, 'Well, we are so pleased to have met you and we'll let you know,' and escorted him out.

Another actor was ushered in to find the star sitting at the desk. Halfway through the interview – without saying anything about it – he quietly tore up the actor's photograph.

Yet another actor found him sitting cross-legged below the desk and he spent the whole interview making additions to the actor's photograph with a felt-tipped pen.

Falling off a log One friend fell on his feet at his first film interview straight out of drama school.

The very first audition I ever went to was for a film called *North Sea Hijack* and it was being held by Alan Foenander at the Park Lane Hotel. I walked in to find a couple of well-known actors laughing easily over coffee and tales of agents. Alan comes out and tells me that, instead of the civil servant I was up for, would I like to read for Roger Moore's right-hand man, Harris, an all-action scuba-diving killer in command of Rog's private army? I said I'd think about it. Well, at least I didn't let the drool show.

I walked in; the director's Andrew V. McLaglen – more used to working with the 'Duke' and with a disturbing tendency to stand on your toes in order apparently simply to see what you'll do. I'm six foot three; he was more like six foot six. I say: 'God you're even bigger than I am!'

There is a pause.

Then he says: 'I like it. Siddown, kid.'

I knew I'd hit Hollywood.

'OK, kid, I want you to read this scene for me. The guy's name is Harris.'

He said it as though he'd given me a great insight into this man's character.

'Do you want an accent?' I ventured.

'No accent.'

I have come to learn that this usually means do it with the accent of the person who asks you, but at that tender age, and with the words of my eccentric Austrian drama tutor – 'Don't be afraid to fall on your arse!' – ringing in my ears, I essayed a cross between Sean Connery and Vincent Price.

'Can you do Scotch?' he asked.

'Scottish accent, yes, OK, fine.' (Billy Connolly meets Miss Jean Brodie.)

'Tell me something, kid. Can you swim?'

'Er . . . actually, yes, I swim very well. I was captain of swimming at school. I beat the school record for the –'

'Kid, I think you just landed yourself a part.'

And so I did. I went on to have a glorious two weeks in Galway, got paid a fortune, and had a 'Ripping Yarns' type time.

Screen tests Somehow these are the stuff of legend and often aren't part of the casting process. After a series of interviews you may be asked to do one – on video and/or film. Like commercial castings you have to be prepared to do instant acting with the script in your hand (which you should look at as little as possible). Usually it will be with another actor (also 'testing' or someone hired for the occasion), but I've heard of actors just having to do their own lines from a piece of dialogue, leaving gaps for responses.

The other thing to remember is that films are largely action-based. (The actual scripted words are often less important – much to the understandable frustration of writers.) In a screen test you could easily be acting out something akin to the fantasy action games you last played at primary school with chairs representing cars and so on.

Digital acting opportunities

These include web-based soaps, virals (web content that is aimed at triggering an online following which builds its own momentum as it spreads – a commercial of sorts), motion capture (translating human movement on to a digital model or animation), and so on. These have been expanding rapidly in the new millennium – and will increase further. The interview and audition processes in these new areas are much as described above – tending more towards the style of those for commercials and films.

8: *Low-pay/no-pay 'work'*

This is commonly foreshortened to 'Lo/No Pay' and can offer opportunities to (a) keep your acting juices flowing, (b) add to your CV and (c) get seen by casting directors and agents who you don't yet know. There are two main areas: Fringe Theatre and Low Budget Films – the latter are often made by students on film/media courses. While both areas may seem to satisfy these objectives, they should be considered with caution as they could easily cost you money, frustrate you and add nothing to your career progression.

This kind of 'work' is usually advertised on websites like Casting Call Pro <www.uk.castingcallpro.com> and Shooting People <www.shootingpeople.org> – see *Actors' Yearbook* for a full list of such sites.

The National Minimum Wage Act (NMW) of 1998 requires that all work (apart from voluntary work for registered charities) be paid at an annually updated minimum rate per hour. In theory, all the 'work' discussed in this chapter should be paid at (or above) this rate. In practice, most of it isn't. There is much passionate debate about how the NMW can be applied in this area. For further insights see <www.actorsminimumwage.wordpress.com>. Also, Equity has advice, guidelines and suggested contracts for use in these areas.

Fringe theatre

The Fringe has grown considerably since the nineties and for many graduates it is their first taste of so-called professional work. However, it is not just the preserve of the newcomer. Many experienced actors are willing to commit time and money to get themselves seen by casting directors and agents. There are also writers and directors anxious to get their work noticed, and there are those who do it simply because they believe in it. From your point of view it is important to assess whether despite the personal costs involved it could have real value for you – personally and professionally.

What is it? In broad terms the Fringe is smaller-scale theatre that operates on the fringes of legitimate activity. Essentially, the idea began at the Edinburgh Festival more than half a century ago. It really started taking off (especially in London) in the late 1960s as an arena for alternative and experimental theatre. The 1990s saw a huge expansion in the number of venues being used and a downturn in the exploration of theatre forms – it became more commercial, much more competitive and not just in London and Edinburgh. (Many venues are listed in *Actors' Yearbook*, which also contains more detailed advice on this area.)

The really confusing thing is that there are several theatres, often regarded as part of the London Fringe, who offer Equity contracts – The Almeida and The Tricycle, for instance. There are also those who are non-Equity, but have huge reputations – such as The Battersea Arts Centre (BAC) and The Finborough. And there are several very reputable companies working on the Fringe who don't pay Equity rates.

What does it pay? The simple answer to this is that, apart from a few productions, you will effectively pay to perform rather than get paid. You should think of participating in a Fringe production as a possible investment in your future. Some companies will pay travelling expenses; others will offer you a share of the profits – a 'profit-share' production. You'll almost certainly be worse off with the latter deal as virtually none of them makes a profit. (A friend once earned just £10, for eight weeks' work, as his share of the profits on a prize-winning production.) The only reasons for being in a Fringe production are that (a) you might be spotted, (b) you fundamentally believe in the production's potential and (c) it could help keep your acting juices flowing.

Will I get seen? Agents and casting directors do scout for new talent on the Fringe. However, many are resistant to travelling too far outside central London unless the venue happens to be close to their homes. The other problem is that there are probably over a hundred Fringe productions on at any one time – plus many more legitimate ones. (The Edinburgh Festival has over 2,500 productions packed into a few weeks.) The agent or casting director has got to be given very good reasons to come and see yours – especially as the quality of Fringe productions is highly variable.

Might it transfer? In the past, unpaid Fringe productions have been known to transfer into paid venues – even into the West End. In recent years, this has become a rarer phenomenon.

Is it regarded as professional work? In general terms it is. However, many experienced directors, agents and casting directors will regard a CV with too much of it with some suspicion. How do they know what's Fringe and what's legitimate? Some very simple maths (combined with a basic understanding of theatre economics) will quickly provide an answer. Almost all venues have less than a hundred seats and can't charge that much – and even a sell-out run will often only cover the physical costs of mounting a production. Even if you don't include the venue, the name of an obscure director will provide another hefty clue. And experienced directors, agents and casting directors know who is who . . .

Also, there is a tendency in Fringe productions for professional standards (and facilities) to be somewhat lacking – and that is sometimes an understatement. Poor technical backup, indifferent front-of-house arrangements and general unreliability are too often the case, almost inevitably damaging the quality of the final product.

Problems to watch out for

The ego trip A number of productions are set up by individuals wanting a starring vehicle for themselves – much like the old actor-managers. It is generally better to avoid such enterprises unless you can be fairly sure that the central ego will not be damaging to your contribution. Ask around for objective advice before accepting a part in such a production.

What else will you have to do? Will you have to do other things – like paint the set, distribute posters, help with the get-in, and so on? You may think that you can make time to do things like this, but are you sure you want to be thus distracted in the last few days before opening night?

Is the script good enough? There really is no point in doing a production that's flawed before it leaves the page.

Can you work well with the director? This is a highly subjective judgement, but since you are not being properly paid, it is important that you feel as sure as you can that it'll be a worthwhile experience.

Can you actually afford to do it? There is no point in taking time out from paid work in order to rehearse and perform a Fringe production unless you really think that you'll get something out of the experience. (It can be worth asking if your rehearsal-calls can be arranged round your work commitments.) Also, check whether your participation will affect your benefits in any way.

Your agent If you have one, will he or she be happy for you to do the production?

Contracts While there is no accepted (by managements) Equity contract for this kind of work (except for a special agreement with The Gate (in Notting Hill Gate, London) and at the time of writing a few others in the pipeline), the Union does have a free set of guidelines which are very useful – and a suggested contract. Some companies issue their own contracts – it is important to read these carefully and check with Equity if you have any doubts.

Will the production get reviews? A good review equals good publicity – important for any production. Some productions in the most prestigious venues get reviewed in national newspapers. However, because there are so many productions at any one time, the press has strict rules (length of run, for instance) about what they will send reviewers to. It is important to note that the perceptiveness of some of the latter is somewhat shallow – that's not sour grapes, it's a fact.

Will the publicity and marketing be sufficient? After the cost of hiring the venue, publicity and marketing represent the next major cost of a Fringe production – and too many productions try to skimp on these. In such a competitive environment these are very, very important.

Does the venue have a good reputation? It is much, much harder to get people into less prestigious ones.

Promises While enthusiasm for a project is wonderful, beware of promises when they seem over the top. Too much optimism can blind people to important practical realities.

If I'm not being paid, can't I just pull out if something better comes along? Legally, you can (unless you've signed a contract – and very few offer these); morally and professionally it's an extremely dubious thing to do without the full understanding of your fellow participants – and you never know who, among them, might gain casting clout in the future.

Is it going to be properly organised? There is far more to putting on a production than most actors realise. Ask questions based on the above and if you don't feel sufficiently satisfied, politely back away – there's no point in being miserable, as well as unpaid, for several weeks.

Setting up your own production

Too many people think that mounting a production is just a matter of getting a few friends together, borrowing some props and costumes, and getting on with it. What about the costs of hiring a venue, a rehearsal space, the publicity and marketing, the author's royalties (if still in copyright), and so on? You may be lucky enough to get some – even all – of these for free, or you might find a rich auntie. However you fund the above essentials, you have got to do a lot of careful planning before rehearsals start. Will the playwright (and/ or translator) allow you to do a production of the play in the first place? Just because a play is in print, it doesn't mean that anyone can perform it. Is the rehearsal room available enough of the time? What is the deadline for getting the poster design to the printers, so that they can get the result back to you in time for the distributors to get them displayed in good time before opening night? And so on, and so on, and so on . . . It is essential to plan and budget with contingency in both time and money – there are always several things that take more time than you'd thought and several things that cost more than you'd thought, or forgotten to budget for in the first place.

Doing it yourself is far more complex than most people realise, but can be incredibly satisfying if you succeed. For a technically simple production you probably need to find at least £5,000 – and that's without paying any of the participants. The chances of recouping this through the box office are very low; the average audience on the Fringe is about 30 per cent. A recent report stated that 'theatres are among the most over-regulated businesses in the UK' – legal requirements like Health and Safety, VAT and performance rights cannot be neglected.

Setting up your own company

If you are dreaming of doing more, there is an incredibly helpful organisation which can guide you – for very reasonable fees. It is the Independent Theatre Council (ITC) <www.itc-arts.org> which runs a comprehensive list of courses covering fund-raising, contracts, marketing and everything else associated with this complex business. You should also get advice from others who've done it before – particularly with regard to publicity and funding applications. (Your local Regional Arts Council, listed in *Actors' Yearbook*, can supply lists of sources of funding.) There is a language called 'application-speak' which you will need help to decipher, and translate your responses back into.

I believe that the most important aspect of setting up your own company is being very clear about and committed to why you are doing it – simply wanting to act is not enough.

The Edinburgh Festival Fringe

There is a real sense that every actor should try this 'Carnival of theatre' experience at least once. (A friend called it 'the biggest theatrical lottery in the world'.) You'll meet lots of new people, make contacts, and it's a great three weeks even if your own production doesn't hit the heights. Even if it does, you probably won't make much money – in spite of all your time and effort.

Advice on mounting a production on the Edinburgh Fringe is available via their website <www.edfringe.com>.

Showcases

The drama schools have been doing these for years, and recently several organisations have been set up to provide the same for non-students. For a fee you get to perform audition speech(es) and/or scene(s) to an audience largely made up of casting directors. (I know of one company that will record your performance on video for distribution.) Some casting directors and agents like these because viewing them takes up less time than a full production. There are others who firmly believe that they need to see more than just two minutes' worth. Once again you should check out any such organisation thoroughly before committing your money.

Note: Sometimes participants are selected by audition to ensure quality control – essentially the company is working like an agent but charging an up-front fee rather than commission.

Low budget films

High quality cameras and editing equipment are now readily accessible in this digital age. However, quality technology is only part of making a good film. That said, some of these films are very good, and who knows where that director will go in the future. At the same time, many are of lesser quality . . . They are far less time-consuming than Fringe theatre and you might get a valuable contribution to your showreel – in spite of earning very little (sometimes losing) money. Many are made by students on film/media courses (at universities or specialist film schools), but not all. Others are made by those trying to get funding for future projects and/or attention at the numerous film festivals around the world – including Cannes. A few have also ended up on television.

Equity does have an agreement with the National Film & Television School (NFTS) <www.nftsfilm-tv.ac.uk> which ensures a small payment and expenses, but (at the time of writing) there are no others using it, although some do pay expenses and very small fees. The Union has also compiled a suggested contract and some very useful advice in a booklet entitled 'Working in Student Films – A Guide'.

Many of the 'Problems to look out for' with fringe theatre productions also apply to low budget films. Quality of script is possibly the most important thing to look out for. Others include:

- Assurances that the film will be submitted for festival screening does not mean that it will be accepted.
- It's worth checking the director's track record. (Is any of their work online?) It has been suggested (apropos student films) that it's only worth committing to those made by students about to graduate as they are the most concerned to get it right. It's also been suggested to me that it is wise to be wary of students doing media studies degrees – as their training and equipment are likely to be limited. It's usually better only to consider films made by students of the specialist film schools. There are details of these in *Actors' Yearbook*.
- Will you get a good quality copy (in a usable format) and will there be a section useful for your showreel?

- Will you be allowed to use an extract on your showreel? And have all copyright permissions been cleared?
- Will it get screened – and will you get a copy beforehand? There's a tendency among such film-makers to lose interest and focus on their next projects after screenings.
- Will it have a sufficient crew and quality equipment – or will it just be the director and a camcorder?
- Will the sound be good enough – a common failing on such films?
- Will travel expenses be paid (or transport provided) – especially to far-flung locations?
- Will start and finish times enable you to use public transport? If not, will transport be provided?
- Will meals be provided?
- Will the working hours be reasonable? Films have a tendency to take a long time to shoot for very little screen time. And will the film-maker guarantee the working days and times in advance? Yes, some over-running is almost inevitable, but they should have planned contingency times to cover this. Just because you're not being paid much (if anything), it doesn't mean that they shouldn't follow professional practice regarding working times.
- Will you be sufficiently credited?
- Will you be expected to supply your own costumes?
- Are there any hazardous circumstances? For example, if you are required to participate in a fight will it be properly supervised?
- Is there Employers' Liability Insurance in place?
- Will you receive an acceptable contract (with contact details) specifying working hours, guaranteeing copy of the result, fee and expenses, etc? If in doubt, check with Equity!
- Will it enhance your CV?

Summary

I have seen many high hopes dashed – sometimes accompanied by considerable financial debt. I've also seen a few significant successes, achieved through considerable persistence, enthusiasm, and careful thought and planning. If you follow the guidelines above, and do your research properly, you too can reap long-term rewards from low-pay/no-pay work – in spite of short-term damage to your bank account.

9: *Other forms of acting income*

Most actors have long had to resort to other kinds of (apparently) unrelated work to bolster their incomes. Bar work, waiting at tables, cleaning, office temping, taxi driving, labouring, painting and decorating, telesales and promotions work are just a few examples. I've also met those who doubled up as teachers, doctors, vicars and solicitors – even a tree surgeon. Some of these jobs obviously require other training, but many use that skill fundamental to acting: communication with those you don't already know using someone else's words. There are a number of websites geared to actors listed in *Actors' Yearbook* which have plenty of temporary jobs using acting skills, and some are advertised in *The Stage*. There are also growing fields of work which utilise acting skills more directly, but not quite in the way you were trained to use them. They could be summarised as helping professionals (in business, social and emergency services) with acting skills to facilitate their work. Because this is a very complex and fast-growing area, it is only possible to give a rough sketch of these areas of work and access to them. There are no generally agreed rates of pay, no trade associations and hardly any standard contracts, just a new and exciting relationship between two very different cultures.

Role-playing

Probably the most lucrative form of temp work (unless you have other professional training) is known as Role Play – that is, using acting and theatre skills to help other professions.

This is the art of taking on a character – without a script, just a detailed brief – and then being that character in a prescribed situation. Medical students, for instance, have long done practice consultations on each other before encountering real patients. However, they (and the many other professions that use this technique as part of training) generally haven't the skill to be fully convincing in what is essentially an unreal situation – especially in extreme circumstances, like being a rape victim, for instance. The actor can bring that indispensable reality, and control it as necessary, or as prescribed by the requirements of the training objectives. Not only that, but actors know the art of accurate repetition.

The world of drama-based training has expanded rapidly in recent years and you will find terms such as 'Forum Workshop', 'Forum Theatre', 'Team Building', and so on being bandied around – essentially, these are all extensions of role-play techniques. You can get more information from the websites of individual companies, some of whom are listed in *Actors' Yearbook*. One such promotes itself with the slogan 'Life can have a rehearsal'. Another says, 'The key is "experiential" learning, which reaches the emotions as well as the intellect.'

Actors are also being used to role-play characters at social occasions such as historical banquets and murder-mystery weekends where a 'murder' takes place and the actors spend the whole weekend in role while the guests try to solve the crime. There is no script, just a carefully worked out scenario. It's very hard work – for the actors.

Presenting at trade shows and business conferences

Any product has to be marketed to the retailers – at trade shows and business conferences. Industries are using actors to help their salesmanship within the trade to give such events more impact. Sometimes actors are simply used as presenters linking various speakers and visual material. At other times miniature pieces of theatre are presented to help in the company's sales pitch – often scripted by the actors themselves. Actors are setting themselves up in companies specifically to provide such a service. They entertain but also aim to get a message across using theatrical techniques.

Enhancing the business person's presentation and communication skills

The actor can teach business people the use of acting techniques to enhance personal impact. This ranges from basic voice lessons to helping managers with essential communication skills in the workplace, using the actor's whole armoury from basic skills, through the fundamental ability to communicate, to the role of amateur psychiatrist.

Presentation
Ask a business person how many speeches and speakers he or she can remember from trade shows and conferences. Too many exhortations

to buy are presented in boring, pedantic detail that require a supreme effort of will on the part of the listener. (Knowing is one thing; showing is very much another.) The trade audience will often go to such jamborees just for the social life – anticipating that the speakers will be boring.

Ask most people if they'd be happy to stand up in front of a crowd and speak on a subject of their own choosing, and they'll freeze up. How many times have you listened to someone talk on a subject and been deeply bored – in spite of how interested you were in the subject? The fact is that most people have no idea how to present themselves, however expert in their subject they may be. Sometimes it is through lack of a good script; more often it is a body tension, a vocal tension, boredom through repetition and/or a basic lack of self-confidence. Acting has techniques to solve all of these problems. Not only that, but in every actor's heart is the need to work and the excitement of working. That excitement is what fundamentally communicates to an audience.

Actors are becoming acting teachers to managers to help in these essential presentation skills. You may not get excited about roofing tiles, for instance, but the person in charge of the company who makes them knows them inside out and could bore you to death for hours on the subject. The actor's job is to find ways of getting that person to communicate their expertise in an exciting way or harness the energy of their convictions.

Communication

Actors are teaching managers to communicate better inside their organisations. Businesses are hierarchical and there is a very definite pecking order of management. A stage production also has a 'pecking order' but when everyone is on the rehearsal floor the boss/workers divide often all but disappears, and first-name terms are the norm. The boss – the director – becomes simply the professional outside eye, standing in for the audience, and the final arbiter in all decision making. Through the teamwork necessary and the creativity inherent in the job of acting, wonderful new ideas can occur spontaneously – simply through working well together. Many businesses don't work like this. The use of first names is limited, orders are passed along a chain of command, and each managerial link is very wary of the higher ones. There is a persistent 'looking over the shoulder' mentality, a tendency to complicate issues for basic job preservation, and so on.

Crucially, teamwork and creativity are restricted by the heavy chain of command. Actors, using the working practices of theatre, are teaching businesses to improve their creativity (and productivity) through better communication.

Getting work in these fields

So how do you get in on these particular acts? First you have to assess your own skills. For instance, do you have the ability to pass on those voice lessons you had at drama school? It's one thing to be able to do it yourself, entirely another to teach it to someone else.

Once you've worked out what you could actually do, try writing to selected local businesses – perhaps choose firms that manufacture something you know a little about already. A lot of the tips in chapter 6 on writing letters will apply, but remember that the *modus operandi* of the commercial world is slightly more formal. For instance, you should address business contacts by their title (Mr/Ms/Mrs/Miss) and not use first names until invited to do so. Also, when you do make contact remember that they are probably among the many who don't understand actors and acting.

Look in *Yellow Pages* <www.yell.com> under such headings as 'Conference and Event Management', 'Corporate Entertainment', 'Party Planners and Organisers' or 'Management and Business Consultants', and in among the puppet shows and debt collectors are companies that use phrases like 'Creative Business Marketing' or 'Business Developments', 'Leisure and Entertainment Consultants', 'Promotions and Entertainment'. It is also worth looking in the Business Resources Directories in your local library and doing searches on the internet.

It is certainly a good idea to get effective business cards designed and printed, and a promotional package (brochure, website, and so on) of what you can offer. This makes you look as though you really know what you are talking about. (This needs a lot of time for thought and a fair outlay of capital.) Make sure that you really do know what you are proposing and what you are going to charge for it. Also be wary of acting jargon. For example, most people outside our profession don't know what 'upstage' and 'downstage' mean.

Business is a conservative world; acting is a fairly liberal one. An actor can take advice or be sent up far more easily than most people. Business people who feel threatened by too much inside knowledge or insulted by their product not being taken seriously will switch off very quickly. Tread carefully and respect their ways. Show them that you can give them what they need and want, not what you think they should have or might be fun. And remember, business people talk to each other as much as actors do. If you wish to tap this market, you need to be businesslike.

Role-play companies

You'll find some listed in *Actors' Yearbook* – intensive Googling will reveal more. Some have information about work for actors on their websites – often stressing the thorough training process necessary, the high-quality improvisational skills required and the importance of organisational awareness. Most seem to have a core team to which they will periodically add – generally actors with good experience.

As an actor you should know how to:

- work well in a team or interact;
- communicate effectively and convincingly even with repetition;
- present yourself well;
- be self-motivated;
- utilise creative instincts;
- respond well to others;
- convey that excitement, that need, that made you become an actor in the first place;
- have at your beck and call all the potent power and influence of drama.

You may also be able to:

- teach acting techniques and skills;
- motivate others;
- transform technical ideas and concepts into potent theatrical form.

You must:

- be organised;
- possess a good, normal corporate suit.

10: *Professionalism: the business of being an actor*

As you progress through your career, you have to be organised and professional. Acting can be an instant business. One day nothing happens and then a few minutes/days/months/years later it can all be happening. You must always be ready but not constantly on tenterhooks. You have to be personally organised or you could significantly harm your employment prospects.

As an actor you are your own business. You are not only your own workforce but also your publicity and public relations office, accountancy division, IT department, transport manager and, above all, managing director. You may well have an agent, an accountant and a friend with a computer, but none of these people can do anything unless you give them clear direction. You are finally responsible for the success or failure of the business.

Organisation of interviews/auditions/castings

Lead times for interviews, auditions and castings – even offers of work (especially for commercials) – seem to be getting shorter as the digital world gets faster. There are a number of aspects you should consider.

Secretaries and personal assistants A lot of the business side of being an actor revolves round these individuals; they are the link to the busy director, agent, casting director, and so on. It is she (occasionally he) who will deal with practical arrangements. You will usually not meet her or, if you do, you may well not realise it was she to whom you spoke on the phone. She, however, will almost certainly remember you if there was anything out of the ordinary in your communications. She is efficient – I've yet to meet one who isn't – and overworked. She doesn't just arrange interviews; she also takes dictation, makes tea and fields phone calls to the boss and to other senior members of staff, and so forth. It is very important not to make her life any more difficult than it is already, as she will have the boss's ear. Her opinions can count. The secretary/PA is an often unconsidered, but not inconsiderable, link in the business of being an actor.

The details of an interview You must always be ready to take down full details of any interview when the phone rings. Make sure there are writing materials (and your diary) constantly close by, so you can take down the details of time, exact location, who will be there, basic details of the part and the production and what will be required of you – all as swiftly as possible. If you are bad at remembering all the questions you need to ask, then devise a checklist which you can fill in. You will probably be offered a specific time – be ready to say 'Yes' or 'I'll phone you back' with the briefest of pauses for thought. If you can't make the time offered, be ready to suggest an alternative. And if that's not possible off the top of your head, don't worry; phone back when you've had time to think. Whatever you do, don't mess about! Remember, that secretary has probably had to make thirty similar phone calls that afternoon. She has probably never been to the interview room itself and cannot be more specific than the postal address. Also, she probably knows no details about the part and the production beyond the brief character breakdown she typed earlier.

Similarly, if the appointment is made via text or email, be simple, straightforward and clear in your response(s). Also, ensure that you (a) read the details carefully and (b) keep a copy in case you forget anything.

Responding If it happens that you have to change your time (or cancel), phone (or email/text, as appropriate) back as soon as possible and make sure that you have your original time and date to hand so that the secretary/PA doesn't have to waste time searching.

You may need other information, but don't keep on phoning (or texting/emailing) back time after time because you've thought of yet something else. Think before you contact again. Is there anything further you should be asking about?

Don't be put off a legitimate enquiry by a brusque response. There may be five other people breathing down her neck at the same time she's on the phone to you. Similarly, emails can appear somewhat blunt when dealing with practical matters.

Finally, bear in mind that a recall won't necessarily take place in the same venue as the original interview; it may be in the same building but not in the same room, or in a completely different place altogether.

Note: It is wise to use the contact mechanism (phone, text or email) that they use.

An interview while you are working If you are supposed to be working elsewhere at the time of a proposed interview, check with your current employer that it will be all right to get away before you accept the appointment. Even if it's only a job to pay the rent, don't think of just 'bunking off'. Don't add to actors' generally untrue image of unreliability.

The best solution is to find a non-acting job that can be flexible and where the employer is sympathetic to some mornings or afternoons being taken off on an irregular basis and at short notice, and to whole weeks or months off while you're acting. If you go for 'temp' work, be clear about how short a notice you can give for not being able to turn up because of an acting interview.

If you are working as an actor, most directors are sympathetic and will let you go if at all possible. But don't put him or her in the embarrassing situation of having to say 'No' because you've asked for an obviously busy time – like a production week. However small a part you've got, your absence will adversely affect too many other people. Except in dire emergency, don't make non-urgent doctor's or dentist's appointments unless you are sure you won't be required for rehearsal at that time. Generally, you should make a request to be absent at least three days in advance – if not more.

Injury and illness It is awful to have to miss the chance of an interview if you are injured or ill. Sometimes it is possible to get another appointment, but most interview times have to be limited because of the costs involved. Of course, whether or not you cancel depends on how incapacitated you are and in what way. If it is something obvious like the spectacularly plastered leg I once saw, then struggle in there and use it as a talking point. However, don't 'milk it' or go to the opposite extreme of trying to ignore it as she did! (Somebody had dropped a stage weight on her foot, which would have been a good talking point.)

My wife got an interview only a few days after she was involved in a car accident. She shuffled painfully along the corridors of Television Centre assisted only by a walking frame – and her own determination. Her face was still showing obvious damage but it didn't affect her spirit and she got the job. That is the central point to consider about whether to go or not. Your body may be affected but is your spirit capable of rising to the occasion?

If you feel that adrenalin will not be able temporarily to restore you sufficiently, it is better not to go. Interviewers are sympathetic but they won't be able to judge much and you will be wasting their time, which could even count against you for future reference. It is much better to turn down the invitation to interview and write a brief, and positive, letter explaining why.

Devious tricks You may hear that 'so-and-so' is interviewing, so you contact them and are politely told that 'the lists are full'. This might well be true, but it may be worth leaving your name or, much better, writing immediately with all your details – don't rely on your previous submission being found. Don't resort to pleadings or plain deviousness. Someone phoned a dear friend of mine – now retired, but in her heyday known over the phone to countless agents and actors for her untiring patience and interview-list compiling. The caller asked: 'Where are the auditions next week? Only I have to meet a friend there.' Why couldn't she ask her friend? Yes, it can be worth gatecrashing, but the caller diminished her chances by trying to pull the wool over my friend's eyes.

It is almost always fruitless to try the same via text or email – it is much, much easier to delete one of these than it is to slam down a phone.

Always be contactable In spite of the many means of communication available, a significant minority still make the mistake of not communicating changes in their 'primary contact details'. (In one case an actor didn't even tell his agent about a new telephone number.) Change of home address is relatively unimportant (but not insignificant), but change of mobile number (and/or email address) is crucial. However, don't rush to tell every contact you've ever made! Most won't instantly update their databases – unless they think you could be immediately (that is, within a few months) useful to them. You should communicate any such change to Spotlight, as they are the final recourse in the search for an untraceable actor. (Equity will not pass on private addresses or phone numbers; they will only forward letters.) I'd also suggest some kind of 'safe house' (family, drama school, or the like) who will always (and reliably) pass on your new detail(s) to legitimate enquirers.

If you change agents, don't rely on your former agent passing on the name of your present one. The majority will gladly pass on the information, but I have been met several times with a dark 'Sorry, we can't help.'

Don't rely on a filing system to match your change-of-address communication with your original. Many organisations completely gut their filing systems more often than you might think.

Fundamentally, it is vital that you are always able to receive a message within a few hours. An interview can crop up at any time. You can easily be subject to very short notice, for all kinds of reasons. Always be on standby, but not on tenterhooks. Being an actor is a bit like being a fireman – without the regular salary.

Voicemails So much professional communication is done by phone that these are very important. You should be clear, have a positive attitude and ensure that you can easily be identified – that is, with your full professional name.

Leaving messages You should ensure that any message you leave is easy for the recipient to understand. Remember, we think faster than we can talk and talk faster than we can write (except those good at shorthand) – think of your voice teachers as you speak. It can also be an idea to repeat your phone number – clearly articulated. Don't leave messages that are too complicated with numerous different contact numbers and times. Your life may be complicated, but don't make it hard for someone else to follow.

Wacky outgoing messages Most of these are facile and off-putting to a professional caller. I know that the child in you is an essential part of your actor's make-up, but this kind of message can make you sound irresponsible – the last thing an actor can be.

Checking for messages You should check at least every day, if not twice. And be prepared for a frustrating nothing.

Responding to messages When responding to a message, don't presume that the person who left it will remember all about you the instant you give your name on the return call. He or she could easily be awaiting several responses and could now be preoccupied with something completely different.

The dreaded phone call Some people have a phobia about making phone calls to people they don't know. There is only one solution: you have to act your way out of it. Try making brief notes about what you need to ask or say. I know someone who suffers from a terrible phone-phobia so he phones a friend first as a warm-up in preparation for a professional call.

It's a good idea to be warm with your 'Hello', or whatever your opening gambit is, when answering the phone. This can ease the way into the conversation, and you might get more from it because you've set yourself up as a friendly sort of person. There is nothing more off-putting than a dull, bored voice answering my well-intentioned call.

Tip: If you're sitting right next to the phone when it rings and it's an unknown caller, don't immediately answer it. Give yourself at least a couple of rings to collect yourself first. Similarly, if you're running for the phone, catch your breath before you pick it up.

Email communications Much of the contents of the previous paragraphs also applies to these. Crucially, you have to remember that you are communicating with someone who doesn't know you, therefore you should ensure that your message is clear.

Also, email is not entirely reliable. It's not just spam and viruses; some simply don't arrive – or take days to do so. There's nothing to beat actual conversation (even if it's only with the secretary/PA) to begin to get the feel of an organisation, so I suggest only using emails if specifically requested and checking your inbox at least once a day.

Always confirm Confirm an appointment if you haven't got an agent and received the details from your flatmate, for example. It is always wise to check those details if they've been passed on verbally unless you feel you can utterly rely on the communicator. Most people not in this profession have no comprehension of how it works and don't realise the importance of taking accurate details. If the invitation is via email, it is still essential that you confirm. Just because you know, it doesn't mean that they know that you know. And there are plenty of other people lining up to take your place if you cannot attend, so let them know as soon as possible: it is an act of ultimate selfishness not to do so, and too many actors are guilty of this.

The irrelevant interview If at the last minute you can't get to an interview or you've got another job which makes it irrelevant, you must communicate that information at once so that there is the possibility that your space can be given to somebody else. Employment brokers may have short memories in many ways, but they tend to remember people who waste their precious time by simply not turning up.

But perhaps not so irrelevant It can be worth going to an interview/audition even if, say, you can't for domestic reasons work that far from home. The director will be doing other productions and a future one might be closer to your home. But tread warily, you may even get an offer. (See 'Turning down an offer', pages 87–8.)

Even if you are committed to another acting job that clashes, it is often a good idea to ask if you can still go along to meet someone you've never met before – you never know what the future may hold – provided he or she is happy to spend time with you.

The crucial thing is to be sure you are not seen to be wasting people's time. Don't go for a musical if you patently cannot sing or if you have two left feet. You have to work out whether you can safely hide unavailability or inability. Be careful!

It is worth going, for example, if you've got just a couple of days' filming that clash – providing it's not at a crucial time during rehearsals. Your having time out can be made a condition of contract. Given sufficient notice, the director might be able to plan things so as to work without you on those days.

Do your homework! Much of the preparation work that I've discussed throughout this book could be summarised under this heading. Sufficient homework is an essential part of success in the work-getting jungle. However, don't get paranoid about it and don't find yourself so encumbered with information that you cannot relax and enjoy.

Casting information

The simple fact is that with the exception of major musicals, most Fringe productions and short films, some children's theatre companies and certain specialist casting, most properly paying managements do not openly advertise their requirements to the profession as a whole. They'd be swamped with too many unsuitable applicants if they did – at least that used to be the argument. A few theatre companies openly advertise their casting breakdowns on their websites and several others will post them out if you send them a sae. (For detailed information see *Actors' Yearbook*.) I applaud such organisations; however, I wonder if some might change their minds if they receive too many unsuitable applicants.

Not every actor has an agent and no agent is privy to the details of every new project being mounted. You can create opportunities for yourself by hunting out what's in the pipeline and writing in advance of others.

Getting reliable information To get reliable casting information you have to contact managements directly about future plans. Most will give you short shrift; a few might be more helpful. However, if the response is along the lines of 'We don't know yet', don't try to ask for hints of possibilities. It can be very irritating for the person you've contacted because any delay in the decision making is holding up almost everybody else in the organisation, and if you are too persistent you will be rubbing salt into the wound. Of course the 'powers that be' have some ideas of what they might or would like to do, but there can be all kinds of hiccups preventing the formal announcement.

The other source of 'reliable information' is Equity's 'Job Information Service', which was launched in 1999 and is freely accessible to paid-up members on their website. All the work included is (at least) reasonably paid (although not necessarily at full Equity agreed rates) and thoroughly checked for accuracy, and the job providers are checked for their record of fair treatment of employees. All this means that there are far fewer jobs advertised than in other information services; however, this is more than compensated for by the accuracy and legitimacy of the information it contains. Since its launch it has gained a great deal of credibility with employers, although that could be jeopardised if too many unsuitable applicants apply.

Other casting information services These are listed in *Actors' Yearbook*. They are usually associated with internet casting directories, cost money, and there are limits to their usefulness. Information about properly paid work is limited. Very few paying managements actually use these services to advertise for actors. In general, it is leaks from 'casting breakdowns', combined with judicious phone calls and combing of forthcoming productions announced, that go into their listings. Essentially their information is of a second-hand nature and is not essentially accurate or still relevant. Writing to try to promote yourself on the basis of what turns out to be misinformation will immediately consign your efforts to the bin, so it's well worth checking before sending of yet another submission.

For instance, I was inundated with letters from young women (and agents suggesting same) to play a character called Jan in an Agatha Christie play. In their various ways they claimed they could brilliantly convey Jan's 'strange innocence and sweetness of manner'. If they'd read the play or even just the relevant stage directions, and not relied totally on the service concerned, they could easily have discovered that the Jan in question was male.

I'm not saying that all such services are inaccurate – some are very useful, doing their best to ensure the efficacy of their information – but there are ones who seem simply out to exploit actors' hunger for any information at all. Check carefully before you commit your meagre funds. It can be an idea to subscribe to one (or more) in groups to cut down the cost.

You!

Your budget Somehow accountancy and acting don't quite fit together. It may be that like so many people (not just actors) your grasp of basic mathematics is not good and you wouldn't know a cash-flow crisis until you were drowning in it. The fact is that as an actor you will have an irregular income, so you will have to work out some way of organising your funds so that money worries don't take over your life and severely affect your ability to sell yourself – let alone work.

Your tax and benefits The actor's tax status has always been a grey area. In the late 1980s the Inland Revenue argued that actors working in theatre should have income tax deducted at source under PAYE (Pay As You Earn, otherwise known as Schedule E). On 6 April 1990 newcomers lost their Schedule D (self-employed) status for theatre work – this also meant they couldn't offset nearly as many professional expenses against tax. (Under Schedule D you are allowed to offset expenses that are 'wholly and necessarily' incurred; under PAYE expenses they have to be 'wholly, exclusively and necessarily' incurred.) In practice this meant that many essential expenses, like photographs, were disallowed. Equity and the managers fought this decision through a test case involving the actors Alec McCowan and Sam West – and won. In 1996, Schedule D for everybody's theatre earnings was restored. Self-Assessment arrived in 1997 and who knows what the future may hold.

The important thing to do is to keep careful records of your professional expenditure and income (remember, employers have to declare what they've paid you to the Inland Revenue) and be prompt with your tax returns. If you find the annual sorting of all your receipts extremely disagreeable, keep weekly record sheets. That will lessen the overall strain at the end of the financial year. If in doubt get an accountant who is expert in the ways of the entertainment industry. You'll find some of these listed in *Actors' Yearbook*.

The whole question of state benefits for actors changes all the time. Equity rises to every change of legislation and its interpretation. Not only do they have a very good Legal and Welfare department, but they also publish an *Advice and Rights Guide* (free to members) which gives good advice on tax and National Insurance contributions.

Your body Do your teeth look OK (especially for television)? Are your hands and fingernails in reasonable condition? Is your body fit and ready for any part? Do you have access to a reasonable range of clothes to cover the many and varied interviews you will attend? Do you have footwear that will not only co-ordinate with these outfits but also leave you with dry feet through the monsoon that suddenly hits on the afternoon of your interview? Think about all aspects of the physical side of your presentation. It is worth investing in clothes, hairdressing, and so on, and they are tax-deductible – as is cosmetic dentistry if you can prove your case.

Your voice It is important to keep this fundamental instrument in good condition – especially if you are a singer. Through your long days of telesales or long nights working in a noisy club, always keep those voice lessons in mind and use your voice properly. It is also worth practising saying your own name so that it always comes out clearly on the phone, especially to voicemails, via entryphones, and so forth.

Your mentality You should be organised, by keeping notes on every submission sent, contact made, and so on, but don't make so much of it that you develop a filing-cabinet mentality. I've known actors for whom self-management has become seriously obsessional and has all but killed off the essential free spirit that is fundamental to an actor's emotional equipment. Your imagination and your instinct can be squashed by excessive devotion to your own organisation. It is not only detailed filing that can do this.

Your psyche You may have left drama school, but you can (and should) keep on learning. Go to classes – there are part-time courses around the country (see *Actors' Yearbook* for details). Learn new skills or revive dormant ones that might improve your work prospects. Take a youth drama group. Go to see plays, read plays, arrange play-readings with friends and perhaps rehearse a few scenes and/or audition speeches. Never sit around moaning – if you've got a legitimate complaint (about your agent, for instance) then do something positive about it. Never let your activity level drop below the point where you can no longer act. Very few are able to rise instantly out of a slough of television, cigarettes and alcohol to get work – in spite of what some may claim. You should honestly be able to respond to 'Any work?' with 'No, but I'm very busy.' And remember, employment brokers can smell desperation.

Your other job Make sure the other job(s) that you do when out of acting work give you sufficient stimulus. It's possible that nothing can replace acting for you, but when you're not earning from it you need to have paid work that will not deaden those essential creative juices. Often a positive attitude to a seemingly mechanical job can do the trick. It is important to have a foot in the 'real' world – don't just live in a world of acting.

Getting stuck It is true that if you keep on working in the same places or media you may not be considered for others. For instance, the director of a straight play can be deeply suspicious of someone who has only done musicals for several years. As a general rule it is better to aim to move around at least to some extent. Some such prejudices are irrational and unfounded, but there is a general truth lurking in the background. Acting is about what you can do with your instincts, energies and imagination as well as with your technical skills. The former (and possibly the latter) will always fossilise somewhat if you work in the same area for too long. The same is true of being stuck out of work.

Professional public relations

Apart from the submission writing and interview round, you will always be on the lookout for a chance encounter with someone of influence. Employment brokers of all kinds, and in all media, can seem elusive – there is too much else to be doing, as I hope is patently clear from the earlier chapters – so think carefully about your social intercourse with them outside the interview room.

Fool's gold It can happen that you phone an organisation, expecting the secretary, but by chance you get straight through to someone with casting clout. Don't think you've struck gold and try to keep them talking to draw attention to yourself unless they really seem happy to chat. You should measure this situation as you would an interview and exploit it carefully. It is an insensitive individual who can just slam the phone down on somebody who hasn't finished a conversation. Concentrate briefly on the purpose of your call and don't be a limpet! Bad behaviour in this area is likely to be remembered and count against you in the future.

'How did I do?' It can be useful to find out how an interview or audition went. Some directors are willing to discuss this but almost never directly with the interviewee. The only way to get this kind of feedback is via your agent. Don't phone the director concerned yourself; you could cause great embarrassment even if you did come over well.

Turning up on spec Don't turn up 'on spec' at the office of someone with casting clout, hoping to meet the incumbent. It is a hard-hearted individual who says 'No!' when you are on the doorstep, and you will put the secretary/PA into an awkward position. I know this kind of hustling happens elsewhere, but that's not the way we like to do things in the UK.

The chance encounter You may be seeing a production that a friend is in and be introduced to the director in the bar afterwards. Don't try to monopolise him or her. Write the next day. The same is true with somebody else's agent, a casting director whom somebody else has invited, and so on. Similarly, you might meet such a person at a party. The same rules apply. Let them have the night off and have a good time! That's what parties are for. They will be aware that you regard them as a potential employer; if you can temporarily make that seem irrelevant, you've scored a lot of points. I introduced myself to an actor whose performance I'd very much enjoyed and told him so. He knew that I was a director and was very appreciative, but quickly and easily changed the subject. It became a delightful chat between two people on mutual interests and concerns. Very shortly afterwards a suitable part came up and I offered it to him. In a sense he'd done an audition speech/reading (the performance) and an interview (our chat). What more did I need to know? The opposite is also true. I have known actors walk deliberately away – as if I had leprosy – in order not to put me in a quasi-interview situation. That is equally alienating.

Another time, another place If you've already met a director, casting director or an agent, don't be unduly perturbed if they don't remember you immediately when you meet in a different context. It's not necessarily a reflection on their attitude towards you. Once, after a long day of auditions, I bumped into an actor I'd interviewed and liked only about an hour earlier. He said 'Hello', but for what must have been a good 30 seconds I didn't know who the hell he was. He was most offended, but as I pointed out he now had a hat on, we were meeting again in a totally different context, and I'd met thirty other actors that day.

Nudge – don't nag A director, agent or casting director gives you a glimmer of probability . . . Not one of those vague 'We'll let you know' remarks, but a definite indication of future positive action on your behalf. You have to be patient – just like a patient – and trust that that glimmer could become action. A periodic reminder (a 'nudge') can be a good idea. However, persistent nagging will turn that glimmer into something only worthy of a toilet.

Being seen around (networking) It is true that being seen in the right places at the right times (press nights, for instance) can create routes to work opportunities. However, they need to be handled discreetly and diplomatically as outlined above – and can be cumulatively costly. I suggest that in attending any actor-related activities you should go with the idea of being involved in the main purpose; let the chance of being seen and meeting those of influence remain a possibility at the back of your mind. If this kind of possibility dominates the proceedings for you, you will almost certainly alienate anybody you seek to impress. (I have so often observed people eking out glasses of wine, cups of coffee, etc. – with their eyes flicking this way and that.) Be aware of chance! It is extremely difficult to create; you can only be aware of circumstances in which it might happen. Only a good agent, with a very good knowledge of what's going on, can guide you in this respect.

Public relations while working

It is not just communications with influential professionals that you need to consider carefully. When in work there are other people to bear in mind.

Learn names! A well-run organisation will send you a list of names before starting a job – cast, crew, and sometimes administrative staff. Try learning them beforehand and aim to establish contact with as many as possible as early as is feasible, without wasting anybody's time. Of course this will be more difficult in the larger organisations; in fact you many never finally succeed in meeting everyone – but word of your positive efforts will get around and stand you in good stead.

Technical staff 'A lot of hard, and sometimes dirty work, and very little of the glory' is the lot of the technical team. An actor's response might be, 'We take the criticisms.' Yes, actors are the front-line troops, but a front line is useless without reliable back-up. You will get better support if you work with them instead of treating them as servants, and news of any misbehaviour travels very fast. Always aim to get to know and work well with everyone involved. The most surprising people can have good ideas to help you, and a few of them will rise to positions where they could employ you – directors (and other employment brokers) have got to start somewhere.

Some actors like to give dressers, cleaners and stage doorkeepers tips or presents at the end of a job. This can be a pleasant gesture to the apparently 'lowliest of the low', but not everybody can afford it and some regard it as patronising. Whatever you feel and whatever your financial situation, they are part of the 'bricks and mortar' of the profession and need just as much care and attention as you do. (In television the equivalents are dressers and make-up artists.)

Always take care of your costumes, leave your dressing room tidy and clear it out properly when the production is over.

Other members of staff Don't ignore, or be offhand with, members of staff not directly connected to the production side – the box office, for instance. A theatre is a tight-knit community; word will get around. Especially, don't get into the traditional 'slagging off' of the administrator and the publicity department. It is unwise to think that an idle barb shot in their direction will do you no harm. These are the kind of people who are close to the director's everyday thinking and might well be asked their opinion of an actor or for a suggestion for casting. Administrative staff work totally different hours from actors, and what they put into their work is often badly misunderstood. (And vice versa.) If you feel you have a legitimate complaint or even a positive suggestion, make sure you place it in the appropriate ear and don't shout it round the bar or backstage. This is also true in the media.

Essential professionalism

Being an actor carries as much responsibility towards other professionals as being a parent does for a child.

A call A 'call' means ready to start at that time, not the time for you to grab a cup of tea. The actor may be last in the organisational chain of command, but that doesn't mean that you can be lax about being ready to start. I know that calls rarely start on time, but there is usually a good reason. Whatever that reason, there should be none for you to be late too. As you are last in that chain you have the potential to hold up all those people ahead of you. If you are just five minutes late and have kept a dozen people waiting, you have wasted the equivalent of one person-hour of working time.

Waiting This invariably happens while everything technical is sorted out (especially in film and television), and the time it takes can be as long as the proverbial piece of string. ('They pay me for the waiting. I do the acting for free.' Burt Lancaster.) Your call includes that inevitable wait and you must be prepared for it. You absolutely cannot be late – keeping the technical crew waiting, even for a few minutes, can cost a disproportionate amount of money.

Responsibility for yourself Acting is not something you can do 'under par'. If you persistently put yourself at risk by indulging in

only true to a certain degree of certainty, or tolerance, however good our measuring instruments are; even the simple act of observation disturbs the observed object. This makes no perceptible difference with everyday objects. It only really matters when observing extremes. (This is not a fanciful abstract idea. The microchip is just one example of its practical application.)

Much of what I have discussed in this book is, I believe, a manifestation of the equivalent in human interactions: for example, the speech that works well for one director but dies a death for another one, sometimes for no apparent reason. If this is the case, and you have faith in your speech and the way you do it, then stick to it. It is your 'absolute' (until some improvement hits you), all the time recognising that its reception is finally beyond your power. In other words, develop a feel for probability to help you through, which is always open to receive a chance bonus or cope with an unforeseen knock.

Some people find this non-deterministic, non-causal concept of life very disturbing. I find it very comforting. It means that we've got little to lose and a lot to gain – especially in the profession of acting where there are too many variables to comprehend fully. And good acting is finally about what you can do beyond the apparent confines of mortal mind and body.

Some other thoughts

'But habit is a great deadener' So says Vladimir in Samuel Beckett's brilliant tragi-comedy *Waiting for Godot*. You might like to respond with Estragon's line earlier in the play: 'We are all born mad. Some remain so.' I am simply using it as a headline because it has a certain ring to it which illustrates my next point. As an actor you have to be continually exploring your art. Sticking only to what you know, especially in your first few years, can deaden those essential instincts that are fundamental to acting. Of course, you will need to fall back on what you know in certain circumstances, but you must always be prepared for that flash of inspiration that can move you on another quantum leap. The need to learn and explore should stay with you, without your becoming obsessive about it. Excessive internal examination is just one route to despair.

Despair As an actor you will often be disappointed, therefore despair is part of the actor's condition. However, it cannot become part of your professional persona. Despair is a cancer that drains essential energies out of not only you but also those around you – and other actors, like relatives, are especially vulnerable. Nobody wants to employ an actor who threatens, however unconsciously, to depress the rest of the company.

On several occasions I have been asked to consider someone who 'has been through a bad time'. I will consider him or her if appropriate, but not on the grounds of charity. I am sympathetic, but it is not an area in which I am prepared to take risks. It has been suggested to me that by giving such people a job I might help in their rehabilitation. This may be true, but I am only an amateur psychiatrist, which could be dangerous, and is there really the time available? Those people and their nearest and dearest have to solve the essential problems. Any work can only be seen as the final stage of the rehabilitation process. Despair is not something that you can act your way out of; only patient effort can destroy it.

Clinical depression requires professional help, but you can help yourself to avoid it overwhelming you by consistently looking for ways to keep yourself buoyant.

Keep buoyant You have to believe that somehow, somewhere, there is acting work for you. You cannot sit back and wait for it; you have to work at getting it, but don't dedicate all your waking hours to this task. Have other things to do and keep in touch with other people, not just with other actors. The everyday events in the local newsagents can provide not only light relief but also valuable character studies. Build yourself a set of activities to cope with the inevitable waiting periods – for an offer (or not), even for an interview. Find a temporary job which gives you contact with other people. Don't feel you are no longer an actor if you are having to spend your evenings serving behind a bar instead of treading the boards.

Waiting can be the principal contribution to an actor's psyche breaking down, and with it his or her ability to function at all. Keep your despair for your lover/mother/cat/budgie/pillow. Learn to handle waiting well; don't allow it to constantly get you down. You have to keep up your survival and fighting energies or you will sink without trace. I have seen this happen too often. Keep buoyant.

Determination The extraordinary example of Nelson Mandela who, after twenty-seven years in prison, emerged almost as if he'd never been incarcerated is an object lesson for us all. I do not exaggerate when I say that you, the actor, will often need to be similarly determined in your quest for work. I've known a number of now well-known actors while they struggled up the greasy pole of success. Some found it within a few years, but it took at least one twenty-five years of determined effort – keeping going in spite of persistent rejections. That determination is not blind; it is also allied with a little cunning. ('The point is to keep going; not to get rotten.' Henri Cartier-Bresson.)

Finally Find your own way of using all this advice. Think of this as a set of guidelines to make your life easier. If you use it slavishly, denying your actor's imagination and instinct, I certainly won't employ you. If you can't find something you wholeheartedly disagree with, then give up now. I am not saying that I don't believe in everything I've written and am trying to cover myself. The greatest exponents of any art (or science) are those who know and understand the rules and then go beyond them. 'Logic controls the excesses of my imagination' was how a man – the nearest to genius I've ever met – put it. The most interesting actors are the ones who cleverly break rules and appear dangerous.

Postscript 'Anybody who thinks he's written the definitive book is a fool.' I caught this statement on Radio 4. I don't know who the speaker was, but I certainly agree. New thoughts and ideas come to me every time I re-read this. Others come from friends and from working with actors and students – an ever-bubbling stream of qualifications, clarifications and illumination. However, there comes the moment when commitment to print is necessary. This will not stop me from continuing to collect material – I will go on enquiring, listening, observing and experimenting. If there's something you'd like to say please contact me via my website. I will continue to receive all comments and criticisms gratefully.

This book cannot create more work, but I hope that it might make whole process of getting it a little fairer.

A brilliant perspective: 'An actor's career is a marathon; not a sprint.'

Bibliography

Books for aspiring, student and young actors

Annett, Margo, *Actor's Guide to Auditions and Interviews* (3rd edition, A&C Black, 2004). A useful guide outlining some of the techniques needed for success.

Dunmore, Simon, *Actors' Yearbook* (Methuen Drama, annually in September). This is the leading contacts directory for training as an actor and finding acting work in all media.

Dunmore, Simon, *Alternative Shakespeare Auditions for Women* (A&C Black, 1997). A collection of fifty less well-known speeches for women.

Dunmore, Simon, *MORE Alternative Shakespeare Auditions for Women* (A&C Black, 1999). Another collection of fifty less well-known speeches for women.

Dunmore, Simon, *Alternative Shakespeare Auditions for Men* (A&C Black, 1997). A collection of fifty less well-known speeches for men.

Dunmore, Simon, *MORE Alternative Shakespeare Auditions for Men* (A&C Black, 2002). Another collection of fifty less well-known speeches for men.

Jones, Ellis, *Teach Yourself Acting* (Hodder & Stoughton Ltd, 1998). A good overview of acting and the profession.

Reischel, Jennifer, *So You Want to Tread the Boards: The Everything-you-need-to-know, Insider's Guide to a Career in the Performing Arts* (JR Books Ltd, 2007).

Scher, Anna, *Desperate to Act* (Lions, 1988). Brilliant, basic advice for those so 'desperate', from a lady who should know.

Shakespeare, William, *Hamlet, Prince of Denmark*. See especially Hamlet's advice to the players (Act 3, scene 2), which is some of the best advice on acting ever given.

Taylor, Malcolm, *The Actor and the Camera* (A&C Black, 1994). Another good 'primer' for the beginner.

Other career advice books for actors

Cohen, Robert and Calleri, James, *Acting Professionally* (7th edition, Palgrave Macmillan, 2009). The 1st edition was published in 1972 and is now regarded as godfather of this genre in the USA.

Hooks, Ed, *The Audition Book* (3rd edition, Back Stage Books, 2000). Excellent reading if you're thinking of trying your hand in the USA. It's also worth looking at Ed's website for his excellent 'Craft Notes' (<www.edhooks.com>).

Messaline, Peter and Newhouse, Miriam, *The Actor's Survival Kit* (3rd edition, Simon & Pierre, 1999). Well worth reading if you're thinking of trying your hand in Canada.

Books for any actor

Bates, Brian, *The Way of the Actor* (Century Hutchinson, 1986). Very interesting insights into the inner workings of the actor's psyche.

Bishop, Nancy, *Secrets from the Casting Couch* (Methuen Drama, 2009). A practical workbook written from the point of view of a very experienced casting director.

Brook, Peter, *The Empty Space* (Penguin, 1990). Written in the 1960s, but still essential reading.

Cairns, Adrian, *The Making of the Professional Actor* (Peter Owen Publishers, 1996). A fascinating study of the history, and possible future, of the art of acting.

Callow, Simon, *Being an Actor* (Penguin, 1995). Autobiographical books by famous actors are generally useless in terms of practical career advice. However, this one – part autobiography and part advice – has a great deal of down-to-earth common sense. His famous 'manifesto' on directors' theatre is spot on.

Churcher, Mel, *Acting for Film: Truth 24 Times a Second* (Virgin Books, 2003). Invaluable insights into the specific techniques involved.

Churcher, Mel, *A Screen Acting Workshop* (Nick Hern Books, 2011). An excellent and comprehensive training course in screen acting which includes a DVD showing the work in action.

Craig, Nicholas, *I, an Actor* (Pavilion Books, 1988). A very funny send-up of the starry actor's autobiography. A must.

Donnellan, Declan, *The Actor and the Target* (Nick Hern Books, 2005). A fresh approach to the actor's art from the artistic director of *Cheek by Jowl*.

Gillett, John, *Acting on Impulse: reclaiming the Stanislavski approach* (Methuen, 2007). An excellent demystification of Stanislavski.

Hagen, Uta, *A Challenge for the Actor* (Macmillan, 1991). One of the best books on acting ever written.

Mamet, David, *True and False* (Faber & Faber, 1998). This book cuts through much of the mythology that surrounds acting.

O'Toole, Fintan, *Shakespeare Is Hard, But So Is Life: A Radical Guide to Shakespearean Tragedy* (Granta Books, 2002).

Rea, Kenneth, *A Better Direction* (Calouste Gulbenkian Foundation, 1989). A very thorough inquiry into directors and the need for more training opportunities.

Rodenburg, Patsy, *An Actor Speaks* (Methuen Drama, 1997). An entirely practical guide with excellent advice and exercises to help develop the performer's voice.

Sanderson, Michael, *From Irving to Olivier – A Social History of the Acting Profession* (Athlone Press, 1984). A very expensive, but nevertheless fascinating, study of the actor's world over the last century.

Sharpe, Edda, and Rowles, Jan Haydn, *How to Do Any Accent: The Essential Handbook for Every Actor* (Oberon Books, 2007).

Shaw, Bernard Graham, *Voice-Overs, A Practical Guide* (A&C Black, 2000). A useful guide which explains and teaches the skills of voicing radio and television commercials.

Shurtleff, Michael, *Audition* (Walker & Company, 1984). An American book which should be read. It contains brilliant insights and thoughts to help any actor.

Spotlight, *Contacts* (Spotlight, annually in October). Contact details for everything you can think of (and more) that relates to the performing arts in general.

Index